W9-ANH-412

WITHDRAWN

Directed by Dorothy Arzner

WOMEN ARTISTS IN FILM

Roswitha Mueller and Kaja Silverman, *Series Editors*

DIRECTED
BY
DOROTHY ARZNER

Judith Mayne

Indiana University Press

Bloomington and Indianapolis

The paper used in this publication meets the minimum
requirements of American National Standard for Information
Sciences—Permanence of Paper for Printed
Library Materials, ANSI Z39.48-1984.

Manufactured in the United States of America

Library of Congress Cataloging-in-Publication Data

Mayne, Judith.
Directed by Dorothy Arzner / Judith Mayne.
p.   cm.
Includes index.
Filmography: p.
ISBN 0-253-33716-X.—ISBN 0-253-20896-3 (pbk.)
1. Arzner, Dorothy, 1900–1979—Criticism and interpretation.
I. Title.
PN1998.3.A763M39   1994
791.43'0233'092—dc20
93-51496

1 2 3 4 5 00 99 98 97 96 95 94

For Terry

Contents

Acknowledgments

MANY INDIVIDUALS and institutions helped me in the research for this book. I am grateful to the Arts Library—Special Collections of the University Research Library at the University of California—Los Angeles, and in particular to Brigitte Kueppers, Ray Soto, and Paul Camp. Virtually all of the new information that I have been able to provide about Dorothy Arzner's career and life comes from the Dorothy Arzner Collection at UCLA; and during my stay in Los Angeles, as well as in subsequent letters and telephone calls, I was given the kind of reception and access that academics dream of. I am also indebted to the UCLA Film Archives, and in particular to Andrea Kalas, for granting me access to many of Arzner's films. Thanks, also, to the Department of Special Collections at UCLA, for access to interviews with Arzner and to the Zoë Akins collection. During my stay in Los Angeles, Vicki Allen-Callahan, John Callahan, Anne Friedberg and Howard Rodman provided me with hospitality and shared my discoveries.

For additional valuable information on Arzner, I am indebted to the Directors Guild of America, and in particular to Selise Eiseman and to Francine Parker; to the Museum of Modern Art Film Library in New York City; to the Library of Congress in Washington, D.C.; and to the New York Public Library at Lincoln Center. I am grateful to the Dance Library at the New York Public Library at Lincoln Center for information on the career of Marion Morgan.

Thank you to the Ohio State University, particularly to the College of Humanities, the Department of French and Italian, and the Center for Women's Studies. Rebecca Thomas, Mollie Driscoll, Christina Lane, and Ami Chitwood provided valuable research assistance.

I am grateful to supportive friends and colleagues, particularly Clare Beavan, Janet Bergstrom, Alan Buster, Teresa de Lauretis, Laura George, Bill Horrigan, Isaac Julien, Lucretia Knapp, Linda Mizejewski, Roswitha Mueller, Jenni Olson, B. Ruby Rich, Kaja Silverman, Jennifer Terry, and Patricia White. Thank you to Dudley Andrew and Lauren Rabinowitz, who invited me to teach a seminar on Arzner at the University of Iowa, and to the students there who took the seminar.

My greatest debt is to Terry Moore, for caring so much about this project, for reading and commenting on draft after draft, and for being so entertaining.

Directed by Dorothy Arzner

Introduction

I NEVER MET Dorothy Arzner. In the several years that I have been research-ing and writing this book, however, I have encountered numerous aspects of Dorothy Arzner. Two factors in particular drew me to Arzner and to this project, and they have remained my primary emphases. First, in the history of the classical Hollywood cinema, Dorothy Arzner was the "great exception"—the only woman director who had a large body of work to her credit, and whose career spanned three decades of Hollywood history. Arzner's film career was not only unique in its own terms; her films are unique. Although many of her films reflect stereotypical Hollywood conventions regarding the representation of women, there is also in Arzner's work a sense of women's independence and a stylistic vision to go with it.

The process of discovering Arzner's films was for me truly eye-opening. As students of feminist film theory know, Arzner's *Dance, Girl, Dance* (1940), features a stunning exploration of women among women, particularly insofar as the pleasures of looking are concerned. While I have long admired other Arzner classics— *Christopher Strong* (1933) and *Craig's Wife* (1936) in particu-lar—I was afraid that these works might prove the exceptions. Instead, I found a body of work that consistently challenges many of our assumptions about the necessary limitations of the Hollywood cinema. I will not claim that Arzner's films are unqualified successes from beginning to end; I am far too suspicious of such a "great genius" theory of authorship. (In any case, the constraints imposed by the Hollywood dream machine were many and they were real, par-ticularly for a director like Arzner who was respected, but only as long as she was able to function productively—i.e., turn a profit—within the studio sys-tem.) But I *will* claim that Arzner's films are consistently provocative, and that they reflect both Arzner's unique achievement and the extent to which she re-mained, throughout her lifetime, the exception in Hollywood. I wanted to ex-plore how relevant it is to speak of feminist concerns in her work, and while I did not expect to discover a fully developed feminist aesthetic, I wanted to see how Arzner's work differed from that of her male contemporaries.

The second issue that drew me to a study of Arzner came less from her films than from the photographs I had seen of her. Arzner adopted a persona that can be best described as butch: she wore tailored, "masculine" clothing; her short hair was slicked back; she wore no make-up; and she struck poses of confidence and authority.[1] If Arzner was a lesbian, I wanted to know, how? That is, what did it mean to *be* lesbian or gay in Hollywood during Arzner's time? I knew that to be lesbian or gay in Hollywood meant being secretive and living in the closet, but this made Arzner even more intriguing, for her image was circulated widely during her career. Hence, assuming that Arzner was a lesbian (and everything I have learned about her suggests to me that she was), the ubiquitous closet was not (excuse the pun) open and shut in her case. For at the very same time that Arzner kept the details of her life private, she flaunted a style that signified "lesbian." Her films are not simply isolated texts; they were (and continue to be) exhibited and received in relationship to her very distinct image.

This is not to suggest, however, that my interest in lesbianism vis-à-vis Arzner's career is neatly and exclusively focussed on the films and the publicity photographs of Arzner that circulated in the popular press. I wanted to know how Arzner lived and what relationship existed between her films and her life. I know that that relationship is impossible to reconstruct in a full and complete way. I acknowledge from the outset that I am interpreting Arzner's life and career. But I do not believe that all interpretations are equal. For whatever reasons, some of which are quite valid, most investigations of Arzner's career do not take lesbianism into account. In general I agree with Edward Turk, who in his research on Marcel Carné discovered how much a disservice was done to Carné's films if the director's gay identity was not taken into account. Turk writes, "By outing Carné, I have helped to pull Carné and his movies *out from* decades of accumulated misperceptions, willful distortions, and vapid commentary. To my mind this is a service to the director and to his artistic legacy."[2]

I thought that I might be regarded as "outing" Arzner, until I discovered that many biographers of Hollywood actresses whom Arzner had directed had no qualms whatsoever about assuming and describing her lesbianism. Charles Higham and Roy Moseley, in their biography of Merle Oberon, describe Arzner as a "famous lesbian."[3] And in his biography of Lucille Ball, Higham claims that Ball was "embarrassed by widespread gossip about Miss Arzner's lesbianism."[4] If necessary, I can "justify" my investigations of lesbianism vis-à-vis Arzner with the same claim made by Turk apropos of Carné's films. For instance (and this is developed further in chapter 7), the importance of dance in *Dance, Girl, Dance* was not just a theme like any other in Arzner's work. For forty years Arzner shared her life with Marion Morgan, a dancer and choreographer who collaborated on several of Arzner's earliest pictures. Throughout Arzner's career, collaborations with women had special significance (screenwriter Zoë Akins and actress Billie Burke come immediately to mind), and the collaboration with Morgan was even more significant in that it bridges so many years, not to mention the supposedly separate worlds of personal and professional life.

What intrigues me more about the "justification" thesis (gay/lesbian sexuality is relevant if it affects the work) is where we draw the line between the "life" and the "work." Films are not isolated objects, and film studies of the last decade have challenged fetishizations of the individual film as the privileged object of analysis. But we have access, with varying degrees of completeness, to films as relatively contained objects. Lives are never so accessible. So, while I was pleased to discover a connection between Arzner's "life" and her "work," I do not want to take easy refuge in what I consider to be a defensive posture concerning lesbianism.

When archivists Ray Soto and Brigitte Kueppers at the UCLA library showed me the boxes of material which would become the basis for a large part of this study, I opened one box to find a large photograph of a luxurious home in (I later discovered) the Hollywood Hills (figure 1). The caption on the photograph read "Home of Marion Morgan and Dorothy Arzner/1930–1951." (The handwriting, I later discovered, was Arzner's own.) If I were attuned to omens, I surely would have read this as a sign. Now I know that such signs are fictions, signs of nothing more than my own projections and the coincidence of opening one particular box first. Nonetheless, that moment of discovery was thrilling; for here was evidence of a home and a life shared by two women. I later discovered that they moved to the desert in 1951, and that they lived together until Morgan's death in 1971.

The correspondence to which I had access made clear that theirs was a loving, committed relationship. The defensive posture I alluded to above would make me want to say that I was thrilled to see a connection between the life and the work. However, that awareness came later. The first thrill was recognizing the relationship, period. And recognition of Arzner's relationship with Morgan seems to me important for more than any imprint one might find on Arzner's films. For too long clichés of spinsterhood, of asexuality, of careers managed at the price of any personal satisfactions, have not only rendered lesbianism invisible, but insignificant and meaningless as well. There, written in Arzner's own hand, was a declaration of her relationship with Morgan.

My initial research into Arzner's work resulted in a chapter in my book, *The Woman at the Keyhole: Feminism and Women's Cinema*, on the feminist reception of Arzner's work and the dynamics of female and lesbian authorship. While I see these two projects as linked, in the present book I seek to bring my analysis of Arzner's career to a larger audience. Readers familiar with the fields of feminist film theory and gay/lesbian studies will see that many aspects of Arzner's career discussed in subsequent chapters coincide with contemporary theoretical concerns. For instance, some feminist film critics and theorists have

Figure 1. Entrance atrium, home of Dorothy Arzner and Marion Morgan, 1930–1951. Arts Library—Special Collections, University Research Library, UCLA.

explored the extent to which costuming is crucial to an understanding of women's relationship to the cinema; as the title of an essay by Jane Gaines puts it, "dress tells the woman's story."[5] I found that Arzner's particular directorial style was consistently revealed by an emphasis on costume, and that changes in female fortune and in women's relationships to each other were often dramatically emphasized through dress and costume.

It may not be particularly surprising that a woman director should be so attentive to costume, but part of what has been so important in the recent feminist emphasis on clothing is the recognition that there are many aspects of film production that have received less attention than others, not because they are less important, but because they are so frequently associated with women.

Costume design was one of the few areas of film production in which Arzner did not work before becoming a director (she was a typist, a script clerk, a screenwriter, and an editor), but it speaks to her appreciation of women's contributions to the screen that costume became so important in her films. It also signals the importance of her relationship with Marion Morgan, who, as a choreographer, did extensive staging and costuming and brought those skills to her collaboration with Arzner.

In the early to mid-1970s, when Arzner's work was brought to the attention of feminists, her films were deemed particularly important for their criticism of Hollywood film "from within." Pam Cook and Claire Johnston described how the universe of the male was "made strange" in Arzner's films, how women's "rewriting" of male discourse subverted the established conventions of Hollywood.[6] At the time that Cook and Johnston's essays were published, film theory was very much preoccupied with the notion of "making strange," with the possibilities of a Hollywood film that critiqued itself and its own assumptions. Cook and Johnston brought a strong theoretical approach to Arzner's work, while other critics of the era were simply delighted to find a woman director among all of the men in Hollywood film history. The tradition of film studies in which I have worked makes me regard the theoretical approach of utmost importance; but in reading and rereading critical assessments of Arzner's work from the 1970s, I find that many critics who do not share those theoretical preoccupations had just as much of value and interest to say about Arzner's career. Put another way, my work on Arzner has made me question the relationship between feminist theory and feminist research.

While working on this book, I was struck by how contemporary theoretical preoccupations also seem to be reflected in Arzner's work. For instance, there has been increasing emphasis placed, both in feminist theory and in gay/lesbian studies, on performance—on the extent to which gender and sexual identities are not fixed essences, but rather are masks adopted and then taken off, if not at will, then at least in radically discontinuous ways. In the 1970s Arzner's work served to demonstrate the "making strange" hypothesis; in the 1990s, it could demonstrate the "performative" hypothesis. Judith Butler's *Gender Trouble* is one of the most quoted sources in this context. Butler says, for example, "Gender ought not to be construed as a stable identity or locus of agency from which various acts follow; rather, gender is an identity tenuously constituted in time, instituted in an exterior space through a *stylized repetition of acts.*"[7] Drawing upon Butler, one could note how the emphasis on performance is indeed a striking aspect of Arzner's films, particularly in terms of how supposedly conventional roles of masculinity and femininity are denaturalized and presented as poses. I find, however, that such an interest in performance can obscure complex issues that do not lend themselves to easy "either/or's" about the nature of identity. I am less interested in claiming Arzner for contemporary theory than in seeing what contemporary theory might learn from Arzner. Hence, my focus throughout this book is on the various texts and images which bear the imprint "directed by Dorothy Arzner."

In terms of academic fields of specialization, this study is indebted to feminist film studies and to the emerging field of gay and lesbian studies. In researching Arzner's career, her films, and her image, I was engaged in a process of thinking and rethinking many of the theoretical foundations of these fields. I have never found it possible (or desirable) to speak of the classical Hollywood cinema as a monolithic institution, yet the economic and ideological restrictions of Hollywood are real. How to engage, simultaneously, with the sheer joy and delight of Hollywood cinema, while acknowledging both the prices paid for the pleasures it offers, and the difference between its legitimate and supposedly illegitimate pleasures? This is, in many ways, the question of female agency that has plagued feminist studies in various ways from the outset, and which has had particular resonance in film studies, given the extent to which the status of cinema as an industry has been so central to the art form.

I would still maintain that one of the greatest contributions of 1970s film theory was textual analysis, the reading and rereading of how film texts (in the 1970s, only individual films; in more recent years, virtually all of the elements that contextualize film reception) both articulate a system and disrupt it. Recent studies in the area of gay and lesbian investigations have taken the notion of symptomatic reading further, revealing both the establishment of compulsory heterosexuality and the various ways in which homosexuality is managed. I have also been influenced by recent rethinkings of what it means to come to terms with an individual life, particularly in those studies in which authors have had to confront the complex and entangled strands of gender and sexuality.

What Blanche Wiesen Cook describes, in her biography of Eleanor Roosevelt, as the "romance of the closet" is particularly compelling: "For some the closet was lonely and disabling. For others it was entirely satisfying and intensely romantic—its very secrecy lent additional sparkle to the game of hearts. The romance of the closet had a life of its own."[8] While it is common for contemporary gays and lesbians to denounce the closet as a vestige of homophobia, I think we have yet to come to terms with our own romances of the closet, from our projections of the present onto the past, to our fantasies of rescue of beloved figures from oppressive institutions. Whatever compromises Arzner had to make in her lifetime, I cannot regard her choices and her decisions as inevitably tragic. Arzner, like all of us, lived fully in a complex and exciting historical period. This is not to downplay homophobia and sexism, but rather to resist making easy divisions between the past and the present.

This book is not a biography of Dorothy Arzner. While I had access to personal papers and correspondence, I never wanted to write a complete biography, definitive or otherwise. This book is intended, rather, as a study in portraiture, in the literal and the figurative senses of the term. I am interested in what kinds of films Arzner made, in how those films and Arzner herself were written about, and in how Arzner was portrayed during her career. In keeping with the importance of portraiture, I think readers should know that the photographs and images that appear in this book are not just "illustrations" that were sought after the completion of the written text, as is often the case with accompanying illustrations. Rather, this study has been guided from the outset by the photographic record of Arzner.

Directed by Dorothy Arzner is divided into three parts. In Part One, "The Cinderella Girl of the Movies," I follow the chronology of Arzner's career, from the beginning of her (very short-lived) typing job in 1919 to her departure from Hollywood in 1943. Chapter 1 traces Arzner's apprenticeship in editing and screenplay writing; chapters 2 and 3 examine her directorial career. In chapter 4, I look at some of Arzner's activities after she left Hollywood, as well as the attention that began to be paid to her in the 1970s. In these chapters, I also discuss Arzner's relationship with Marion Morgan, and I suggest how that relationship affected Arzner's career. Throughout these chapters, I pay particular attention to how Arzner's films were received as examples of the "woman's film," and how Arzner herself was received as a "woman's director."

Part Two examines a selected group of Arzner's films, following thematic and stylistic preoccupations in her work. Arzner's attention to women's lives was accompanied by a focus on the influence of social class, particularly insofar as working women are concerned. Chapter 5, "Working Girls," takes its title from the 1931 film that is virtually unknown today, but which is as worthy of attention as Arzner's better-known films. In addition to *Working Girls*, I discuss how women's work emerges in *Nana, The Bride Wore Red*, and *First Comes Courage*. In chapter 6, "Odd Couples," I look at the precarious status of heterosexuality and the suggestions of other types of couples in *Christopher Strong* and *Craig's Wife*. Chapter 7, "Dance, Girls, Dance," takes its title from Arzner's best-known film, and here I argue that in *Dance, Girl, Dance*, as in *The Wild Party*, dance becomes a privileged metaphor for both women's aspirations and women's communities. In these three chapters, I focus on films that are currently in distribution; with the exception of *Working Girls* and *First Comes Courage*, all are available on video. *First Comes Courage* is still available in 16mm. I hesitated to discuss *Working Girls* at all, since for most readers the film is unavailable for viewing, but it is such an important film in relationship to Arzner's career that I felt its inclusion was a necessity.

In Part Three, I examine how the "image" of Dorothy Arzner has been assessed and appropriated, both in her own time and currently. During Arzner's career, stories about her appeared frequently in the popular press. Chapter 8, "Looking for Dorothy," details how Arzner's appearance was described—for described it was, often in deliberate, hilarious, and symptomatic detail. The

Figure 2. Marlene Dietrich, at the home of Dorothy Arzner and Marion Morgan. Arts Library—Special Collections, University Research Library, UCLA.

conclusion, "Lesbian Detection," looks at how Arzner's image has surfaced in the last decade in lesbian representation.

I previously noted my thrill in discovering, as a quite literal entry into the Arzner archive, the photograph of the entrance to the home Arzner and Marion Morgan shared in Hollywood. My account of seeing that photograph conveys the sense of discovery I encountered, again and again, as I learned more about Arzner. But I do not want to give the impression that I see myself as one of those fictional characters who is miraculously presented with a key that unlocks all the secrets of another's past. There were a number of snapshots of various individuals in one of the boxes at UCLA. Most of these snapshots showed Arzner at home with various acquaintances. One snapshot promised truly exciting possibilities: Marlene Dietrich, sitting (I assumed) in Arzner and Morgan's yard, holding a cat (figure 2). Since Dietrich's death, several detailed biographies have appeared, and I have scoured them all, looking for some mention of Dorothy and Marlene. Even with the taboo of lesbianism apparently broken (everyone, from Dietrich's daughter Maria Riva to biographers Steven Bach and Donald Spoto, has something to say about Dietrich's lesbian affairs),

I have yet to find a single acknowledgment of a friendship, an acquaintanceship, or an attachment between the two. I freely admit my disappointment, but at the same time I think it is a good thing to have this photograph of Dietrich to situate next to the one of the entrance to Dorothy and Marion's home; it reminds me that no individual life is completely knowable by anyone else.

PART I

The Cinderella Girl of the Movies

"It can't be done," they told her—the wise-acres did.
But there is a well known little poem about the man who did what others said
couldn't be done.
So she did it—Dorothy Arzner did.

—Cecil Carle, "The Cinderella Girl of the Movies,"
Southern California Alumni Review, December 1927, p. 9

1

Apprenticeship

ON DECEMBER II, 1926, an article in the *Los Angeles Daily Times* announced: "Lasky Names Woman Director." Dorothy Arzner was not the first woman director in American film history, and the author of the article mentions Lois Weber and Ida May Parks as her predecessors. However, Dorothy Arzner's career was unique: Arzner was virtually the only woman of her era who endured. She established a substantial body of work in a Hollywood film career that began in 1919, when she started working as a typist at Famous Players-Lasky, and ended in 1943, when illness forced her, the only woman of her era to succeed as a director, to abandon her final film. Her directorial career spanned fifteen years and produced sixteen films which bear the credit "Directed by Dorothy Arzner," not to mention several others completed for, and credited to, other directors.[1]

Arzner's unique career was due not only to her ability to succeed where few women had before, but also to her management of her career. Arzner worked her way through the various stations of film production, and she became adept at many of the most important parts of filmmaking, like editing and screenwriting. Her film career began in 1919 when she visited the set of Paramount studios at the invitation of William De Mille. During World War I, De Mille had been head of the Los Angeles Emergency Ambulance Corps, in which Arzner was a volunteer (never making it overseas). That her career began at Famous Players-Lasky (which would eventually become Paramount) was thus a fortuitous coincidence of contacts rather than a consciously plotted strategy. But as coincidence would have it, Famous Players-Lasky was the most successful film studio of the time. "In 1920," writes film historian Douglas Gomery, "Famous Players stood at the acme of the US movie industry."[2]

According to Arzner, this introduction to film production made her decide not only to become a film director, but to pursue that goal by learning virtually every stage of the film production process. She began by typing scripts, a job that lasted only three months; by her own account, Arzner was a horrid typist (often relying on the good will of colleagues who typed her scripts for her). As she later told the tale, "I was a terrible typist. There was a big, redheaded Irish girl . . . who was a wonder at typing. She took pity on me and did more than half of my work. But for her I wouldn't have lasted a week."[3] Nonetheless,

Figure 3. Dorothy Arzner, ca. 1926. Arts Library—Special Collections, University Research Library, UCLA.

Arzner's first film job allowed her to learn first-hand about the preparation of a good film script.

Another factor made the movies a particularly attractive endeavor. After graduation from high school in 1915, Arzner had entered the University of Southern California with the hopes of studying medicine, but a brief sojourn in a doctor's office convinced her that a medical career was not for her. She found that people were always talking about their troubles and their sicknesses, and this was boring. "I wanted to heal the sick and raise the dead instantly," she said. "I didn't want to go through all the trouble of medicine. So that took me into the motion picture industry."[4] If motion pictures offered another way to "heal the sick and raise the dead," they also provided an entry into a particularly attractive modern career. Arzner described a conversation with two friends after her studio tour with William De Mille: they thought that since the movies were a modern business and Dorothy was a modern girl, a film career was tailor-made for her.[5]

A modern career for a modern girl, and an alternative to medicine: Arzner accepted these rationales to explain her interest in motion picture production. What else about Dorothy Arzner prepared her to occupy such a unique position in the history of motion pictures? She grew up in comfortable upper-middle-class surroundings, one of two children (her older brother died when she was quite young). Her year of birth is listed alternately as 1897, 1898, and 1900. According to one anecdote, her birth records were destroyed in the San Francisco fire, and she decided to list 1900 as her official birthdate, thus defining herself quite literally as a "modern" woman, fully a part of the twentieth century. The earlier dates are, however, more realistic. Arzner was born in San Francisco, and her family moved to the Los Angeles area in 1906, after the infamous earthquake.

Her parents operated several restaurants, including one that provided early commentators on Dorothy's career with a ready-made myth of how she happened to become a motion picture director. Louis Arzner was the manager of the Hoffman Café, a restaurant frequented by movie and theatre professionals. Some writers were eager to invent for Dorothy a life-long desire to make movies because of her childhood experiences. One tale repeated several times in the popular press went as follows: At the far end of the Hoffman Café was an alcove with a round table, screened from the main dining room by a velvet drape. Here various members of the film community congregated—Charles Chaplin, Mack Sennett, D. W. Griffith, and James Cruze. Of this distinguished group, silent-film director Cruze, known in particular for westerns, is undoubtedly the least known today; however, he had, as we shall see, an enormous influence on Arzner's career. The story continues: "One day the small Dorothy, peeping through a slit in the velvet curtain, was surprised by James Cruze, who laugh-

Figure 4. Dorothy Arzner, at the age of 1 year. Arts Library—Special Collections, University Research Library, UCLA.

ingly led the little girl to the table and introduced her. Once inside the magic circle, the child remained, and each day found her absorbed in their talk of acting, writing and directing."[6]

The incident may have had bare-bones truth embroidered for the sake of legend, but Dorothy begged to differ insofar as any childhood dream of motion pictures was concerned. True, she had been around actors and directors during her childhood, but if anything, the contact dissuaded her from a moving-picture career. Actors were always throwing her up in the air, she said. For the most part, however, she had little contact with the patrons of the restaurant. If there was any connection between the Hoffman Café and Arzner's choice of career, it was the desire to be financially independent of her father, not to carry on a family tradition of association with stars and directors.[7]

Despite that desire for financial independence, it is crucial to appreciate the extent to which Arzner was able to make some career choices unavailable to other women—and men—precisely because of her father's financial provisions for her. Arzner was cognizant that, while she wanted her financial independence, the fact that her father *had* provided generously for her financial welfare meant that she could take career risks, knowing that she had an independent income to fall back on. "I had a loving father," Arzner said in 1975, "so I wasn't dependent on the job and in that way I was able to be more independent than men with four children."[8] Indeed, despite the large number of successful films in Arzner's directing career, there were large chunks of time during which she was not working. *Nana*, for instance, was released in February, 1934, and although several directing and producing deals were announced in the years that followed, Arzner did not direct another film until *Craig's Wife*, released in September 1936. Similarly, *The Bride Wore Red* was released in September 1937, and Arzner did not direct again until 1940 (*Dance, Girl, Dance*), and then again in December, 1942, when she was signed on as director of what would become *First Comes Courage* (released in 1943).

I do not want to suggest that these breaks are signs of failure in Arzner's career, even though after *The Bride Wore Red* she did have difficulty finding work. Rather, they emphasize that she could be selective about directing projects, due in large part to her independent income. In addition, Arzner invested her own income quite wisely, so that her departure from her directing career in 1943, necessitated by a serious illness (pneumonia, contracted during the filming of *First Comes Courage*), was also facilitated by her wealth. To be sure, other factors intervened as well. Arzner suggested once in an interview that the infamous Louis B. Mayer of MGM studios had blackballed her after the failure of *The Bride Wore Red*, and in any case she herself was unsatisfied with the results of the film.[9] Arzner is the one who made the decision to retire as a Hollywood director after *First Comes Courage*, but she always said that Hollywood left her, as well: "I went out with the big studio era. I wouldn't say that I left it. I think it left me also."[10]

Given Arzner's characterization of herself as a modern girl, and given her commitment to making her own living, it would be easy to assume that career always came first for her. She loved her work and the independence that it gave her. Arzner was always professional, devoting long hours on the set. But she

Figure 5. From Arzner's family album: Dorothy Arzner as a teenager. Arts Library—Special Collections, University Research Library, UCLA.

had other interests, and she always made clear that motion picture directing was not her only passion.

Arzner graduated from a private girls' school, Westlake, in 1915. Her stepmother sent her there because she was concerned about young Dorothy's tomboyish ways—as evidenced, perhaps, by Dorothy's dressing up as "Garth" (see figures 6 and 7). A profile of her, published in the school's magazine in 1982, notes that Dorothy was active in art, drama, tennis, and the school yearbook.

Figure 6. From Arzner's family album: Dorothy dresses up as "Garth for a Night." Arts Library—Special Collections, University Research Library, UCLA.

In an essay published in the school yearbook in 1915, Dorothy writes: "Life is full of beginnings; we start something new each and every day. Most beginnings are small and seem trivial, but in reality they are full of significance. . . . Each act and each thought is like a building block, all going toward the completion of the perfect structure. . . . Let us not be satisfied with ourselves; climb

Figure 7. "Garth for a Night." Arts Library—Special Collections, University Research Library, UCLA.

Figure 8. Dorothy Arzner's graduation photo from the Westlake School, 1915. Arts Library—Special Collections, University Research Library, UCLA.

higher. Do not be earthbound!"[11] Several such "building blocks" characterized the next several years of Dorothy's life. She spent two years at the University of Southern California (1915–1917) preparing for a medical career, but she left school to join the volunteer ambulance corps, which led, indirectly, to the fateful meeting with William De Mille.

What, then, were the events that led to the momentous announcement of Arzner's contract to direct? After typing scripts for three months, Arzner worked on an Alla Nazimova production holding script, i.e., maintaining continuity between production and script. Her brief stint with Nazimova's company has not received much attention in any account of Arzner's career. To be sure, later encounters with directors like James Cruze provided more sustained, long-lasting, and influential effects on Arzner's career. Despite the lack of information about Arzner's work with Nazimova's company, their encounter deserves attention. The film Arzner worked on was *Stronger Than Death*, which was released in January, 1920.[12] The film was co-directed by Charles Bryant, Nazimova's husband, and Herbert Blaché, husband of the pioneering French director Alice Guy Blaché. Here, as with most of Nazimova's pictures, one assumes the two men to have been directors in name only; Nazimova was notorious for overseeing and controlling virtually all aspects of the production of her films.[13]

Nazimova was notorious in other ways as well, primarily for the openness of her lesbian attractions and relationships. Her adaptation of Oscar Wilde's play *Salome* (1923) is legendary not only for its remarkable sets and costumes, but also for the rumored insistence on Nazimova's part that only gay and lesbian actors participate in the film.[14] The list of her supposed affairs goes on at some length, including Natacha Rambova, the wife of Rudolf Valentino.[15] While Nazimova is known primarily today for her flamboyance, she was an enormously successful actress, and however brief her film career, she stands as an early example of a woman who insisted upon creative autonomy and control in her work. Arzner's brief association with Nazimova provides a fascinating encounter between two women who fashioned independent careers for themselves in the film industry.

Born in Russia, Nazimova came to the United States in 1905, and she soon became known as the foremost performer of Henrik Ibsen's dramas. Her film debut occurred in 1916, when a play in which she had toured, *War Brides*, was adapted to the screen for her. At the peak of her career, she was one of the highest paid film performers. Her films tended to emphasize the exotic and the excessive, thus earning decidedly mixed reviews from the critics. Her final film was released in 1925, and she returned to the New York stage. Some years later she came back to Hollywood to appear in supporting roles in films like *Escape* (1940) and *Since You Went Away* (1944). Aside from her personal flamboyance, Nazimova is known for her association with Rudolf Valentino and Natacha

Rambova; Valentino played the role of Armand Duval in *Camille* (1921), a role that helped to launch his own film career, and Rambova was the set designer for *Salome*. Curiously, one of Nazimova's later roles was in the remake of *Blood and Sand* (1941); its 1922 version starred Valentino and was edited by Arzner.

There is no question that Nazimova was a temperamental actress whose flamboyance offscreen tends to be remembered more than her work onscreen. Indeed, her most visible legacy today is not her work, but rather the Garden of Allah, her palatial home (later turned into a hotel), legendary for the supposed wild parties and quintessential Hollywood excess that went on there.[16] But Nazimova also deserves reconsideration as an early pioneer of women's cinema. In 1921 she was quoted as describing the "element of spontaneity" in motion pictures as "their principal charm." "I find in them an everlasting source of stimulating pleasure," she said, "but ever I am in pursuit of that something new, something different." One such pursuit of the "new and different" was her desire to produce a play that would be all female, from the cast, to the director, to the staff.[17] Nazimova was committed to feminism and to equal rights for women. She was a member of the National Woman's Party, which she joined in 1923, and she served as founder of the actresses' council.

It is not completely clear how Arzner got her job with Nazimova's company. One fan magazine described Dorothy's encounter with Nazimova as follows: "With the nerve of a movie trade paper ad solicitor at Christmas time she invaded the sacred precincts of Alla Nazimova's dressing-room. And came out a full-fledged script girl."[18] Arzner's period of employment with Nazimova's company may have been brief, but the episode was significant to Arzner's career, at the very least because it exposed her to another example of female independence and autonomy—even if it was a somewhat negative one. Arzner was critical of Nazimova's ego, acknowledging that while she learned from holding script for her company, she preferred Paramount. Arzner noted that Nazimova was a "temperamental star" who made a habit of arriving in the late afternoon while her company was on set early in the morning. "I was around actors a lot," Arzner said, "so I was not impressed by the acting off screen, as it were."[19]

Information that Arzner's relationship with Nazimova was more than professional comes to us from director George Cukor, a man whose career intersects with Arzner's in many interesting and sometimes curious ways. In an interview with Boze Hadleigh, one of the few interviews in which Cukor speaks (albeit in many cases indirectly) about his own identity as a gay man in Hollywood, Cukor makes a brief comment about Nazimova as the "stage manager" of Rudolf Valentino's marriages. Cukor continues: "Alla had many distinguished female lovers, including our Dorothy Arzner."[20] Throughout the various stages of the interview, Cukor refuses to confirm whether specific individuals are indeed gay, thus conforming to the standard code of conduct among gay men and lesbians of his time, that is, that public declaration of one's sexuality was not only inappropriate, but dangerous. That the information about Arzner (who is referred to by Hadleigh as a lesbian director) is so forthcoming suggests, at the very least, that Arzner's lesbianism was quite well known. Well known, that is, within certain defined limits—the limits of the gay and lesbian community, and those familiar and/or comfortable with it. Cukor's brief forthrightness about Arzner needs to be understood not as an "outing", but rather as an acknowledgment of what was known within very specific circles.

The encounter on the set of *Stronger Than Death* between the twenty-one-year-old newcomer to the film business and the flamboyant forty-one-year-old Russian actress provides plenty of grist for the fantasy mill. And the more one learns of how many participants in the Hollywood dream factory were gay, lesbian, or bisexual, the more difficult it becomes to sustain the myth of universal heterosexuality, despite how feverishly Hollywood films and publicity outlets were then, and still seem to be, devoted to that myth. In the case of Arzner and Nazimova, the lack of details about their relationship makes it impossible to say with any certainty what effect it had on their respective lives. But in a general way, the encounter between the two women dramatizes encounters that marked Dorothy's entire career. My point here is not that all working relationships disguised romantic ones, but rather that within Hollywood, Arzner developed and nurtured, and was nurtured in turn, by her relationships with women.

Adrienne Rich has theorized a lesbian continuum, an approach to lesbian existence less concerned with the absolute separation of the lesbian from the heterosexual, and more concerned with the identification of the ways in which what we call "lesbian" characteristics inflect and inform the lives of women who might otherwise consider themselves thoroughly heterosexual—from the importance of all-female communities in women's lives to the intensity of female friendship.[21] Rich's postulation of a lesbian continuum has been controversial, particularly in that it contains the risk of denying the specificity of lesbian experience. Those controversies, particularly as they pertain to *contemporary* lesbian existence, are beyond the scope of this book; however, I would argue that Rich's lesbian continuum is useful in historical terms, when we are confronted with women, like Arzner, whose lives conform to many, if not all, contemporary definitions of lesbian life. More to the point, Rich's lesbian continuum ranges from self-identified lesbianism to close friendships between women, and attempts to define lesbianism as one moment in the history and fabric of relationships among and between women. I believe we do a disservice to Arzner's life and career if the evidence of lesbianism is not seen in relationship to the close bonds with women that characterized her approach to her life and her career. In other words, a lesbian continuum characterizes Arzner's life and career.

Hence, the next stage of Arzner's apprenticeship to motion pictures was influenced by yet another woman. Arzner's experience with typing scripts and holding script for Nazimova led to her interest in cutting and editing, an interest which was encouraged by cutter Nan Heron. Arzner told Kevin Brownlow: "She was cutting a Donald Crisp picture, *Too Much Johnson* [1920]; I watched her work on one reel and she let me do the second, while she watched and guided every cut. On Sunday I went into the studio and assembled the next reel. On Monday I told her about it and she looked at it and approved. I finished the picture under her guidance."[22] Heron recommended to Crisp that Arzner hold script and cut his next picture. Thus began Arzner's illustrious career as a cutter and editor (the difference between the two roles is primarily one of status and responsibility: cutters are supervised by editors).[23]

Arzner worked as a cutter at Realart, a subsidiary of Paramount, and eventually became chief editor. As Arzner described it: "I cut something like thirty-two pictures in one year at Realart. . . . I also supervised the negative cutting and trained the girls who cut negative and spliced film by hand. I set up the film filing system and supervised the art work on the titles. I worked most of the day and night and loved it."[24] Indeed, Dorothy's passion for her work was obvious to her co-workers, including the actress (and later screenwriter) Bebe Daniels. Daniels described spending evenings with Arzner in the cutting room, a process that "taught me more about writing for motion pictures than anything in the world could have taught me." "Every night," Daniels said, "I'd trudge up there and work with Dorothy until seven or eight, then I'd go home with my nails full of glue. I remember saying to Dorothy that I didn't want to bore her by coming up all the time. 'Bebe,' she said. 'I love this.' "[25]

Arzner worked at Realart until she was called back to Paramount, in 1922, to edit *Blood and Sand*, an experience she described as the "first waymark to my claim to a little recognition as an individual."[26] *Blood and Sand* (1922), directed by Fred Niblo and featuring Rudolph Valentino in his first star billing, is a tale of a handsome bullfighter (Valentino) caught between his virtuous wife and a heartless vamp. The bullfight scenes feature masterful cutting from stock footage of Madrid bullfight arenas to close-up shots of Valentino. Arzner not only cut the film, she also was in charge of the filming of the bullfight shots of Valentino on a nearby ranch.

The bullfight scenes in *Blood and Sand* are sophisticated integrations of stock and original footage. The film demonstrates not only Arzner's skill, but also her resourcefulness. Arzner saved Paramount an enormous amount of money through her skillful use of stock footage. Her experience on *Blood and Sand* established her reputation for remarkable efficiency and—especially—equally remarkable economy. Indeed, anecdotes appear throughout her directorial career exemplifying this resourcefulness, from the rectangular mask set into her megaphone so that a single object could be used to call directions and frame a scene simultanously, to the use of a fishing pole to allow mobility of the microphone in Paramount's and Arzner's first sound film, *The Wild Party*. She regularly brought her pictures in under budget, and throughout her career provided a model of economy (*Craig's Wife* was used as an example of how an "A" picture could be made on a "B" picture budget).[27]

Arzner's work on *Blood and Sand* led to yet another fortuitous coincidence as well. While it is true that Arzner's most sustained collaborations were with women (particularly writers and actors), there were also influential men in her life, such as director James Cruze. Arzner was working on the final editing of *Blood and Sand* when, unbeknownst to her, Cruze walked into the room on his way to an adjoining projection room. He paused behind her and exclaimed "My God, who cut that picture?" When Arzner replied that she had, he offered her the opportunity to cut *The Covered Wagon*.[28] Arzner's association with Cruze was an important part of her apprenticeship. After *The Covered Wagon* (1923), she worked on several other Cruze pictures, including *Ruggles of Red Gap* and *Merton of the Movies*.[29] After working for smaller companies as a scriptwriter (including Columbia), Arzner worked with Cruze again on *Old Ironsides* (1926) as both editor and scriptwriter.

Both *The Covered Wagon* and *Old Ironsides* are historical epics. *The Covered Wagon* traces the trials and tribulations of a wagon caravan as it travels to Oregon in 1848; *Old Ironsides* tells of the triumph of the battleship Constitution against pirates threatening U.S. trade in the early nineteenth century. The two films were important in Arzner's career in demonstrating her skill as an editor and in providing her with the experience of location shooting, in what was an almost exclusively male environment. While honing her already considerable editing skills, she learned how to work with a large cast and crew. *The Covered Wagon* was shot in Nevada and Utah, with a cast of thousands. According to Arzner, the Cruze company was known as a "Wild West" company, with plenty of drinking and gambling, and she was told that she wouldn't last long on the set. She not only endured, she thrived: an experience repeated in the on-location shooting for *Old Ironsides*. James Cruze was an enormous influence on Arzner as well, less because of his particular style as a filmmaker (Arzner's own films were very different from those that she had helped Cruze make), and more because of the professional interest he took in her. Arzner once said of him, "I owe him a tremendous lot. . . . He always treated me as though I were his son, without any frills but with a sort of comradely friendship."[30]

While Arzner's work on *The Covered Wagon* and *Old Ironsides* marks the ascent of her career, the latter film marks the descent of James Cruze's career. *The Covered Wagon* was a huge success, and it was expected by all concerned that *Old Ironsides*—another historical epic, made by the same director—would follow suit. *Old Ironsides* was an expensive production and used a new technique that producer Jesse Lasky called "magnascope": the selective use of wide screen projection to dramatize the size of the ship. Lasky attributed the film's unexpected failure to poor timing: "Had it been shown soon after the First World War, or after the first rumblings of World War II, it might have ridden on a wave of national patriotism to set new records, as did my later picture *Sergeant York*. But in 1926 it was just stale history, apathetically received and soon forgotten."[31]

James Cruze received much of the blame for the failure of *Old Ironsides*, and his contract with Paramount ended in 1928, just a year after Dorothy Arzner's first film was released. Cruze's career is significant in relation to Arzner's in several ways. Arzner learned early on from her association with Cruze how precarious the director's position is, and how the bottom line is always financial. Throughout her own career, Arzner spoke glowingly of James Cruze, and the loyalty he inspired in her was typical, since he preferred to work with a small, stable production unit. Richard Koszarski suggests that Cruze's commitment to such production practices was in part responsible for the demise of his career ("this approach did not suit the developing production practices of the studios").[32] Yet Arzner herself inspired the same kind of loyalty in many of those with whom she worked, from cinematographers to screenwriters to actors.

There is some irony in that in terms of temperament and professional behavior, Arzner had much more in common with Cruze than with the one woman in charge of her own company with whom she worked, Alla Nazimova. But such irony is typical of Arzner's apprenticeship, as well as of her later career in Hollywood. I would argue that one of the advantages Arzner had, among the many disadvantages of being a woman in a man's world, was that she was not a "woman" in any one-dimensional or stereotypical sense of the term. Arzner's butch persona complicated any easy alignment of the fact of being female and the acquisition of femininity. Nothing about Arzner fit the stereotype of female sexual objectification that was quickly becoming standard in Hollywood cinema. To be sure, other gendered roles emerged (as "son" to Cruze, for example) to describe her. Nonetheless, Arzner had more flexibility vis-à-vis gendered roles than other women in Hollywood at the time.

While Arzner was certainly not in a position of authority in any way comparable to that of Cruze, the experience of concentrated and extended location shooting had to have been enormously valuable to a young woman learning the ropes of the business. With *Old Ironsides*, she was one of few women aboard a battleship with 3,000 men, and according to a newspaper notice, "every one of the 3,000 tried to save her when the mast fell during one of the scenes, killing one actor and injuring seven."[33] However, Arzner's own descriptions of her experiences with the Cruze company and the photographs of her on location are not always totally compatible, for while Arzner emphasized how protective and gentlemanly the men of the company were toward her, the photographic record of the two films suggests a woman who was so boyish as to inspire

Figure 9. Arzner on the set of *Old Ironsides*, 1926. Arts Library—Special
Collections, University Research Library, UCLA.

comradeship as much as protection in her male colleagues. Arzner's youth (she
was in her twenties) and petite physical size may well have inspired the kind of
attention usually described as chivalrous or gentlemanly, but from the outset
of her career, Arzner did not fit easily or comfortably into gendered dichotomies. She was always seen as a *woman*, but a woman with a flexible gendered
persona, whose masculine clothing well suited her.

Arzner's most elaborate memento of her silent film days is a photo album
from the shooting of *Old Ironsides*, and throughout the photographs she appears to be fully a part of the crew. Actresses and other female studio employees
were also on location, but Arzner's presence was nonetheless distinct (see
figures 9–11). Compare, in this context, the photographs of Arzner on location
in *The Covered Wagon* and *Old Ironsides*. A cast photograph from the Western
epic shows men in cowboy outfits (including Cruze) and women in dresses;
there, off to the right, sitting cozily with one of the women, is Arzner—clearly
a woman, and just as clearly unlike any of the other women on the set (figure
12). With *Old Ironsides*, pictures of Arzner in her sailor's costume with the

Figure 10. Arzner on the set of *Old Ironsides*, 1926. Arts Library—Special Collections, University Research Library, UCLA.

actors depict a woman who is like, and at the same time distinctly unlike, her male colleagues. Before the production of these films, Arzner had already begun to sport a distinctly butch style—pants and jackets, sensible shoes, short hair brushed back, and no make-up—which then lent itself quite well to the cowboy costumes of *The Covered Wagon* and the sailors' dress for *Old Ironsides*.

Figure 11. Arzner on the set of *Old Ironsides*, 1926. Arts Library—Special
Collections, University Research Library, UCLA.

Now one can assume that there was no requirement that Arzner dress in either
cowgirl or sailor costume for the two films. The fact that she did, and that the
attire meshed so well with her butch style, speaks to another quality Arzner was
learning—the acquisition of her own personal style as a future film director.
Indeed, right from the beginning of Arzner's film career, she had a flair for

Figure 12. Arzner (far right) with the cast and crew of *The Covered Wagon*, 1923. James Cruze is standing in the second row, fourth from left. Arts Library—Special Collections, University Research Library, UCLA.

style that was not assimilable to either conventional male or female modes of dress in Hollywood.

I find the photographs of Arzner on the sets of these two films extremely provocative, in two senses of the term. First, they are provocative in the sense that these images of Dorothy challenge any easy fit among sex, gender, and sexuality; they are troubling in that they suggest masculinity, yet problematize it. This simultaneous quotation and subversion of masculinity is the essence of butch style. Second, the photographs are provocative in that they play upon a kind of visual pleasure[34] that thrills, not at the objectification of the female body, but at the possibilities of crossing boundaries between supposedly opposite terms: male/female, masculine/feminine, heterosexual/homosexual. In describing Arzner's flexibility in relation to gender and sexual stereotypes, it can be too easy to dismiss or downplay the enormous influence of sexism and homophobia in Hollywood. Thus, I want to maintain both senses of provocation in assessing Arzner's career—the liberating potential she represented, as well as the threat.

Arzner's work with James Cruze, like her editing of *Blood and Sand,* reveals technical expertise and dedication to her craft. There is little in *The Covered Wagon* or *Old Ironsides,* however, to suggest the kinds of preoccupations concerning communities of women or the fragility of the heterosexual couple, which would become visible in the films she would direct. Ironically, few of the films Arzner went on to direct demonstrate the sophisticated technical expertise evident in the Cruze films, particularly insofar as editing is concerned. Indeed, the range of the films is quite different, and one cannot help but wonder if Arzner's directorial assignments reflected more a stereotypical gender dichotomy than her early career did.

This is in no way a criticism of Arzner's work as a director, nor is it a confirmation of the view that Arzner was a better editor than director.[35] But it is curious that a woman so adept at editing should never really use those particular skills in quite the same way again in her career, despite the fact that she personally supervised the editing of her films. I have discussed how Arzner's physical presence challenged gender dichotomies, and yet another such dichotomy is evident in the shift from her editing career to her directorial one. Action, adventure, and historical epic characterized Arzner's editing projects, features far more generally associated with male directors and male audiences. Indeed, only when Arzner began *directing* films was the category of the "woman's film" applied to her work. One can only wonder what kind of further challenges to gendered roles and dichotomies might have resulted if Arzner's talents as an editor had had a more direct, visible influence on the films she directed.

True to her desire to learn everything about the motion picture industry, Arzner worked as a screenwriter as well. In particular, she wrote screenplays for Columbia, then considered a "poverty row" company, in the mid-1920s. One of the films for which Arzner wrote the screenplay (adapting a story by Adela Rogers St. John), *The Red Kimono* (1925), suggests that her apprenticeship period in motion pictures included not only the development of her technical expertise, but also her engagement with certain themes that eventually would be the focuses of her own films. *The Red Kimono* was produced by the widow of actor Wallace Reid, whose death, attributed to drug addiction, caused one of several scandals for Paramount in the early 1920s.[36] The film was directed by Walter Wang. After her husband's death, Mrs. Reid became involved in a number of morally uplifting causes, and this particular film is adapted from Adela Rogers St. Johns's reporting of a murder trial that occurred in 1917.[37]

Mrs. Reid appears at the beginning of the film, reading newspapers in an archive. She tells her audience that the story they are about to witness is, unfortunately, common. The film tells the story of Gabrielle, a young woman who is drawn into prostitution by a suitor named Howard, who later abandons her. While most of the events in the film follow the real story as reported by St. Johns, Arzner's particular vision is evident throughout. Early in the film, a scene takes place in a bordello, where Gabrielle mourns the departure of Howard. Sister prostitute Clara, described in the titles as a " 'girl' next door," comforts her. While the primary focus of the scene is Gabrielle's misery, the strength of the bond between the two prostitutes is also foregrounded. In particular, close-ups of the two women's intertwined hands emphasize their connection. As the film progresses, close-ups of hands function as details to signify emotional intensity, but if the desired goal was only to suggest the common degradation of prostitutes or the mournful state of Gabrielle, then these frequent close-ups of the women's hands exceed that goal by emphasizing the positive bonds between women.

This is not to say, however, that in *The Red Kimono* (or in Arzner's later works) relationships between women are romanticized or idealized. Rather, those relationships acquire specific class contours, and are portrayed as dynamic, complex, and conflict-ridden. For example, in *The Red Kimono*, Gabrielle goes after her departed lover and kills him. After she is acquitted by a sympathetic jury, a wealthy and hypocritical society woman takes Gabrielle under her wing in order to publicize her own good works. The society woman presents Gabrielle to her female friends at a reception. Virtually every cliché of the objectified female is present here, from close-ups to an emphasis on the power associated with the look; but there is one important exception—those who objectify Gabrielle are all women. *The Red Kimono* demonstrates not only the importance of "female bonding" in Arzner's cinema, but also and especially the complexities and the conflicts in communities of women, from bordello to high society.

While I think Arzner's writing gives a better sense of her future films than does her editing, the experience of working with James Cruze on *The Covered Wagon* and *Old Ironsides* was crucial to her future. After *Old Ironsides*, Arzner was prepared to leave Paramount to accept an offer writing and directing at Columbia. As Arzner told the story (several times), when she left Paramount she wanted to say goodbye to someone important. When studio boss B. P. Schulberg was unavailable, she passed Walter Wanger (head of Paramount's Long Island studio) in the corridor and told him of her plans. Wanger immediately contacted Schulberg, who assured Arzner she could remain in the scenario department until directing possibilities came along. Arzner was adamant that she wanted to be "on the set in two weeks with an 'A' picture. I'd rather do a picture for a small company and have my own way than a 'B' picture for Paramount."[38] Paramount acquiesced and Arzner soon began directing her first feature.

Of all of the anecdotes about Arzner's career, this one—of being offered a director's job only when she threatened to leave Paramount—has been repeated most often by others, as well as by Arzner herself. At the beginning of this chapter, I mentioned the anecdote so often told about Dorothy's aspirations for a cinematic career, based on camaraderie with the film folk from her father's restaurant. Just as Arzner was annoyed by that anecdote, so was she angered by another one which began circulating early in her career to explain her first directing contract. It was said that Cruze and another director went to Paramount officials on her behalf and asked that she be given a chance. It says much about Arzner that the two myths she most often sought to correct were those that depicted her choices and desires as shaped by male authority figures. In Arzner's own scrapbook, the stories that attributed her career to either the influence of the Hoffman Café or the intervention on her behalf of Cruze inspired her to cross out lines and write "untrue!" in the margins.

And so, on her own initiative, Arzner was signed to direct for Paramount. Her apprenticeship in the editing room, on the set, and with the script was now completed, and would serve her well.

2

Successes and Failures

ARZNER'S DIRECTORIAL DEBUT, *Fashions for Women*, was released in April 1927 to mostly positive reviews. This film was also the first starring role for Esther Ralston, who had been featured in *Old Ironsides*. The simultaneous launching of the careers of these two women provided a model for what was perceived, throughout Arzner's career, as one of her strengths: her role as a "star-maker." As star-maker, Arzner was entrusted with supervising the passage of actresses like Ralston from supporting to starring roles. Almost without exception, the stars "made" by Arzner were women. One suspects, of course, that the role of star-maker provided a niche for Arzner as the only woman director of her time. In other words, it was assumed that as a woman director Arzner would empathize better with her actresses and elicit the kind of performance needed to assure their star status.

Fashions for Women is a light comedy, set in Paris, in which Ralston plays two roles, Celeste de Givray, a fashion model, and Lola Dauvry, a cigarette girl in a café, who is recruited to impersonate the fashion model. De Givray is in need of a face-lift, and her agent creates a publicity stunt. He picks the cigarette girl to substitute for de Givray at a fashion show. The agent plans to have de Givray show up—with her new youthful appearance—and denounce her imposter. The film plays upon a tried and true theme of American cinema, the simultaneous lure of impersonation and disguise, with the appropriate romantic mix-ups thrown in. For Lola, in her impersonation of Celeste, falls for a wealthy man, but he—unaware of the impersonation—learns unsavory facts about the "real" Celeste and is ready to break off the relationship. By the conclusion of the film, of course, all has been resolved and the happy couple—Lola and the wealthy man—emerges victorious.

Reviews of the film were not unanimously positive, but virtually all of them mention Arzner's skill as a director as well as Ralston's beauty. Indeed, some reviewers give top billing to Arzner's direction, largely due, of course, to Arzner's unusual status as a woman director. Praise for Arzner's direction ranged from the exuberant ("Woman Director Delivers Delightful Photoplay") to the qualified (" . . . considering the ungrateful story she had to contend with, Director Dorothy Arzner, Paramount's first woman director, did fairly well").[1] While the quality of the screenplay was a matter of disagreement among re-

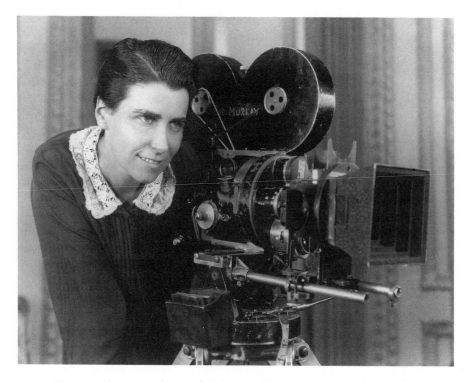

Figure 13. Arzner on the set of *Fashions for Women*, 1927. Arts Library—Special Collections, University Research Library, UCLA.

viewers, Arzner's resourcefulness—one of her most enduring qualities—was noted by at least one reviewer, who congratulated the director who "was forced to labor under extreme difficulties [Arzner completed the film in less than two weeks] in order that the production might be completed within a certain period."[2]

Whatever the limitations of *Fashions for Women*, the picture was a commercial success, and on the basis of that success Arzner was signed to a long-term contract at Paramount. B. P. Schulberg, then associate producer at Paramount (and the man responsible for signing on Arzner to direct *Fashions for Women*) was quoted as saying: "In *Fashions for Women*, Miss Arzner more than fulfilled our every hope. Facing the responsibility, not only of a first picture under her own guidance, but of conducting a new star through her first starring vehicle, she made a picture which shows every indication of being one of the outstanding box-office successes of the year. . . . This is what we expected Miss Arzner to do, and it has been a real pleasure to extend a new contract to her."[3]

Arzner's next picture, *Ten Modern Commandments*, also starred Esther Ralston, and was released in July 1927. Ralston plays Kitty O'Day, who works as a maid at her aunt's boarding house in New York City. A down-on-his-luck song-writer, Tod Gilbert, arrives at the house, and Kitty promptly falls in love with him and determines to help him sell his music. Kitty manages to meet Broadway producer Mr. Disbrow (clearly based on Flo Ziegfeld), who agrees to buy a song by Tod if she will agree to pose as Disbrow's ladyfriend, in order to keep the petulant and overbearing female star of the production away from him. A variety of complications arise: first, when Tod disappears, and later when he mistakes Kitty's pose for a genuine affair. Kitty must find Tod to sign the contract. Eventually Kitty herself goes on stage in order to perform Tod's song, which is, of course, the hit of the production. The "ten modern commandments" of the film's title are actually one: "Get Your Man," displayed in bold type backstage (and providing, as well, the title of a future Arzner film).

As with *Fashions for Women*, Arzner's direction of Ralston was praised, and in some reviews Arzner's role once again received top billing over Ralston's. One reviewer commented that Arzner "seems to get along well with Esther Ralston. She has put the blonde actress through a really human performance, with straightened hair, and clothes that aren't too perfect."[4] The *Variety* reviewer even recommended that Ralston's future as a star performer be entrusted to Arzner: "From the manner in which [Arzner] did the megaphoning here she might be teamed with Miss Ralston and given latitude in the selection of story for this star. If this is done, Miss Ralston should prove to be a great draw for Paramount, which she is not today, though coming along nicely."[5] Yet another reviewer praised Arzner for revealing the talent that had previously been invisible in Ralston's career: "Miss Ralston, under the exclusive direction of men for her first few pictures, was regarded almost solely as a model, or a pretty figure on which to hang clothes and parade in front of the camera for pretty and attractive shots. . . . Miss Arzner has done what her men directorial rivals had failed to do, that is, see the humor and the charm of Esther Ralston's character and sucessfully transfer them on to the screen."[6]

Given this praise for Arzner's work with Ralston, it is surprising to learn that their collaboration was troubled from the start. Indeed, Arzner's first experience as star-maker was far from agreeable. In Ralston's autobiography *Some Day We'll Laugh*, published in 1985 (six years after Arzner's death), the actress describes her relationship with Arzner on the set of *Old Ironsides* as "friendly and courteous." But once they worked together as director and star, problems arose. Ralston attributes tensions on the set of *Fashions for Women* to Arzner's desire to make scenes that were more sexually explicit than Ralston would have liked. Ralston also alleges that, on the set of *Ten Modern Commandments*, yet another problem arose, in that she was the object of unwanted attentions by Arzner: " . . . with Arzner trying to get me to sit on her lap between takes and insisting on patting and fondling me, I began to freeze up and resent her at-

Figure 14. Dorothy Arzner and Esther Ralston, 1927. MOMA Film Stills Archive.

tentions."[7] In addition, Ralston claims, Arzner took sadistic pleasure in making her do an excessive number of takes of a particularly difficult scene in which the heroine attempts to choke the prima donna Broadway star while a number of exhibitors were watching. "I could just see Arzner chuckling and saying to herself, 'Okay, miss smarty pants, swell-headed new star, here's where we find out who's the boss on this set.' "[8]

After the humiliating experience on the set of *Ten Modern Commandments*, Ralston claims, "I went back to New York and had a long talk with [producer] Jesse Lasky about Arzner, and I never had to do another film with her again."[9] Paramount had indeed intended to feature Ralston in an Arzner-directed film, *The Glory Girl* (later released as *Figures Don't Lie*), but the project was turned over to Edward Sutherland.[10] It is, of course, impossible to validate or to deny Ralston's claims. It is equally impossible to gauge how much Ralston benefited, or did not, from her insistence that Arzner not direct her again. This much *is* certain: Ralston's career did not take off; she was a popular actress, but she never achieved the kind of stardom anticipated for her.

Arzner was more discreet in her references to difficult actresses. Several times during her career (the first in 1929), Arzner referred to the fact that

Figure 15. Dorothy Arzner and Esther Ralston, 1927. Arts Library—Special Collections, University Research Library, UCLA.

women made her life more difficult in Hollywood than men did. Specifically of actresses, and most likely Ralston, Arzner said: "On some occasions I have detected a certain antagonism in the women I was directing, but I believe this was due to the fact that a woman director was a novelty."[11]

More crucially, Ralston's claims raise once again the question of lesbianism, of how influential it was on Arzner's work on the set, and of how extensively and publicly Arzner was regarded as a lesbian. That Arzner dressed in butch style was noted, sometimes directly and sometimes indirectly, in a variety of articles about her (see chapter 8). Frequently her style was explained away as the required disguise for a woman in a man's world. The failure to distinguish between "dressing like a man" (in order to "make it" in a man's world) and "dressing butch" (in order to make a statement in a lesbian world, or to make a lesbian statement in a "man's world") may lead to an assumption that "clothes make the man," and that, therefore, Arzner probably exhibited the sexually harassing behavior for which males in Hollywood are notorious.

Photographs (many of which are reproduced in this book) imply that not all of Arzner's relationships with actresses were as inharmonious as that with

Ralston. Often there *is* a lesbian suggestiveness in the interaction captured in photographs between Arzner and her actresses, especially in the looks that are exchanged between them. Regardless, in the situation with Ralston, given Arzner's tenuous position as that rarity—a female director—it seems unlikely that she would make her directorial debut by harassing her female star. What seems more likely is that *any* attention on Arzner's part would be interpreted as a sexual advance, particularly by the legions of women (and men) who imagine all lesbians as predatory.

Additionally, of course, there is the factor of potential rivalry, both between competing actresses and between actress and director. Arzner may have been relieved of any directorial duties vis-à-vis Ralston, but she went on to direct one of Ralston's rivals, Clara Bow, who had a much more successful screen career than Ralston. As coincidence would have it, one of the more striking images evoked in Ralston's memories of Arzner—the director's attempt to persuade the actress to sit on her lap—is replicated in a publicity photograph of Arzner and Clara Bow, whose collaboration did not provoke any bitterness on either the actress's or the director's part. It is possible that, later in life, when Ralston wrote her autobiography, she felt a bit envious about Bow's more successful collaboration with Arzner, as well as her more successful career in general. Another possible source for Ralston's feelings about Arzner, is that, despite the positive reviews for Ralston in *Fashions for Women* and *Ten Modern Commandments*, Arzner consistently received "star" billing in the press due to her unusual role as Paramount's first woman director.

At the very least, however, Ralston's account suggests not only that Arzner was known as a lesbian, but also (to make an obvious point) that her presumed sexual identity posed a threat to some. Yet curiously, Arzner's supposedly hostile and unsolicited flirtatious behavior towards Ralston occurred at the very same time that Arzner was forging what would become a lifelong relationship with Marion Morgan. Morgan was responsible for both the fashion shows in *Fashions for Women* (the film's highlight, according to several reviewers) and the choreography in *Ten Modern Commandments*. Morgan was frequently on the set of the very pictures where Ralston claims she was receiving unwanted attentions from Arzner.

Like Dorothy, Marion Morgan was a modern woman, although the path she followed began quite differently. Morgan was at least ten years older than Arzner, and she had been married and had a son. Morgan was drawn to the film industry, not to pursue a career as a director or an actress, but rather to extend her already successful career as head and founder of the Marion Morgan Dancers, a troupe which performed interpretive dances, usually based on themes drawn from classical legend and antiquity. A 1919 performance, for instance, depicts Attila and the Huns as they battle and pillage their way through Italy. A Milwaukee reviewer described the performance as "quite the most beau-

Figure 16. Dorothy Arzner and Marion Morgan, ca. 1927. Arts Library—
Special Collections, University Research Library, UCLA.

tiful thing of the year," and provides this description of the first scene of the performance in which a princess dances with her maidens: "The bared limbs of the dancers look as if modeled in marble while the fluttering diaphanous draperies float gracefully around them."[12]

Like Arzner, Morgan was a California native. She was a physical education instructor at the Manual Arts High School in Los Angeles, and in 1910 she began directing dance programs during the summer school of the University of California at Berkeley. Her dance troupe was composed of former female students, all of them Californians. The Marion Morgan Dancers appeared on the vaudeville stage for a decade, from 1916 to the mid-1920s, touring throughout the United States. Morgan also established her own dance school, offering instruction in "Greek, Interpretive, Egyptian, Oriental, Character and Dramatic" dance.[13]

Elizabeth Kendall has suggested that interpretive dance and the early movies shared a close relationship: "In California in the teens, dance and movies were especially close. They looked alike; they favored the same antique costumes and mannerisms, and they shared some performers." Furthermore, dance, like the cinema, offered not only new images, but new conceptualizations of the human body. As Kendall says, "dance was technology too, a re-thinking of the human anatomy in terms of modern rhythms."[14] Marion Morgan's dancers began working in Hollywood in the mid-1920s, at a time when, in response to renewed interest in dance, films regularly incorporated dance numbers. A 1926 article in the *Los Angeles Sunday Times* noted that a "new popular wave" of dance had hit the movies, and that Marion Morgan was being kept busy "rushing from one picture to another, inserting dance sequences."[15] The Marion Morgan Dancers appear as participants in a "Bacchanalian Revel" in *Don Juan* (1926), a café production number in *Up in Mabel's Room* (1926), a "Moorish Bacchanalian Orgy" in *A Night of Love* (1926), and an "Indian Jazz Ballet" in *The Masked Woman* (1926).[16]

The elaborate staging and costuming central to Morgan's dances characterized her creative endeavors for the cinema. Morgan worked on Arzner's first four films. In addition to the fashion show in *Fashions for Women* and the choreography for *Ten Modern Commandments*, Morgan designed a series of waxworks tableaux for *Get Your Man* and choreographed scenes in *Manhattan Cocktail*. William Kaplan, assistant director on *Fashions for Women*, confirmed the collaborative relationship between Arzner and Morgan: " . . . she had Marion Morgan to help her with the fashion show. . . . "[17] With the advent of sound, however, Morgan's film career, insofar as dance and choreography are concerned, ended. How much this abrupt end was due to personal choice, how much due to changes in the film industry, is unclear. While the development of sound film offered many opportunities for dancers, the kind of dancing Morgan represented—interpretive, modern dance with an emphasis on pantomime and tableaux—was more compatible with the silent era of filmmaking. In 1930, Marion and Dorothy moved into a spacious, elegant home in the Hollywood Hills. They were companions until Marion's death in 1971. Since Morgan's dance troupe apparently disbanded at around the same time she moved in with Arzner, it would appear that Morgan's subsequent activities—extensive travel in Europe and graduate education—were made possible by Arzner's financial successes.[18]

The facts of Arzner's relationship with Marion Morgan cannot prove or disprove the interactions that occurred between Arzner and other women. However, the existence of this relationship does dispel a common misconception about Arzner. Arzner was often depicted in the popular press as a woman for whom career came first. While she was certainly devoted to her career, she insisted that the film industry was never her sole focus or interest. Because Arzner never married a man, it was far too convenient to assume that she had no personal life to speak of. But of course she had: the problem was that her personal life was unspeakable in conventional terms. Recognition of the signi-

Figure 17. Dorothy Arzner with the Marion Morgan Dancers, on the set of *Ten Modern Commandments*, 1927. Arts Library—Special Collections, University Research Library, UCLA.

ficance of Dorothy and Marion's relationship can thus challenge not only homophobia, but also the tendency to assume that women with successful careers necessarily sacrifice any other satisfactions.

The spirit of collaboration so central to Arzner's career as a film director was nourished also by her relationship with Marion Morgan. Arzner's often-praised abilities as a star-maker and as an expert editor were enormously important, but so were other abilities that are less often acknowledged, like her use of mise-en-scène and choreography, abilities directly influenced by her collaboration with Morgan. Costuming, staging, and performance are central motifs, technically and thematically, in Arzner's films. I am suggesting, of course, that the real-life relationship was built in part on shared passions and interests that spilled over into Arzner's films. Dance, in particular, has a privileged status in some of Arzner's films, particularly in *Dance, Girl, Dance* (1940). Informed by the life-long collaboration between the filmmaker and the dancer, the exploration of relationships among women through different kinds of dance in this, arguably Arzner's most successful film, also makes it her most personal

Figure 18. On the set of *Manhattan Cocktail* (1928), (from left) Georges Bruggeman, Marion Morgan, and Dorothy Arzner. Arts Library—Special Collections, University Research Library, UCLA.

one. Dance is a vital connection between Arzner's life and her work, a connection through which the desires and conflicts of female communities are experienced.

It has always been tempting to attribute some of Arzner's success as a star-maker to her affinity with her women stars. Arzner and Morgan's collaboration suggests a more precise basis to that affinity, one based on female creativity as manifested in dance and fashion, on the one hand, and film, on the other. It is too easy, and too simplistic, I believe, to regard the development of images of women in Hollywood by image-makers like Arzner purely in terms of the increasing, and increasingly monolithic, objectification of women. To be sure, it is important to recognize how thoroughly the history of Hollywood cinema has been shaped by patriarchal assumptions and sexist practices. But it is equally important to recognize that those assumptions and practices are not absolute. Arzner's career in Hollywood, particularly through her collaborations with a variety of women artists, suggests a perspective on women's relationship to the classical cinema that challenges any monolithic definition of man as subject, woman as object, now from the vantage point of women who actually *did* contribute actively to the film medium.

Arzner's and Morgan's collaboration continued through two more features. As with the fashion show in *Fashions for Women*, Marion Morgan's waxwork-museum tableaux (featuring her dancers) in Arzner's next picture, *Get Your Man* (starring Clara Bow), received particular praise. According to the *Variety* reviewer, the waxworks tableaux were the highlights of the film.[19] Bow plays Nancy, a young American in Paris who keeps encountering a young man (Robert) at various sites, including the wax museum, where they are locked in and forced to spend the night. In the morning, Robert tells Nancy that he is engaged to be married, and that the wedding will take place that week. Nancy moves quickly to fake a car accident in order to enter the home of Robert's fiancée; after a series of adventures, she wins him away from her rival.

Get Your Man was well received. Arzner's association with Clara Bow was productive for both actor and director, and so respected was Arzner's work that she was entrusted with directing Bow in her first talking film— *The Wild Party*. Before making the transition to talking pictures, however, Arzner directed one final picture that belongs to the transitional period from silent to sound film. *Manhattan Cocktail* (1928) contained no dialogue, but did include synchronized score and vocal performances by the star, Nancy Carroll. Marion Morgan choreographed and staged the opening prologue in which the tale of Theseus and Ariadne is recreated. (Theseus enlists as one of a group of youths to be sacrificed to the Minotaur; he marks his passage with a thread, kills the monster, and returns to flee with his beloved Ariadne.) Theseus and Ariadne are represented by Fred (Richard Arlen) and Babs (Nancy Carroll); the Minotaur, by the Broadway monster they escape. Along with their friend Bob (Danny O'Shea), they embark on Broadway careers after their graduation from college. Renov, an evil Broadway producer, complicates their plans, and Fred and Babs leave the stage for a presumably happy life as a married couple.

The Wild Party marks a new stage in Arzner's career. Its success confirmed her reputation as a competent and resourceful director, as well as a "starmaker." Clara Bow was Paramount's most valuable commodity (in every sense of the word), and the fact that Arzner was entrusted with the direction of her first sound film was indicative of the respect she commanded. Also in *The Wild Party*, one sees evidence of the preoccupations evidenced in *The Red Kimono*—

Figure 19. Clara Bow and Dorothy Arzner, 1929. Arts Library—Special Collections, University Research Library, UCLA.

female communities and female bonding—as well as a number of touches that would become important to Arzner's later work (see chapter 7 for a detailed discussion of the film). Although Arzner is best known for her work with female stars, *The Wild Party* demonstrates that she was no slouch insofar as male actors are concerned. For the part of Gil, Arzner cast Fredric March in one of his first leading film roles after a successful career on the New York stage. March went on to be featured as the male lead in three more Arzner films.

The film received mixed reviews. *The Wild Party* was regarded as rather inconsequential fluff, but of course the film had been conceived as little more than a star vehicle for Clara Bow. Arzner still received attention as virtually the only woman director in Hollywood, but understandably, reviews of the film were much more concerned with Clara Bow's first talking role. While one re-

Figure 20. Dorothy Arzner and Clara Bow, 1929. Arts Library—Special Collections, University Research Library, UCLA.

viewer spoke of Bow's voice as a "smooth contralto, vigorous and natural," another pointedly remarked that while her voice was "fairly clear," it nonetheless had "a harsh tonal quality that is not very easy on sensitive eardrums."[20] Arzner's direction was still commented upon, and one assessment waxes as enthusiastic about her as ever:

> The feminine Columbus has just made one of the most important discoveries of the year—a revelation which will prove more interesting to millions of people the world over than would the finding of a new comet with a tail 90,000,000 miles long.
>
> For this woman, Dorothy Arzner, has discovered a new star in Hollywood!
>
> She has disclosed that Clara Bow, fiery red-haired star of the silversheet, is an even greater stellar light in talking pictures than she was on the silent screen.[21]

As was typical for Arzner by this point in her career, her direction of her actors garnered her particular praise: " . . . Dorothy Arzner has made it thoroughly entertaining and has smoothed out the spots in the story which have a distasteful scenario smack. Besides this she has taken care of Clara Bow to the star's own advantage."[22]

Although recognition of Arzner's success with actors certainly helped her career, the resourcefulness she first exhibited in *Blood and Sand* (with her use of stock footage) also surfaced in *The Wild Party* and this factor, too, was important to her career. For example, Bow was terrified of her first sound performance, and in order to make her movements on the set more natural, Arzner devised what is reputed to be the first fishpole microphone to allow flexibility of placement. Whether in the form of facilitating the speed of production, bringing films in under budget, "smoothing out spots in the story," or highlighting the unique abilities of her actors, Arzner was an enterprising director, always committed to getting the job done. Constantly singled out as the only woman director, Arzner needed to prove her competence, and competence was far more important than brilliance or originality in making her career possible.

While I think an early screenplay—such as *The Red Kimono*—is far more indicative than some of Arzner's earliest directorial efforts of the particular female signature she would bring to her later work, nonetheless her preoccupations with female communities and female connections would never have found their way to the screen had Arzner not proven herself in the cutting room. Her remarkable ability to learn virtually every stage of film production was essential to her success as a "modern girl," seeking a career and financial independence.

Like film critics in Arzner's time, contemporary feminist critics have brought particular attention to Arzner's role as a star-maker of female actors.[23] Yet, just as this single aspect of Arzner's career provided an inadequate explanation for Arzner's success in practical terms, so, too, can it be too easily fetishized in theoretical terms. It is, perhaps, tempting to reverse the popular cliché of the male director as Svengali, the female star as Trilby, and therefore to assess Arzner's career as director largely through her work with actresses. Esther Ralston's accusations, in this context, are one extreme, and extremely negative, view of the female Svengali; the other extreme consists of the more sympathetic, largely feminist accounts of Arzner's subversion of the gender dichotomy of Hollywood. I think that it is a mistake to overemphasize Arzner's role as star-maker, and too easy to focus on one relationship—actor and director— as the unique or even primary basis of Arzner's directorial career. Relationships with women functioned in a complex way at virtually every stage of the production of Arzner's films—from her close collaboration with the writer, to her first-hand knowledge of the editing room, to her collaboration with Marion Morgan.

This certainly is not to diminish Arzner's reputation as a star-maker, but rather to resist the reduction of Arzner's career to this one factor. It is interesting to compare her developing career with those of Esther Ralston and Clara Bow, the two actresses with whom Arzner was paired more than once during her first directorial efforts in Hollywood. It was reported that when Arzner first visited William DeMille and informed him that she wanted to work in motion pictures, he asked to see her profile, thinking, of course, that any young woman who wanted to work in motion pictures wanted to be an actress. While Arzner's work as a director situated her behind the scenes, she nonetheless managed to strike poses in her directorial role, suggesting that performance was indeed part of her career. But there is little in Arzner's life to suggest that an acting career was ever one of her dreams, even though play-acting and dress-up seem to have been a part of her youthful repertoire.

For Esther Ralston and Clara Bow, however, such dreams were very much a part of their formative years: Ralston because she grew up in a family theatrical troupe, and Bow because she sought escape in motion pictures from a childhood of poverty and suffering.[24] Both Ralston and Bow were from poor, struggling families, and the sudden wealth afforded them due to their Hollywood careers was overwhelming. On one level, then, the aspirations of director for Arzner, and actress for Ralston and Bow, demonstrate the different effects of class privilege. Even more important, the intersection of these three women's lives in Hollywood is suggestive of the complicated ways that the American cinema of the time responded to the ambitions of women.

In different ways, these three women embodied myths of modernity for women, an image most strikingly conveyed in Clara Bow's famous incarnation as the "It" girl, the woman with sex appeal, for whom the pleasures of sexual conquest are just as tantalizing as they are for men. While Ralston's roles were more conventional, she too embodied modernity, in the sense that a Hollywood career gave her (as it gave Bow) financial success that far surpassed anything dreamed of by the conventional male breadwinners in their families. As modern women, however, both Bow and Ralston suffered the contradictions of their modernity, largely through a series of exploitative and generally disastrous relationships with men (where financial and romantic intrigues were inevitably entwined).[25] Like Bow and Ralston, Arzner was "modern" through her career and her financial success. For Dorothy, however, it would not appear that being a breadwinner provoked any crises; rather, the contradictions of modernity for her came from spending the majority of her adult life in a committed relationship that didn't happen to be a heterosexual marriage.

Arzner's role as "star-maker" vis-à-vis Ralston and Bow thus conceals a number of other factors having to do with social class and with the contradictory elements of modernity for women. While neither Ralston nor Bow had entirely successful careers in the sound era, Arzner thrived, and she was soon entrusted with the direction of yet another female star, who brought to Hollywood sound films experience on the Broadway stage—Ruth Chatterton.

After the success of *The Wild Party* (1929), Arzner's career reached its highest point, at least insofar as the respect and power afforded her were concerned.

Figure 21. Dorothy Arzner, ca. 1929. Arts Library—Special Collections, University Research Library, UCLA.

Two feature films appeared in 1930, *Sarah and Son* and *Anybody's Woman*, both starring Chatterton. While *Sarah and Son* was not Chatterton's first starring film (she shared star billing with Fredric March, who was appearing in his second film for Dorothy), and although in her two years in Hollywood she had appeared in successful films (for example, *Madame X*), under Arzner's direction she achieved wide acclaim.

Arzner's work with Chatterton carried on the tradition she had already established in her brief directorial career: the ability to work well with actresses. In addition, a new form of collaboration was born with *Sarah and Son* and

Figure 22. Dorothy Arzner and Ruth Chatterton, 1930. Arts Library—Special Collections, University Research Library, UCLA.

Anybody's Woman, for these were the first collaborations between Arzner and writer Zoë Akins. Arzner insisted throughout her career on the importance of the screenwriter: "No director will have a good script or a good picture unless he has a good writer. I bow to a writer at all times. In fact, I have tried to always keep a writer on the set with me. That's how much respect I have for them."[26] Zoë Akins provided the most sustained example of what the collaboration between director and writer could accomplish.

Akins had achieved acclaim as a playwright, beginning with *Déclassée* (1919), which was produced in New York and starred Ethel Barrymore. Akins was a prolific author; adaptation of her plays to the screen began in 1924. A native of Missouri, Akins moved to California in 1928, and by 1930 she was under contract to Paramount, and the collaboration with Arzner began. Their collaboration was conceived by Paramount in order to showcase Ruth Chatterton—four of Akins's first five screenplays were written expressly for Chatterton, and Arzner, of course, was entrusted to bring her developing skills as a star-maker to Chatterton's career. Akins's enduring collaboration with Arzner produced not only *Sarah and Son* and *Anybody's Woman*, but the screenplays for *Working Girls* (1931) and *Christopher Strong* (1933). The other director with whom Akins sustained a collaborative relationship was George Cukor, especially when Akins moved to MGM in the mid-1930s. Akins's work with Cukor includes *Camille* (1936), arguably her greatest Hollywood success in terms of box office and critical reception. Additionally, some of Akins's plays were adapted by others to the screen and have become classics, such as *Morning Glory* (1933), for which Katharine Hepburn won her first Academy Award, and *The Old Maid* (1939), featuring Bette Davis and Miriam Hopkins.[27] That Akins worked so well with two gay directors may well be a matter of coincidence.[28] As we shall see, Arzner's and Cukor's paths crossed more than once during their respective careers. In the Arzner-Akins collaboration, a strong attention to women's lives and women's friendships made for a strong bond between the director and the writer.

Sarah and Son is a wrenching, melodramatic tale of mother love. Chatterton plays a German immigrant who works as a domestic in New York and performs a vaudeville act with an ex-truck-driver. She had hoped to bring her younger sister to the United States, but in the midst of a performance she receives a telegram announcing that the sister has died. In her grief, she marries her vaudeville partner, who turns out to be a cad. He abandons her, enlists in the Marines, and in retaliation against his wife's criticisms of him, gives up their son for adoption by a wealthy couple.

Sarah continues to perform, now with an ex-opera-singer. Some time later, the duo are touring hospitals to entertain soldiers, and in one of several extraordinary coincidences typical of the melodramatic genre, who should die before her eyes but her ex-husband. Before dying, he utters the name of the couple to whom he gave their son—Ashmore. Sarah visits the Ashmores and demands her son, but they insist that their son could not possibly be her child. They threaten to have her committed to a mental institution if she persists.

Years pass; Sarah returns to Germany and trains to become an opera singer. She returns to New York to achieve great success, and uses that success to try to find her son. Fredric March plays Howard Vanning, a sympathetic attorney who falls in love with Sarah. As yet another melodramatic coincidence would have it, his sister and her husband are the adoptive parents of Sarah's son. After the Ashmores try to pass off a servant's child as their adopted son, and Sarah recognizes that the child is not hers (her own son has a distinguishing birthmark), she agrees to go to the country with Howard Vanning. Lo and behold, Bobby, her son, has run away to the very spot, and Sarah and son are reunited.

Sarah and Son was an enormously popular film, and on the whole—with some exceptions made for its excesses and its required suspensions of disbelief—it was critically praised. It made several "ten best films" lists that year, and Arzner was singled out for praise. Many critics saw the role of Sarah as Chatterton's best to date, particularly because of the subtle changes in accent she adopts as she moves from recent immigrant to successful, cosmopolitan opera singer. As with Arzner's previous films, mention was occasionally made of the director's ability to rise above the melodramatic formula. Perhaps most significant, *Sarah and Son* gave a particular inflection to the notion of "woman director" and the "woman's film." Several critics noted that *Sarah and Son* was made by women: "It is very much a woman's picture—adapted by a woman, Zoë Akins; directed by a woman, Dorothy Arzner; and enacted by a woman. . . . Here is a motion picture which will grip every woman in the audience and hold her in its thrall throughout its length."[29] Or, in the inimitable prose of *Variety*, it was an "all-femme film."[30] Some critics even noted that the editor and the production assistant were women.

Most mentions of the female collaboration at the heart of *Sarah and Son* are positive: "The film is rather a triumph for the women. Dorothy Arzner directed it and Zoë Akins wrote the continuity".[31] Occasionally, however, the female point of view was cause for complaint. Commenting on the conclusion of the film, when Bobby chooses his biological mother over his adoptive one, one critic observed that the film "surrendered to sentiment. . . . For seventy-one of its seventy-three minutes the piece is mature, restrained and believably dramatic. Then it ends on a note of hysteria which I am inclined to blame upon the fact that its continuity was written by a woman, Zoë Akins, and directed by another of the sex, Dorothy Arzner." This critic also notes—perhaps making the first in a long chain of such complaints during Arzner's career—that the men in the film are "spineless," "mere puppets" (thus predating by over forty years Andrew Sarris's comment on the "spectacular spinelessness" of the men in Arzner's films).[32]

That Arzner's position as a female director was unusual and worthy of mention had been a given in reviews of her films. The suggestion was made that as a woman, she was better able to work with female actors, and more capable of understanding the nuances of women-centered dramas. But with *Sarah and Son*, something changes. One observer, after calling Dorothy "the second woman director in celluloid captivity," regards *Sarah and Son* as a major step forward for her:

> I've been waiting and waiting for her break. Not that she didn't direct the baby dolls pretty well, but I could never get hopped up on baby-doll pictures. But at last they have handed her a real story, a bunch of fine dramatic artists, and was Dorothy equal to it? Well, you must see this picture if you would be convinced that a woman can turn out as fine a bit of workmanship as any man. In fact there aren't half a dozen men in the whole caboodle who could have done as well.[33]

The critical reception of *Sarah and Son* is marked by a notion of the woman's film that is both expansive (having to do with virtually every level of the production process, as well as with a "real story") and limited. One suspects that after several noteworthy films to her credit, Arzner was no longer in the position of having to prove herself, at least not to the extent that she was in her earlier silent films or in her first sound film. Is it possible, then, that the very notion of a woman's film, made by, about, and for women, was a way of codifying Arzner, of reconciling her to a notion of business as usual in Hollywood? If Arzner had been previously praised for her ability to rise *above* her material, here she is assumed to be fully of a piece *with* the material.

The reception of *Sarah and Son* also suggests that the dimensions of Arzner's position as a woman director in Hollywood were changing. Interestingly, those changes work in two different ways. On the one hand, the emergence of a woman director and a genre known as the woman's film at approximately the same time provides a safe, stereotypical way to channel any challenge that Arzner might represent, whether as a woman—period—or as a woman who did not resemble the Hollywood ideal of femininity. On the other hand, *Sarah and Son* marks the beginning of the kind of complex collaboration that would characterize the best aspects of Arzner's career, that between woman director and woman writer, as well as that between director and actress.

Between her two major releases of 1930, *Sarah and Son* and *Anybody's Woman*, Arzner also directed a segment in Paramount's variety/revue film, *Paramount on Parade*, which featured eleven Paramount directors in charge of a number of skits featuring stars like Clara Bow, Ruth Chatterton, and Maurice Chevalier. The revue format had been used previously by Warner Brothers (*The Show of Shows*) and MGM (*The Hollywood Revue*), and Paramount's was a relatively late entry to the genre. Arzner was in charge of the "Gallows Song" segment in which Dennis King sings "Nichavo" against a gallows background. Additionally, Arzner worked on two films released in 1930 for which she received no directorial credit, but which she completed: *Behind the Makeup* and *Charming Sinners*. With both of these films, Arzner had entered into a collaborative process with stage director Robert Milton, who received official director's credit. For a brief time the two formed a team of producer/director. As Arzner explained their collaboration, "Robert Milton was a fine stage director, but he didn't know the camera's limitations or its expansions. Because I did know the technique so well, I was asked to help him." Noting that she did not receive screen credit, Arzner continues: "I merely helped with the technical work. He directed the performances. I blocked the scenes for camera and editing."[34]

One cannot help but wonder how much this collaboration depended upon Arzner's status as a woman in Hollywood—not to put too fine a point on it, whether a male director would have been so modest about his contributions or so willing to remain an (officially) uncredited part of the production. Such modesty was not new to Arzner; she told how, early in her career, she made the mistake of *not* wanting her name to appear on screen:

> I was so averse to having any comment made about being a woman director, that in my first contract I asked that I didn't even have screen credit on the picture, because I wanted to stand up as a director and not have people make allowances that it was a woman. So I later found that was a great mistake, because my name was lost down with the trademark . . . [35]

To be sure, Arzner's early experience with modesty is not identical to the arrangement made with Robert Milton; by 1930 she was an established director, even if one still singled out by her anomalous status as a woman. However, the collaboration *does* highlight one of the most distinctive aspects of Arzner's career, and one that may well constitute overcompensation on her part, that is, a willingness on her part to accept conditions that might not have been acceptable to her male colleagues. I do not want to overstate the argument for such overcompensation, since Arzner's financial independence enabled her to refuse conditions that she found unacceptable—something she did only two years after the collaboration with Milton, as we shall see. Yet at the same time, Arzner did not want to be identified as a "woman director," and this sometimes led her to make excessive compromises, such as the above mentioned refusal to allow screen credit.

As the collaboration with Milton suggests, Arzner was known not only for the resourcefulness mentioned previously, but also and especially for her ability to take over difficult projects and to carry them through to completion. This ability did not always work to her advantage; she may have completed *Nana* (taking over direction from George Fitzmaurice and basically restructuring the entire film), but the film was not the success that producer Sam Goldwyn had anticipated. *Dance, Girl, Dance* was also a film project that had already begun when Arzner was brought in as director; in that case, though, the ability to rethink and refashion a project initially conceived by another led to a film that may not have been a success at its time of release, but which is rightly lauded today as Arzner's most original contribution to the screen.

Arzner's next solo project was *Anybody's Woman*, also starring Chatterton and written by Akins. Despite the identical collaborative team, *Anybody's Woman* had more in common with Arzner's earlier directorial efforts than with *Sarah and Son*. Clive Brook plays Neil Dunlap, a lawyer whose wife leaves him to marry a wealthier man. He finds that, as the result of a drinking spree, he has unwittingly married an ex-chorus-girl, Pansy Gray, played by Chatterton. Pansy has been fond of Dunlap ever since he successfully defended her against charges of indecent exposure on the stage. They move to his home town, and she is mocked and snubbed by his well-to-do friends, with one exception—a man who has earned his wealth the hard way. This friend falls for Pansy, and Dunlap finally realizes his true feelings for his wife. He does so only after believing that she has betrayed him, and the moment of recognition comes from an interesting but forced device—she speaks her true feelings for Dunlap while sitting next to an electric fan, and her voice carries into his room!

Anybody's Woman was not as highly regarded as *Sarah and Son*, but the film was nonetheless a critical and popular success. Chatterton was one of Paramount's most popular stars, and the presence of Clive Brook in this production assured additional popularity. Once again, it was noted that the men in the film are weak. "The story," one critic noted, "has distinct feminine feeling, the men making a poor showing."[36]

Arzner relocated to New York City and Paramount's Long Island studios to direct her next project, *Honor among Lovers*. The film starred Claudette Colbert and Fredric March (in his third film under Arzner's direction, after *The Wild Party* and *Sarah and Son*). March plays Jerry Stafford, a businessman in love with his secretary, Julia Traynor (Colbert). He proposes setting her up in an apartment and taking her on a cruise. She, panicked at the thought that she actually might accept such an arrangement, marries someone else. Arzner is at her best in directing films that play not only on the differences between men and women, but also on class difference; *Honor among Lovers* is no exception, particularly given Julia's position (snobbishly pointed out by several characters in the film) as Jerry's employee. The man she marries turns out to be a louse (as husbands often seem to be in Arzner's films), and he embezzles from one of the accounts that Jerry has entrusted to him.

Julia, desperate, goes to Jerry and offers to take him up on his previous offer if he will cover the funds lost by her husband. Hence, the film plays on repetition and reversal of the illicit affair versus the legitimate marriage. This time, it is Jerry who refuses the offer, but he nonetheless writes the check. The husband, Phil, is suspicious when Julia reports what happened ("He gave me that check and made me feel contemptible for assuming he would accept anything in return"), and in a drunken state he visits Jerry with a gun, intending to shoot him. Jerry talks him out of it, but the gun goes off accidentally and shoots Jerry. Jerry attempts to pass off the gunshot wound as self-inflicted, but the police don't buy it. Phil, when questioned, breaks down and implicates Julia. Eventually, all is set right; Phil is acquitted of any wrongdoing, but he loses Julia, while Julia and Jerry are finally reunited.

Once again, Arzner's direction of the actors was praised—without sarcastic comment about her male characters. *Variety* noted that Arzner brought a welcome comic touch to the material: "Actually no heavy dramatics at any point, it evidently having been Dorothy Arzner's purpose to achieve results more delicately. In this she has been unusually successful, aided no little by excellent dialog and a brilliant cast."[37] Critically and commercially, however, the film was only a mild success.

The same cannot be said for Arzner's final film of 1931, *Working Girls,* which was a financial disaster. The film never had a national release. Once again scripted by Zoë Akins, this was perhaps the most daring and innovative film Arzner ever made, and its virtual invisibility is a shame. If Arzner rarely took bold artistic risks in her films, *Working Girls* may well provide the rationale, since this effort cost Arzner dearly. This is not to suggest that *Working Girls* is a forgotten masterpiece, but rather that it contains, as much or more so than any other single film in Arzner's career, many of the touches that appear scattered throughout her films. (Detailed discussion follows in chapter 5.)

The commercial failure of *Working Girls* was due to a combination of factors. It was not given the kind of publicity that other films directed by Arzner had received, and here there were no famous stars—whether established or rising—to sell the film, something that distinguishes *Working Girls* from virtually every other film made by Arzner up to that stage in her career. Arzner also had to battle with the censors over the film's explicit treatment of pregnancy (and therefore sex) outside of marriage, which, of course, was not particularly welcome by the studio. Nonetheless, why *Working Girls* should have been treated so shabbily by Paramount, when virtually all of Arzner's films had done well by the studio, remains something of a mystery.

With *Merrily We Go to Hell* (1932), Arzner returns to a comedy of the couple not too different from *Honor among Lovers.* Fredric March and Sylvia Sidney star in a cynical romantic tale based on a best-selling novel, *I, Jerry, Take Thee, Joan,* by Cleo Lucas, adapted for the screen by Edwin Justus Mayer. Jerry (March) is an alcoholic writer, and Joan (Sidney) is a wealthy, yet innocent, socialite; they meet when Jerry's corkscrew lands on Joan's head at a party. Despite Jerry's alcoholism and his continuing obsession with a former love, Claire, Joan falls madly in love with him, and they marry against her father's wishes. Jerry has a play produced, and Claire stars in it, provoking Joan's jealousy and subsequent departure from Jerry. Jerry gives up his drinking, but he is reunited

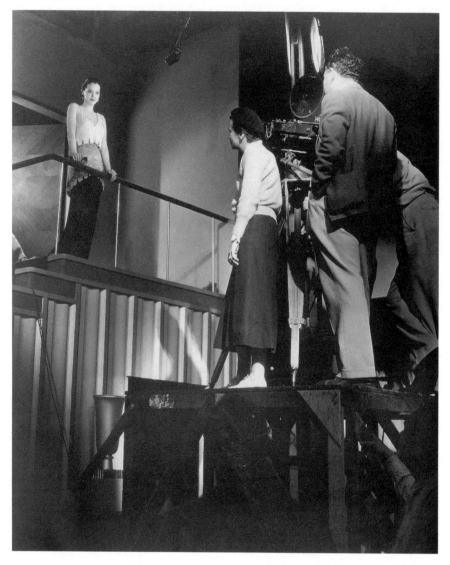

Figure 23. Sylvia Sidney and Dorothy Arzner on the set of *Merrily We Go to Hell*, 1932. MOMA Film Stills Archive.

with Joan only after she gives birth to their child, who dies. Jerry joins her at the hospital—barging past Joan's father—and in one of the more ironic conclusions to any of Arzner's romances, Joan calls Jerry her "baby."[38] (The ending echoes *The Wild Party*, where Fredric March and Clara Bow are reunited, with Bow's Stella embracing her professor and calling him "my savage.")

Merrily We Go to Hell received mixed reviews, and exceptionally in this case, when the actors' work is praised, it is despite Arzner's direction, not because of it. As one critic noted of Sidney's and March's performances, "their sincere attempts at characteristics are something more than plot, dialogue, continuity or direction deserve."[39] Yet one thing remained constant in reviews of this film, as with all of Arzner's previous ones: a preoccupation with the very fact that it was directed by a woman. One critic, who found the film close to disastrous, was perplexed by its director. "If this is an example of the highly vaunted 'woman's touch' in the movies," he writes, "what the feminine fans demand is wilder parties and heavier drinking."[40] In what may well be the only wildly enthusiastic review of the film, one critic notes that it represents a project with "plenty of meat" in it, in sharp contrast to Arzner's previous films:

> When one considers the high quality of the women novelists in this country, one is astonished that there have been no more women motion picture direc-tors. But one is forced to admit that a dainty flavor of fudge and cucumber sandwiches hitherto has marked the offerings of Miss Arzner, the industry's lone woman megaphone wielder. Often her pictures were entertaining, but usually they were self-consciously womanly."[41]

These opposing viewpoints illustrate the gender paradox in which Arzner was caught. For whether her films were too "self-consciously womanly" or not quite womanly enough, they were judged in terms their "directed by a *woman*" status.

However mixed the reviews, *Merrily We Go to Hell* was a genuine box office success—one of the most financially successful films of the year. *Merrily We Go to Hell* ran into some problems with the censors—first, the Hays office objected to the title, and then, in Ohio (and perhaps elsewhere) certain scenes were cut. Interestingly, the public objected to the censorship, and the cut scenes were restored. *Merrily We Go to Hell* was Arzner's last film for Paramount Studios.

Although her contract was renewed in March of 1931, Arzner refused the following year to accept a pay cut that was demanded of Paramount person-nel.[42] Paramount underwent a major reorganization in the early 1930s, and the man who had been responsible for Arzner's first contract as a director, B. P. Schulberg, ended his career as head of production in 1932. It is difficult to say with certainty how much Arzner's decision to leave the studio had to do with the cooler reception afforded her films—especially *Working Girls*—in her last years there. Once again, however, the fact that Arzner had an independent in-come meant that she had the freedom to leave the studio. It also meant that, whatever her reasons for leaving Paramount, money would likely have been the least of them. Regardless, 1932 marks the beginning of Arzner's career as a megaphone for hire.

3

The Independent

IN THE YEARS following Arzner's departure from Paramount, she directed fewer films. While under contract to Paramount, in the space of six years (from 1926 to 1932), she directed ten films, in addition to her segment in *Paramount on Parade* and the films she completed for other directors. In contrast, in the remaining ten years she spent as a director, she had six films to her credit, one of which (*First Comes Courage*) was completed by another director. After leaving Paramount, she worked on an independent basis, and her next film assignment was to direct Katharine Hepburn in *Christopher Strong*, an RKO film initially produced by David Selznick and then assigned to Pandro Berman. Once again Arzner worked with Zoë Akins on the script, adapted from a popular British novel by Gilbert Frankau.

It is hard to imagine few pairings more logical, and more enticing, than Arzner and Hepburn. Both women represent spirits of independence, and, in different but related ways, their personae departed sharply from the stereotypical views of femininity typical of Hollywood. But discussions of their relationship, most of them from biographies of Katharine Hepburn, suggest that they did not get along. Sheridan Morley writes that "Arzner disliked the way that Hepburn would always be speaking up for the 'little people' on the set against her often autocratic and very demanding way of working."[1] Anne Edwards describes a "competitive rivalry" between Arzner and Hepburn, one exacerbated by Zoë Akins's participation on the film ("Zoë Akins represented everything nouveau riche that Kate hated").[2] Gary Carey reports that Hepburn looked forward to making a film with a woman director, "but the making of the film turned out to be an unpleasant experience."[3] According to Michael Freedland, Arzner and Hepburn did not get along, and the "result showed in the film."[4]

Charles Higham, who offers the most detailed description of the encounter between the two women, says of the collaboration, "For Arzner, making the picture was a challenge. As a woman in a man's business, she dared not have any failures; she would have been 'let out of the club.' This made her directing of the film purposeful and grim; she took little or no time getting to know Kate on a personal level; they didn't really hit it off."[5] Arzner supposedly complained to Selznick that Hepburn attempted to interfere with her direction. Some problems during the production of the film were far beyond the control

Figure 24. Dorothy Arzner, 1933. Arts Library—Special Collections, University Research Library, UCLA.

of director or star. Akins's husband was quite ill at that time, leaving Akins distracted; and Hepburn came down with influenza.[6]

However Arzner and Hepburn might have felt about each other personally and professionally, *Christopher Strong* was an important, vital contribution to the development of Hepburn's screen persona. In her autobiography, *Me*, Hepburn speaks more positively about her work with Arzner than her biographers have: "Dorothy was very well known and had directed a number of hit pictures. She wore pants. So did I. We had a good time working together."[7] Nonetheless, the fact that neither actress nor director was eager to work with the other again suggests that this was not a collaboration made in heaven. Arzner had the opportunity to direct *Morning Glory*, scripted by Zoë Akins and starring Hepburn, but she turned it down. As much as one would like to imagine an ideal collaboration between Hepburn and Arzner, the actress found that working with gay male director George Cukor offered her the most sustained and successful collaboration of her career.

Christopher Strong was Hepburn's second film, and her first star billing (see chapter 6 for a discussion of the film). Her first film had been *A Bill of Divorcement* (1932), directed by Cukor, and she worked with Cukor again in *Little Women* (1933), *Sylvia Scarlett* (1936), *Holiday* (1938), *The Philadelphia Story* (1940), *Keeper of the Flame* (1942), *Adam's Rib* (1949), and *Pat and Mike* (1952). Cukor and Hepburn's collaboration was one of the most successful between star and director in Hollywood history, and Cukor's direction provided an ideal showcase for the Hepburn persona. These facts seem to me less interesting for what they say about the relative worth of *Christopher Strong* than for what they suggest about the status of gay and lesbian directors in Hollywood, specifically, and the influence of gay and/or lesbian sensibilities on Hollywood, more generally.

The classification of Cukor as a "woman's director" was a homophobic (and sexist) way of denigrating his enormous talent. Nonetheless, the description of Cukor as a "woman's director" describes an affinity between director and star which, when read "against the grain," suggests how vital gay sensibilities—the fluidity of gender roles, the importance of costume and performance, the centrality of style—have been to the development of Hollywood cinema. But are "gay sensibilities" the same, or even similar to, "lesbian sensibilities?" It is interesting in this context that any notion of a lesbian presence in Hollywood tends to follow the classic gender divisions of performance, and usually is discussed only when actresses like Dietrich or Garbo or Hepburn, who have ambiguous sexual personae, appear in scenes with explicit lesbian connotations (the famous kissing scenes in *Morocco*, *Queen Christina*, and *Sylvia Scarlett*, respectively).

On the other hand, gay readings and gay sensibilities are much more expansive, and are not limited to literal onscreen depictions of gayness: Cukor is just as important to the gay male history of Hollywood as Rock Hudson; James Whale is just as important as William Haines—and Haines's career as a decorator was more easily readable in gay terms than his career as an actor, thus proving the point. There is, I believe, much more willingness to associate the gay male presence in Hollywood with a style and an attitude, and to be much more restrictive when it comes to lesbians, as the examples mentioned above, all very literal representations of lesbianism, illustrate. One of the important features of Arzner's career is the way lesbianism affects her films in diffuse ways. There are no lesbian plots, no lesbian characters in her films; but there is constant and deliberate attention to how women dress and act and perform, as much for each other as for the male figures in their lives.

The differing connotations of "woman's director" as applied to Arzner and Cukor are also instructive. In Cukor's case the term was a code for "homosexual," clear enough to those who understood it and innocent for those who chose not to. But for Arzner, being known as a "woman's director" meant a multitude of things, from her own gender, to the failures and/or successes of her films, to her treatment of male characters, to her compatibility with actresses. Describing her as a "woman's director" could hardly be read as code, at least not in any direct sense. If anything, the term functioned as much to repress lesbian implications about her as to suggest them, since by emphasizing over and over again that she was a *woman* director, the fact that she might be something else *besides* a woman is deemphasized. But at the same time, all of the other "woman's directors" were men, and most of them were gay. Thus, in Arzner's case the label of "woman's director" defined her simultaneously as a woman's director because she was a woman, and a woman's director because she was like other woman's directors, all of whom happened to be male, and most of whom (like Cukor) happened to be gay. Being a woman and a "woman's director" is a little like being a lesbian: one is assumed to be a woman acting like a man acting like a woman.

There has been a tendency in recent writing about gays and lesbians in Hollywood history to adopt a long-standing and, in my view, problematic distinction between the threatening potential of gay men versus lesbians. This distinction assumes an easy division between men and women, and assumes as well that gay men are far more threatening to the Hollywood status quo than lesbians are. In his recent biography of Marlene Dietrich, for instance, in which her love affairs with men and women are detailed, Donald Spoto notes that "it was of course always easier for two women to have social variations on the so-called Boston marriage, which could be interpreted as simply a warm friendship; men, on the other hand, could never be so open, and their careers were jeopardized by even temporal cohabitation."[8] Spoto's assumption that lesbianism offered "easier" alternatives than male homosexuality may be problematic, but at least he acknowledges lesbians, unlike other recent biographers who speak of "gay Hollywood" as if lesbians simply did not exist. And that is precisely the problem—assumptions tend to be made about lesbians based on ignorance of lesbianism, without considering the extent to which assumptions about gender, as well as sexuality, enter into play.[9]

Arzner's and Cukor's differing relationships with Katharine Hepburn offer the opportunity to consider how "womanly" characteristics—whether of a director or of his/her films—functioned vis-à-vis the relative visibility and invisibility of gay men and lesbians in Hollywood. In Cukor's case, "woman's director" was a fairly easily decipherable code; in Arzner's, it was contradictory and confusing. When a film was overly sentimental, it was because of Arzner's "womanly touch," but when it was appropriately so, then again the "woman's touch" was responsible. In chapter 2, I noted the gender paradox that characterized some reviews of Arzner's films, where male attributes either affirmed her status as a director, or made her suspect as a director. The same paradox holds true for the "womanly" side of the equation. The most explicit reference to possible lesbianism in reviews of Arzner's films occurs via comments on the male characters and her supposed disdain for them, something once again attributed to her "woman's touch."

Cukor's homosexuality may have threatened his status as a Hollywood director, but he was still able to take risks and to make decisions that were available only to men. Patrick McGilligan tells the anecdote of how Cukor astonished Paramount officials by fighting for screen credit in 1932, when he was virtually an unknown director. Cukor left Paramount for RKO after the incident; at about the same time, Dorothy left Paramount, period. In other words, Arzner's position in Hollywood was distinctly different from Cukor's, not because lesbianism was less threatening, but because the status of *any* lesbian in Hollywood is complicated by gender politics.

Consider, for example, director Robert Aldrich's characterization of Arzner's success, recounted in Vito Russo's book *The Celluloid Closet*: " . . . an obviously lesbian director like Dorothy Arzner got away with her lifestyle because she was officially closeted and because 'it made her one of the boys.' "[10] What does it mean to describe Arzner as "one of the boys"? Most obviously, it reflects the assumption that lesbians are women in drag, and that women desire women the same way heterosexual men desire women. And most problematically, it assumes that "one of the boys" is not really a woman, and therefore not treated like a woman in her career. As reviews of Arzner's films amply demonstrate, she was never really one of the boys. And despite Arzner's success in Hollywood and her praise for her co-workers, she too experienced the effects of sexism.[11] Any eagerness to define Dorothy as "one of the boys," for whatever reasons, can offer only a completely distorted view of the obstacles she encountered as a peripheral member of the boys' club. Cukor's membership in that club may have been peripheral as well, but never to the extent that Arzner's was.

There is no single actress (like Hepburn with Cukor) with whom one can identify the quintessence of the collaborative process vis-à-vis Arzner, although her wonderful work with Clara Bow comes close. But a comparison of Cukor and Hepburn's collaboration to Arzner's work with Hepburn *does* put into relief

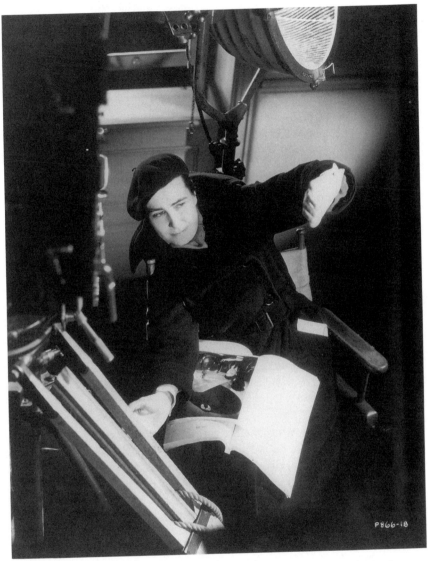

Figure 25. Dorothy Arzner on the set. Arts Library—Special Collections, University Research Library, UCLA.

the extent to which, throughout Arzner's career, the most striking examples of successful collaboration tend to be with those actresses who are more immediately classifiable as "femme"—Clara Bow, Ruth Chatterton, and especially Billie Burke. With Hepburn (and later, Joan Crawford), the meeting of two butches just did not work well. Just as the phrase "woman's director," vis-à-vis

Cukor, alludes to, yet represses, the gay sensibility so important to Hollywood cinema, the same phrase, applied to Arzner, alludes to and represses the importance of contrasts and connections between women, by implying that all women are the same. I have already mentioned how important the "lesbian continuum" is to an understanding of Arzner's career in Hollywood, and the phrase is equally applicable to Arzner's collaboration with actresses. Among lesbians, the styles of butch and femme play on the various performative qualities of gender and sexuality, and in Arzner's films, such qualities extend to a complex and dynamic interrogation of relationships between and among women.[12]

During the changes in Dorothy's film career—from Paramount director to independent, and from greater to lesser successes—her relationship with Marion Morgan remained a constant. Their home in the Hollywood Hills remained their base, even though Morgan travelled extensively during the early 1930s. Her letters and postcards to Dorothy during trips abroad are chatty, informative, and affectionate; they illustrate the strong bond between the two women. In the summer of 1933, Marion travelled to Massachusetts, and wrote: "Dear—Someday we must tour these New England towns together—so restful, quaint, and secure. Saw the Plymouth Rock—Love dear—Marion." In that same year, Marion travelled to Austria and the Soviet Union, signing her postcards with translations (often fractured) of "Love" and "I love you" in the language of whatever country she was in, a custom she continued during her trips abroad in 1934 and 1935.

Marion pursued another interest in the early 1930s as well; she graduated from the Yale School of Drama in 1934. At Yale, Marion met and befriended George Brendan Dowell, who remained a life-long friend of both Marion and Dorothy. In collaboration with Dowell, Marion's career entered yet another phase: the duo co-authored two stories, which were the bases of screenplays of two films starring Mae West: *Goin' to Town* (1935) and *Klondike Annie* (1936).

The postcards sent from Marion to Dorothy during her three extended trips (1933, 1934, 1935) provided me with the most detailed picture of their relationship, although it is admittedly a very partial one. Marion wrote regularly to Dorothy, and she alludes to similarly frequent letters from her companion. The connection between the women is evident throughout, whether the context is one of sadness or joy. Marion had suffered the tragic loss of her son, Roderick, and she tells Dorothy she "can rest against [her] when in trouble."[13] While in Vienna in 1935, Marion sent Dorothy a postcard depicting a Tyrolean costume, and refers to an outfit she has gotten for her; "You will be very striking in this! Ich liebe dich."[14] That Dorothy and Marion were connected by a shared passion for art and introspection is evident in the correspondence, but there are also allusions to unnamed conflict and turmoil. Marion concludes one card with the following: "Nothing matters to me now except a raising of consciousness—a gigantic task when one has the human mind to deal with, not only one's own but the onslaught of contacting minds. . . . To give me peace keep up the mental work, it will somehow lead to harmony. We both have a path to travel—I still love you—Marion."[15]

At the very least, Morgan's cards to Arzner give concrete shape to Arzner's own insistence that Hollywood was never her sole and abiding interest, and certainly not the exclusive passion of her life. This is particularly important to remember through the series of film projects that followed the completion of *Christopher Strong*—from *Nana*, to the announcement of jobs that never came to fruition, to the autumn of 1936, when *Craig's Wife* was released. The three-year span from *Christopher Strong* to *Craig's Wife* was a far from satisfying period in Arzner's professional life. By insisting on the relevance of her connection with Marion Morgan, and the interests that they shared, to an assessment of Arzner's career, I am suggesting that the career cannot be understood purely in terms of contracts, completed projects, and reviews. Arzner's own approach to her career as one element of her life challenges any artificial separation of the worlds of personal and professional life. Indeed, if the separation is even remotely applicable to Arzner, it is the former aspect that remained a source of strength, sustenance, and continuity much more than the latter. To some extent, of course, Arzner herself insisted upon the division between work and personal life, but this was a necessary strategy to protect her privacy, not to mention her career.

The apparent stability of her personal life was not reflected in her professional life, then, after the lackluster box office performance of *Christopher Strong*. In 1933, she was hired by United Artists to take over *Nana*, a production that had been beset with difficulties from the beginning. Conceived as a star vehicle for Anna Sten, a Russian actress who had worked in France, and who was groomed by Sam Goldwyn for superstar status à la Dietrich or Garbo, *Nana*'s production was halted when George Fitzmaurice, the original director, was dismissed. Goldwyn then tried to hire George Cukor to direct, and once again Arzner's and Cukor's career paths intersected, if only indirectly. According to Goldwyn's biographer, Goldwyn had some hesitation about Cukor's tendency "to put lace panties on every scene"—about as obvious and homophobic a reference to Cukor's homosexuality as can be imagined. But Cukor refused the offer, much to Goldwyn's irritation, and the producer turned to Arzner, another "woman's director." It would appear that the Hepburn connection was at least partially responsible for the move from Cukor to Arzner, since Arzner had completed *Christopher Strong* at RKO, where Cukor, at the time of Goldwyn's request, was editing *Little Women*.[16]

Despite Arzner's success in advancing the careers of Esther Ralston, Clara

Bow, and Ruth Chatterton, she could not produce the desired effect with Anna Sten. While the film opened to huge crowds in New York City—due largely to the publicity efforts made on Sten's behalf—enthusiasm dwindled quickly, and the film was regarded as something of a dud. Reviews were not uniformly bad, however; some critics praised Sten as living up to her advance publicity. "Mr. Exhibitor—you have been asked for many months now, to 'hail' a new star whom you have not yet seen," begins one advance review. " . . . That star is Anna Sten. We have seen her in her first picture and are of the opinion that you have not been deceived."[17] For once, the actress received consistent top billing in the reviews, rather than the fact that the film was directed by a woman. Given the elaborate build-up by Goldwyn (Sten was called the "Million Dollar Discovery"[18]), this is not surprising; but from another perspective, it is interesting that Dorothy should have been overshadowed in her status as the sole woman director only when such elaborate efforts had been made to promote a female star.

At least Louella O. Parsons, however, mentioned what had become standard commentary about Arzner's direction—her ability to work with women. "As for Dorothy Arzner, in my opinion she is one of the best directors for our women stars. She understands feminine psychology, and that is important."[19]

Feminine psychology notwithstanding, Sten never enjoyed the success that Goldwyn had hoped for. It needs to be stressed, however, that Arzner was asked to intervene in a most difficult situation. While I do not think the film equals Arzner's best efforts, it isn't quite as dreadful as some critics have suggested, and it contains some quintessential Arzner touches—like the emphasis, from the start, on Nana's close relationship with Satin, another prostitute (see chapter 5 for an analysis of the film).

Nana was released in February of 1934, and in October of that year, Arzner achieved yet another distinction: she was signed by Harry Cohn as an associate producer at Columbia Studios. Although Arzner was to begin her producing career with two films, *Maid of Honor* (described as a "typical Arzner yarn with a great woman's role"[20]) and *A Feather in Her Hat*, the projects never materialized under her auspices, and her career as producer really existed only on paper. Yet Columbia signed her to another contract, this time to direct what would be one of Arzner's most successful films, one that made up for some of the disappointments of the early 1930s— *Craig's Wife*.

Based on George Kelly's Pulitzer Prize-winning play, the film had many familiar Arzner elements and provided more evidence of her purported talent with actresses (see chapter 6 for a discussion of the film). The decision to cast Rosalind Russell in the potentially unsympathetic role of the woman who marries for a house rather than a husband reflected Arzner's skill at sizing up the potential of her actresses, and Russell was uniformly praised for her portrayal.

Stardom soon followed. Yet even though Arzner's work with Russell suggests, again, her abiliity to launch actresses' careers, Russell herself did not seem to regard the role as quite so crucial. Indeed, even Arzner acknowledged that Russell only reluctantly accepted the role of such a "meanie" (in Russell's words). In Russell's autobiography, *Life Is a Banquet*, there is no mention of Arzner, and very little mention of *Craig's Wife*. Rather, Russell regards *The Women* as her breakthrough role, even while noting that *Craig's Wife* was her first starring role. In response to the question, "What film do you think made you a star?" Russell replied, "That's easy. *The Women*, made from the Clare Boothe Luce play in 1939."[21] Once again, Arzner's career as a star-maker crosses paths with that of George Cukor, who directed *The Women*.

Although *Craig's Wife* was the only film in which Arzner collaborated with screenwriter Mary McCall, their work together on the film illustrates the emphasis Arzner placed on the writer's input. McCall was under contract to Warner Brothers and was loaned to Columbia to write the screenplay for *Craig's Wife*, largely, she said, because of her reputation for writing dialogue. When she began working with Arzner, she was stunned to discover "that there were directors who felt that writers were part and partners in an enterprise." Together, Arzner and McCall went over the script, discussing every line in detail. McCall described her work with Arzner this way: "She also had the peculiar notion that a writer might be of some use on the set. This was again all quite new to me. At the end of each rehearsal she turned and said 'how was that for you?' and I couldn't believe it."[22]

McCall also described a particular incident on the set of *Craig's Wife* that illustrates Arzner's respect for both the writer and for the collaborative process. "Toward the end of the second day, I decided to crowd my luck; an actor had read a line straight and I thought it was more of a question. Dorothy turned to me and said 'how was that for you?' and I said, 'well I did think it was more of a question than a flat statement.' She said 'say it for me,' and I said it, and she got the actor over and said, 'I think it would be better if you made that line more of a question.' This was the happiest day of my life." So unusual was Arzner's respect for the writer that McCall said, "Dorothy Arzner changed my life."[23]

Craig's Wife marked yet another kind of collaboration in Arzner's career, this time with William Haines. Arzner disagreed with the film's producers on how the set should look, so she and Haines went to the studio after hours and transformed the set. Arzner had insisted in her contract for *Craig's Wife* that she have complete directorial control, but one area in which Harry Cohn, then head of Columbia, objected was in set design. With the assistance of Haines, Arzner adopted a very theatrical, Greek-inspired look for the sets. As a result, the sense of the Craigs' house as a stage on which to perform, rather than a home in which to live, is accentuated. The choice of Haines is interesting, too, for he was well known in the gay community of Hollywood; indeed, Haines's successful acting career had been terminated due to a gay scandal, and afterwards he fashioned for himself a successful second career as an interior decorator.[24]

Craig's Wife was by and large regarded as a "quality" picture. According to Arzner, it was not a huge box office success when it was released, but because it received good reviews, it eventually became a successful film for Columbia. The usual contradictory implications of Arzner's status as a "woman's director" applied; one reviewer praised Arzner for bringing Kelly's "biting" play to the screen "with no feminine softening of the harsh outlines and no sentimentalizing over the characters that make up the domestic drama," while another noted that "it's a woman's picture from start to finish," and still another that "the women will be stirred by it, for it represents a splendid job of depicting one of the most unhappy members of their breed. . . . "[25]

Curiously, a criticism levelled more than once at Arzner's direction was that the adaptation of play to screen was too literal: "The adaptation follows the original rather too closely," said one reviewer; and another: "Perhaps out of respect for Mr. Kelly's fine play, perhaps out of lack of initiative, the film does not strike away definitely enough from stage technic."[26] Arzner herself noted that Kelly did not think her adaptation resembled his play, but evidently the preservation of significant portions of the play was enough to convince many critics that the adaptation was more literal than it actually was.[27] One critic did note a change in focus in Arzner's adaptation: "Whether when the play was first produced a decade ago Mrs. Craig's fanaticism was given a psychopathic aspect, is a matter of question, but Dorothy Arzner's direction of the film version . . . hints at the possibility, and by that hint makes the study the more believable."[28]

After *Craig's Wife*, true to form as a trouper willing to step in to finish projects begun by others, Arzner completed a film that would introduce her to Joan Crawford, *The Last of Mrs. Cheyney* (1937), which was begun by (and credited to) Richard Boleslavsky. This film led to a contract to direct with MGM, which resulted in a single film: *The Bride Wore Red*. If *Craig's Wife* compensated for some of the disappointments of the early 1930s, *The Bride Wore Red* marked the beginning of the end of Arzner's directorial career. Starting with *The Bride Wore Red*, continuing with *Dance, Girl, Dance* (1940), and concluding with *First Comes Courage* (1943), it became increasingly clear that Arzner's directorial philosophy clashed with studio heads and producers. For as committed as Arzner was to collaboration, she also believed that this collaboration had to follow the director's lead.

Initially intended for Luise Rainer, the lead in *The Bride Wore Red* eventually went to Joan Crawford. It is tempting to read the collaboration between

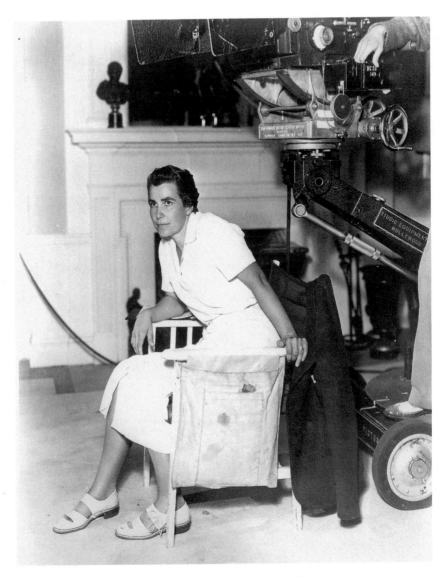

Figure 26. Dorothy Arzner on the set of *Craig's Wife*, 1936. MOMA Film Stills Archive.

the two women positively, particularly given Crawford's admiration for *Craig's Wife* (she starred in a 1950 remake, *Harriet Craig*, which is much more faithful to the spirit of Kelly's original play) and her continuing association with Arzner long after Arzner's Hollywood career had ended (Arzner directed some Pepsi-Cola commercials at Crawford's request in the 1950s). Crawford's own reputa-

Figure 27. John Boles, Dorothy Arzner, and Billie Burke on the set of *Craig's Wife*, 1936. Arts Library—Special Collections, University Research Library, UCLA.

tion as sexually ambivalent (at the very least) would seem to make a perfect match with Dorothy. But the collaboration was not a happy one, according to at least one of Crawford's biographers. Bob Thomas says that "Joan looked forward to working with a woman director, but by the end of filming, Crawford and Arzner communicated only through written messages. . . . "[29]

Figure 28. Dorothy Arzner, ca. 1937. Arts Library—Special Collections, University Research Library, UCLA.

The continuing contact between director and star for more than two decades would suggest that some bond was forged between the two women, although Crawford seemed more eager to maintain the connection than Arzner did. In any case, *The Bride Wore Red* was a bitter disappointment for Arzner, and the experience of working at MGM was none too pleasant, either (see chapter 5 for a discussion of the film). Irving Thalberg had died in 1936, leaving the notorious Louis B. Mayer to define the essence of an MGM picture. Crawford's own career was at a crossroads, and as Alexander Walker points out, Mayer's preference for "wholesomeness, family sanctity, love for one's mother, respect for one's father" did not "enhance or advance Crawford's career."³⁰ Sure enough, *The Bride Wore Red* also proved to be a hindrance to the development of Crawford's career. The film was released in September 1937, and in 1938 Crawford received the dubious distinction of being labeled "box office poison."³¹

If the imprint of Louis B. Mayer on *The Bride Wore Red* was no help to Crawford's career, it was disastrous for Arzner's. Ferenc Molnár's play (*The Girl from Trieste*) was about a prostitute who attempts to leave her profession, only to discover that the members of the respectable social class to which she aspires are far nastier and more malicious than the members of her own. Mayer insisted that the play be rewritten as a Cinderella story, with the prostitute changed to a cabaret singer and a happy ending ensured.³² Arzner believed strongly that the director should make such decisions, but Mayer proved to be more tyrannical than even Harry Cohn at Columbia. Mayer's interference with Arzner's direction is one thing; his hostility toward her after the picture was completed is yet another. Mayer was well-known as a sexist and a homophobe, and in the aforementioned scandal involving William Haines, Haines became a casualty of Mayer's beliefs. Arzner's resistance to Mayer's control, as well as her identities as female and gay, makes the hostility between them seem inevitable.

Many years later, Arzner acknowledged that Mayer had been a significant part of her decision to leave her directing career. She attributes his influence to her refusal to direct scripts that she found inferior:

> He sent me two or three scripts. One had Rosalind Russell playing three parts. It was silly. Then I did 'The Girl from Trieste' which turned out to be synthetic and plastic. I refused to do the next two or three scripts and I was suspended. Mayer put out the word that I was difficult, and you know how producers talk to each other. I think that was the reason I left.³³

But somewhat more cryptically, she suggests in the same interview that his hostility toward her was more than professional. In a discussion of Charlie Chaplin, she says: "Yes, it was so unfortunate that he was blackballed but then we were all blackballed at some time. . . . " The term "blackballed" may be general, but it summons up images of prejudice and exclusion. Mayer's may well have been the deciding vote cast to keep Dorothy out of the "boys' club" of Hollywood.

The Bride Wore Red was poorly received, and the very synthetic qualities that disturbed Arzner were noted by the critics as well. One critic described the film as having "no dramatic conviction," and said that Arzner was unable to "give a vapid Cinderella pipe dream more than a handsome pictorial front."³⁴ Another reviewer complimented the moviegoers who disliked the picture, which "flopped resoundingly."³⁵ And once again, the concept of a "woman's picture" was alluded to, now negatively, to explain the failure of the film: "If

Figure 29. Dorothy Arzner on the set of *The Bride Wore Red*, with George Zucco and Joan Crawford, 1937. Arts Library—Special Collections, University Research Library, UCLA.

anything at all, it is a woman's picture—smouldering with its heroine's indecision and consumed with talk of love and fashions. Tall talk, mostly."[36]

Arzner did not direct again until 1940, when she stepped in to take over an RKO production, supervised by Erich Pommer, after Roy Del Ruth, the initial director, left. *Dance, Girl, Dance* was not a hit at the time, but it has become, justifiably, Arzner's best-known film today (see chapter 7). For once, she was able to bring her own unique vision to material initially conceived and developed by others. Based on a story by Vicki Baum, the script was co-authored by Tess Slesinger and Frank Davis. When Arzner was brought in to work on the production, she made some changes in the script. As she put it, "No one seemed to know what the script was all about. So, to nail it down, I decided what should be said from the script at hand with some rewriting. I decided the theme should be 'The Art Spirit' (Maureen O'Hara) versus the commercial 'Go-Getter' (Lucy Ball)."[37]

Dorothy would direct only one more film after this one, so it is appropriate

Figure 30. Dorothy Arzner, ca. 1937. Arts Library—Special Collections,
University Research Library, UCLA.

that she stepped back into her lauded role as star-maker, now with Lucille Ball.
One reviewer declared, "If RKO accomplishes nothing else with the venture
. . . it has informed itself that it has a very important player on the lot in the
person of Miss Ball, who may require special writing. But whatever the requirements, she has the makings of a star."[38] Arzner was not entrusted with the
launching of Ball's career; Ball had appeared in many films by 1940, the year
Dance, Girl, Dance was released (including a bit part as a dancer in Arzner's

Figure 31. Dorothy Arzner, ca. 1938. Arts Library—Special Collections, University Research Library, UCLA.

Nana). But *Dance, Girl, Dance* made visible the enormous star potential of Lucille Ball.

However warmly *Dance, Girl, Dance* has been received in recent years, its reception in 1940 was lukewarm. Hence, Dorothy's return to directing after the distressing experience with MGM was less than triumphant. She would return to Columbia to direct her last film, an adaptation of a novel entitled *The Commandos*, by Elliott Arnold. The film, later called *First Comes Courage* (1943), follows the adventures of a female spy (played by Merle Oberon) in Norway (see chapter 5). Arzner became gravely ill with pneumonia during the filming of *First Comes Courage*, and the film was eventually completed by Charles Vidor. The film was neither a commercial nor a critical success. Arzner thought that it suffered from poor timing, i.e., that the vogue for patriotic spy films had passed, although this explanation does not seem convincing when contemporary films like *Casablanca* were successful. Joseph B. Walker, the cinematographer on the film, said that despite Arzner's record, " . . . all her experience couldn't pull the weak story together." Halfway through the filming, said Walker, Charles Vidor arrived: " 'Arzner's off the picture,' he told me

Figure 32. Dorothy Arzner at home, ca. 1940. Arts Library—Special Collections, University Research Library, UCLA.

curtly. 'Cohn thinks the thing's a dud. He's not about to spend any more money on it. My orders are to finish it in fast order.' "[39]

Arzner always said that, even though she made the decision to leave Hollywood, she also felt that Hollywood had left her.[40] *First Comes Courage* exemplified Arzner's sense that she no longer really belonged to the film industry; she may have agreed that the picture was made at the wrong time and the wrong place, but, in a more general way, she felt that the kind of pictures she was interested in making were no longer encouraged or supported in Hollywood. Throughout Arzner's career, the notion of a "woman's director" had been ambivalent, lending itself to multiple meanings, often contradictory ones. Ambivalence and contradiction notwithstanding, her kind of woman's film no longer had a place, and after *First Comes Courage*—the first film in Arzner's career, ironically enough, to have been completed by another director—she never directed in Hollywood again.

4

After Hollywood

A NY ACT OF interpretation is a reconstruction, a piecing together of fragments in an attempt to find meaningful patterns and connections. In the
previous three chapters, my major focus has been how Arzner's career was
shaped by the various meanings associated with her status as "woman director."
My goal in this book is not a definitive, biographical study of Arzner, but rather
a study of Arzner's work and of the Dorothy Arzner image that includes some
biographical elements. Now to some extent, even in the most exhaustive biography, gaps are inevitable; no single life is accessible in all its detail or complexity
to the researcher. Such gaps are perhaps more visible in a study like mine, since
I have been inspired to some extent by biographical details of Arzner's life and
career, as well as by other factors—the films themselves, contemporary feminist
theory and criticism, and the complexities of gay and lesbian life in Hollywood.
However, acknowledging that gaps exist does not necessarily mean they become
irrelevant. I have argued, for instance, that it was necessary for Arzner's own
survival that she separate her personal life and her career, but that her relationship with Marion Morgan nonetheless inspired and influenced her work. In
some sense, then, I have attempted to bridge the *apparent* gap between the
spheres of Arzner's private and professional lives, but I have also attempted to
make clear the tentative, hypothetical quality of such "bridges."

Despite the gaps inevitable in any project that involves reconstructing the
past through the life of an individual, I believe that it is possible to create an
accurate portrait of the complexities of Arzner's career in Hollywood from
1919 to 1943, to appreciate how important her example was, and to understand
what a vital contribution she made to the cinema. After 1943, however, for the
purposes of my study, the gaps are larger, the patterns and connections more
difficult to trace.

Aside from the lack of documents and information, there is an obvious
reason for these gaps, this difficulty; Arzner really *did* leave Hollywood. She
left in spirit in 1943, and she left physically in 1951, when she and Marion Morgan moved permanently to their desert home in La Quinta, California. Arzner
may have continued to participate in film-related activities, but if one is cen-
trally interested in Dorothy Arzner, Hollywood Director, then for all intents
and purposes the study should conclude in 1943.

And yet, the very fact that Arzner participated in a variety of other activities, related directly or indirectly to the cinema, is significant for an understanding of her career in Hollywood. It may be tempting to view her departure as a defeat, particularly given her own (even though admittedly sketchy) comments about being blackballed by Louis Mayer. I think it more appropriate to see Arzner as a woman who decided that the Louis Mayers and Harry Cohns of Hollywood were more trouble than they, or Hollywood films, were worth. Fortunately for her, she had the financial means at her disposal to make such a decision. However many limitations were imposed upon Arzner because of her status as woman director, it is a grave mistake to see her primarily, much less exclusively, as a victim. She negotiated her life in Hollywood—and afterwards—in creative and complex ways. And while Arzner was somewhat publicity-shy, especially in the 1970s, it is also a mistake to think of her as having retreated into solitude or isolation. In other words, Arzner may have left Hollywood, but the work that she continued to do is nonetheless important to an understanding of *her* notion of meaningful work and activity.

Even after making her last Hollywood film, she never completely left the cinema or the world of performance. She made training films for the Women's Army Corps during World War II, shortly after the experience of *First Comes Courage* and after her own health had improved after a horrible bout with pneumonia. Arzner directed a series of short films, and she also trained a staff of four women to cut and edit them.[1] Karyn Kay and Gerald Peary summarize this experience:

> Arzner had great fun making these shorts, for her actors were the Samuel Goldwyn stock company, including some of her old *Nana* cast. These documentaries were never shown in theatres nor in general release, but were restricted to WAC training situations—How to Groom Oneself, etc. Apparently they were successful, for the government offered Dorothy Arzner an appointment as Major. She turned it down, because, as she says, "I never wanted to be in the Army."[2]

At about the same time, Arzner developed a short-lived but enormously interesting radio program entitled *You Were Meant to Be a Star*. The program aired weekly, and Arzner, with the assistance of a (male) emcee, presented a series of "scenes," supposedly drawn from real life. In the introduction to each episode, Arzner explains that there is an affinity between real life and motion pictures, from which she has developed her theory that "you were meant to be a star." Arzner then contrasts a scene from everyday life with a parallel scene from the movies in order to demonstrate how individuals might "perform" more successfully the roles of real life. The goal, Arzner explained, was to demonstrate how the "acted" scene could be seen not only as "good performance, but as an index to better living."[3] The supposed basis of the material was mail

Figure 33. Dorothy Arzner with two members of the Women's Army Corps, 1943. Arts Library—Special Collections, University Research Library, UCLA.

received from the listening audience—with the two most interesting letters chosen to be the two scenes of the week. Arzner plotted the scene as it really happened in the life of one of her listeners, and then chatted with the performers to solicit their opinions of how the characters they played might have behaved differently.

For instance, several programs focus on the dilemma of the jealous wife who suspects that her husband is seeing his secretary. Arzner recreates a scene between husband and wife, at the dinner table with the wife complaining bitterly about the secretary, and the husband remaining stubbornly, and equally bitterly, silent. Arzner yells "Cut!," then turns to the wife, identified fictitiously as Mrs. Jane Blake, and asks, "What have you gotten yourself into? By all standards, that was a very bad performance!" A discussion between actress/character and director ensues, with Arzner pointing out that Mrs. Blake was "not a star in that situation." When the actress notes that Mrs. Blake was disturbed by her jealous suspicion, Arzner points out that this is precisely the problem. According to Arzner, Mrs. Blake should have mentioned the secretary's name casually, all the better to observe her husband's reaction.

Arzner asks the actress how Mrs. Blake could avoid antagonizing her husband; the actress returns to her first line of the scene ("I always thought you had good taste in women") and suggests another "take": "You know, Bob, I think you have wonderful taste in women." As a result of this change from defensiveness and hostility to feigned sweetness (and manipulation), the entire conversation between husband and wife is replayed in both senses of the term—performed differently, and with different results, because in the second version the husband decides, spontaneously and enthusiastically, to spend the evening with his wife. Arzner concludes the performance with these words to Mrs. Blake: "We don't presume to guarantee that your situation would turn out exactly like this, but we have tried to give you the motivating thought and action that would make you a star in your own world."

Virtually all of the scenes recreated in the program concern women's roles, even when an episode begins by focussing on a man's dilemma. One episode begins with a man complaining about his wife's attentions to another man who, it turns out, is planning a business deal with the husband, but believes that it is important to evaluate clients in terms of their wives. The husband receives from Arzner the same kind of suggestions that Mrs. Blake did in the previously discussed episode. But after the husband says that a comment from his wife put him on the defensive, attention is quickly focussed on her as the primary performer. Arzner thus suggests that the wife should assume her responsibilities as the one who sets the appropriate tone.

This constant return to the woman as central performer could reflect simply the intended female audience of the radio program, but more generally it reflects a theme consistent with Arzner's films and with Hollywood cinema in general—that performance is the female domain par excellence. In later chapters I will suggest that female performance is one of the most complex aspects of Arzner's film work, in that it is represented critically and positively at the same time. *You Were Meant to Be a Star* shows a preoccupation with performance and with the female condition that may not always be critical, but which can nonetheless be read easily as a demonstration of the ideology of performance.

Other episodes of *You Were Meant to Be a Star* sound like plots from Hollywood films—a housewife who feels underappreciated by her family, a mother concerned about her daughter's affection for an older man, and endless variations on the theme of the jealous wife. The bottom line, the moral, if you will, is always the same—women are chided by Arzner ("I thought you told me you wanted to be a star in your own world"), and advised on how they can perform well ("A husband never strays far if a wife plays her role with grace and charm").

You Were Meant to Be a Star was entirely an Arzner creation, and while her references to fan mail and requests for advice may well have been grounded in fact, the situations recreated tend to repeat certain formulas. To be sure, some formulas occur in real life, but several scenes recreated in the show begin with exactly the same opening line: "I thought you had good taste in women." My point here is not at all to discredit Arzner's relationship with her listening public, but rather to insist upon how thoroughly the program was her creation. It does not require too much imagination to see in this, one of Arzner's first post-Hollywood productions, as it were, a reflection of her own directorial career. There may be something hokey about the constant attempt to draw moral lessons from the world of performance, but there is something quite touching about these little essays as well. For in each case, Arzner advises her female listeners to perform, as if at the core of the scenarios is a recognition that to be "female" in the world is always to act a part.

Some specific connections exist between these scenes and Arzner's own film career. Some of the fictional names she gives her characters are drawn from her own films—like Mrs. Frazier, a selfish mother (Mrs. Frazier was the neighbor played by Billie Burke in *Craig's Wife*), or the Strong family, as in *Christopher Strong*. Other scenarios are replays of Arzner's own films, whether the scenarios concern a jealous wife (*Christopher Strong, Craig's Wife*) or a woman threatened by her daughter's attraction to the wrong man (*Christopher Strong*). To be sure, these scenarios are not specific to Arzner's films, but were common Hollywood plots. But that may well be the point; from the basic material of Hollywood plots, Arzner recreates scenes that function both to replay her own Hollywood past, and to suggest yet another relationship between spectator and performance—the same kind of detached observation that Arzner herself suggests to Mrs. Blake. In the process of creating *You Were Meant to Be a Star*, Arzner herself was creating her own detachment from Hollywood, a detachment characterized simultaneously as evaluation and independence.

Selected episodes of *You Were Meant to Be a Star* were the only professional "texts" by Arzner to which I had access in order to account for the years between her departure from Hollywood and her death in 1979. Capsule director biographies give some information about Arzner's activities during these years, and since MGM was one of the last studios for which she worked, MGM's bio of her provides what sketchy official information exists about her activities. This is ironic, since Arzner's experiences with MGM and Louis Mayer in particular were decisive in her disaffection with the film industry. Arzner updated her own studio biographies, and the next five years of Arzner's life provided a hiatus from anything having to do with Hollywood. Arzner described the years from 1945 to 1950 as follows: "I took time out to look at the world and beyond it away from Hollywood, but here is the next chapter of my activity."[4] Just what looking "at the world and beyond it" entailed I do not know, although travelling with Marion Morgan was certainly a part of it. The "next chapter" included a wide range of activities, but accounts available to me were, once again, sketchy.

Arzner's own film-related activities took three forms during the 1950s and early 1960s: teaching, theatre production, and the direction of Pepsi-Cola commercials for Joan Crawford. In 1951, Arzner developed a course in film production at the Pasadena Playhouse. In 1959, she began a teaching career in the Motion Picture Division in the Theater Arts department at UCLA, which she continued until 1963. Her most famous student was Francis Ford Coppola, who praised Arzner for giving him encouragement when he sorely needed it. I imagine Arzner as a gifted teacher, although I say this less from any evidence offered by her students (beyond Coppola's praise) than from a philosophy of life that emerges in some interviews. Arzner spoke of the need, in teaching, to preserve youthful arrogance; "you must preserve the young ego that thinks it knows so much," Arzner said. She also spoke of the desire of her students for job security, but added that "the most secure thing you can have is to embrace the insecurity of life."[5]

Through her involvements in stage productions, Arzner maintained her collaboration with playwright Zoë Akins and actress Billie Burke. In the early 1950s, Arzner produced several plays in California, including *HATS OFF! Miss Smith*, Akins's *The Swallow's Nest*, and Irving Phillips's *Mother Was a Bachelor*. Burke starred in all three productions.[6] Arzner's work for the Pepsi-Cola company began in 1958, at the request of Joan Crawford; Arzner directed fifty commercials and served in an official capacity as "consultant" to the company.

One other interesting brief mention on Arzner's bio is that she was, in 1961, Director of the Religion in Science Foundation. There are few mentions of religion in interviews with Arzner or in official documentation of her career (one suspects, of course, that this was an area she considered private). Correspondence between Marion Morgan and Arzner includes a number of postcards from the home of Mary Baker Eddy, the founder of Christian Science, and Morgan's descriptions of her visit suggest that she and Arzner shared that interest. My own sense of Arzner, after several years of researching her, is that she was a deeply spiritual person, perhaps in the sense of a commitment to organized religion, but even more so in the sense of a meditative and conscious awareness of the activities of life. The most interesting interview with Arzner to which I had access was conducted in the early 1960s; here Arzner articulates an approach to her career that reflects a commitment to living in the moment, to being conscious of the present: "I'm afraid I have no goals. I think that it's in the doing that I'm living in the present moment. I don't see goals, I don't know about them at all, I'm just working at life itself wherever I find it and doing the best job I can with it".[7]

It seems entirely fitting that a woman always living in the present moment would find the stillness and calm of the desert appropriate to her needs and desires. Aside from the activities outlined above, I know little else of how Arzner spent her time after 1951, when she and Morgan moved to the desert community of La Quinta, except that frequent references to her roses in later interviews and profiles suggest that she was a devoted gardener! One of her greatest personal challenges was the prolonged illness of Marion Morgan, who died in 1971. Letters of condolence from friends, family, and former colleagues make clear that their circle of loved ones was extensive, and that their devotion to each was respected and admired.

For all the attention paid to Arzner as the lone woman director during her career in Hollywood, she fell into oblivion fairly quickly once she departed. But that changed in the early to mid-1970s, largely because of a renewed interest in women and film, sparked by feminist activism in a variety of forms. In 1973, *Action*, the publication of the Directors Guild of America, published a special issue on the female director that included an essay by director Francine Parker on Arzner's work. Parker's essay, as well as Nancy Dowd's more general article on the woman director in the same issue, suggests that the reconsideration of Arzner was simultaneously a discovery of a woman director and a discovery of a director; as Dowd put it, "Dorothy Arzner is, quite simply, an important American director."[8] This is not to say that Arzner's distinct contributions as a woman were downplayed, but rather that attention was drawn to the fact that Arzner was successful as a filmmaker on anyone's terms. Hence, Parker evaluates Arzner's career both in terms of Arzner's philosophy of the director's role that involved both authority and collaboration, and in terms of Arzner's unique female vision (" . . . woman has a different point of view on life. And the world does take on a rather startling and surprising look when observed through the eyes of a skilled, talented, hard-working, learned and thoroughly unintimidated female").[9]

In January 1975, a tribute to Arzner as "Pioneer Director" was sponsored by the Directors Guild of America. Organized by the Committee of Women Members of the DGA, the tribute paid homage to the first female member of the organization—in the words of *Variety*, Arzner was "DGA's first femme member."[10] The tribute was co-moderated by Francine Parker and Mary McCall, author of the screenplay for *Craig's Wife*, who had been so grateful to Arzner for her recognition of the importance of the writer. The distinguished panel exemplified the spirit of collaboration so central to Arzner's career, with representatives from virtually all areas of film production. Robert Wise, who edited *Dance, Girl, Dance*, praised Arzner's insistence on the director as the creative center of the film: "You're one of the pioneers of that area, of the director having control over his films . . . something we of the Guild have fought for all these years."[11]

If the DGA tribute marked the importance of Arzner's contribution to

Figure 34. Dorothy Arzner at the Directors Guild of America Tribute, 1975. Arts Library—Special Collections, University Research Library, UCLA.

the history of Hollywood cinema, other acknowledgments in the 1970s were concerned more specifically with her status as a female artist, and with her films as investigations into female experience. One of the most important phenomena in the development of women's film culture in the 1970s was the growth of film festivals devoted to exhibiting the works of contemporary women directors and recognizing the contributions of women directors of the past. Such festivals offered the opportunity to "see" women's cinema in several senses of the term—literally, of course, but also in the sense of "revision" as Adrienne Rich defines the term: "the act of looking back, of seeing with fresh eyes, of entering an old text from a new critical direction. . . ."[12] The DGA tribute recognized Arzner's unique contributions within Hollywood cinema; feminist film festivals recognized her importance as a woman whose vision extended beyond that of Hollywood.

Feminist investigations of the importance of Arzner tended to follow one of two paths. Some feminist critics found in Arzner's work detailed and engaging narratives that put women center stage, while others were more enthusiastic about how Arzner's films interrogated the dominant codes of classical Hollywood cinema. Karyn Kay and Gerald Peary were two of the most active critics in creating feminist interest in Arzner's work, and they argued that Arzner's best films offered detailed, complex portraits of women. In more general terms, Arzner's example was an important corrective, then, to views that the "woman's film" and the "feminist film" were necessarily incompatible. Molly Haskell articulated beautifully the conflict inherent in Arzner's position:

> Arzner's films move forward with the jerky unpredictability of a vision not quite resolved into a style. Without rationalization, I think we might see this as an expression of the discomfort of a woman who feels herself an artist in an alien land, but is nevertheless trying, always, to bridge the gap: between Hollywood and her artistic aspirations; between the romantic conventions and her own feminist sensibility.[13]

This interest in Arzner in Kay and Peary's and Haskell's work developed at about the same time as contemporary feminist film theory, which problematized the notion of film as a vehicle for portraits—complex or otherwise—of women. Arzner was an equally important example for these feminist theorists, for whom the classical Hollywood cinema was less a code to be adapted to feminist ends than an institution to be critiqued in feminist terms. The best-known proponents of Arzner as a woman who managed to subvert Hollywood from within are Claire Johnston and Pam Cook. Both Johnston and Cook wrote influential essays praising and analyzing the ways that, in Johnston's words, the "discourse of the woman" in Arzner's work "render[s] the dominant discourse of the male fragmented and incoherent."[14]

The recognition of Arzner by women active in the Directors Guild of America established an important connection between Hollywood's present and past, and feminist interest in Arzner's work—no matter how wide the range—similarly acknowledged the importance of understanding women's relationships to film history. Feminist interest in Arzner tended to reflect larger assumptions about women and the classical Hollywood cinema. At one extreme is Andrew Britton's assessment, in his study of Katharine Hepburn, that Arzner is the unproblematized *auteur* of *Christopher Strong*. For Britton, *Christopher Strong* functions as a "critique of the effect of patriarchal heterosexual relations on relations between women." Hence, Britton suggests, the classical Hollywood cinema lends itself to feminist ends. At the opposite extreme, Jacquelyn Suter's analysis of the same film evolves from the assumption that whatever "female discourse" there is in *Christopher Strong* is subsumed and neutralized by the patriarchal discourse on monogamy central to the film.[15]

If the classical cinema described by Britton is remarkably open to effects of subversion and criticism, the classical cinema described by Suter is just as remarkably closed to all but patriarchal meanings. Claire Johnston's and Pam

Cook's readings of Arzner's films suggest, if not a mean between the two extremes, then at least the need to understand the classical Hollywood cinema and Arzner's place within it as contradictory; that is, as open to effects of subversion, perhaps, but in a mediated way. Hence, Johnston's and Cook's readings of Arzner's films are reminiscent of how Roland Barthes, in *S/Z*, describes Balzac's novella *Sarrasine* as representative of a "limited plurality" within classical realist discourse.[16] Johnston and Cook have argued that the strategies of Arzner's films open up limited criticisms of the classical Hollywood cinema by locating the "discourse of the woman" center stage and thereby problematizing those devices (particularly the male gaze and male-centered narration) that would be naturalized in other films. Johnston's description of the scene in *Dance, Girl, Dance*, where Judy (Maureen O'Hara) confronts her audience and tells them how she sees them has become something of a privileged moment in feminist film studies.

It may well be that the enormous theoretical attention paid to that ubiquitous entity, the classical Hollywood cinema, has had a contradictory effect on explorations into Arzner's career. Feminist film theory developed at approximately the same time as theories of the cinematic apparatus, with the attendant implication that woman's relationship to the classical Hollywood cinema could be only a negative one. While I am less persuaded than some as to the interpretive or historical validity of the cinematic institution understood monolithically, the recognition of the power of that institution remains one of the most important contributions of 1970s film theory. It is one thing, however, to acknowledge that dominant cinema places a series of constraints upon whatever experiences or pleasures the cinema offers; it is another thing altogether to assume that the dominant cinema is a static, unchanging entity.

Indeed, through Arzner's experience in Hollywood, it would appear that the classical Hollywood cinema changed dimensions radically during her career. Perhaps it comes as no surprise that Arzner's most successful film, *Dance, Girl, Dance*, was made when she functioned as an independent director, not under contract to a single studio; indeed, the experience of *Dance, Girl, Dance* stands in sharp contrast to Arzner's experiences with producers Louis B. Mayer and Harry Cohn. But Arzner had the most opportunity and the most flexibility early in her career, from the time she began editing at Paramount to the conclusion of her directing contract there. During that time, she established collaborative relationships with other women, from actresses to choreographers to screenwriters. The advent of the studio system on a large scale, particularly with power located in the hands of producers like Mayer and Cohn, was disastrous for Arzner's career, but the studio conditions under which her career began, at Paramount, were most advantageous. In other words, Arzner's "exceptional" status as the (nearly) lone woman director may prove some rules about Hollywood and women, but it challenges other stereotypes.

Dorothy Arzner died on October 1, 1979, at the age of 82, in the La Quinta home she and Morgan had shared. Obituary after obituary concludes with variations on the same chilling words that have characterized death notices of those who live on the margins: "She leaves no known survivors." "Miss Arzner leaves no survivors." "There was no funeral and she leaves no survivors."[17] However much I—like many contemporary gay men and lesbians—want to mourn these words, they are cause for neither mourning nor pity. In any case, renewed interest in Arzner's life and career—a renewed interest that began, happily, before her death (but in relation to which she was not always the happy recipient!)—is perhaps the best survival strategy and the best celebration of her achievements.

PART II

Films for Women Made by Women

From a news story on *Craig's Wife*:
There is a film which will be shown all over the country next week that raises a
very interesting point for women filmgoers.
It is a film which has been made for women and it has been written and
directed by women. Although there are one or two men in the cast . . . they are
there only because they help the women to express their points of view.

— R. Ewart Williams, "Film for Women Made by Women"

5

Working Girls

CONTEMPORARY INTEREST IN Arzner's career and her work has focused largely on how she, as a woman director in Hollywood, conveyed women's lives, desires, and experiences on screen. Arzner's work did indeed focus primarily on women's lives, women's friendships, and women's communities. But women are never identified in a simple or isolated way in Arzner's work. For instance, I suggested earlier in this book that Arzner's screenplay for *The Red Kimono* is indicative of her commitment not only to the exploration of the connections between women, but to those connections as they are shaped and complicated by social class. In this chapter I will examine how the attention to social class and women's lives is foregrounded in four of Arzner's films— *Working Girls* (1931), *Nana* (1934), *The Bride Wore Red* (1937), and *First Comes Courage* (1943). As the title of this chapter indicates, each is concerned with women's working lives.

It is significant that the attention to social class, in Arzner's films, is given especially to working women. To be sure, in early films like *Get Your Man* (1927), American and European definitions of social class are juxtaposed, with attendant differences in sexual morality. Clara Bow's character exploits these differences to her benefit, as if to suggest that the brash, entrepreneurial attitude towards love that she embodies is symptomatic of an approach to social mores quite different from the European aristocratic values with which she clashes. More typically, however, it is through jobs and careers that women's encounters with social class occur. *Sarah and Son* and *Dance, Girl, Dance* use women's careers on stage to explore the differing class associations of vaudeville versus opera (in *Sarah and Son*) and burlesque versus ballet (in *Dance, Girl, Dance*). In *Honor among Lovers*, the obstacles to romance between Julia (Claudette Colbert) and Jerry (Fredric March) are specifically those of social class, since Julia's status as Jerry's secretary puts her outside the wealthy circles in which he circulates.

As coincidence would have it, the four films discussed here have something besides the working girl in common. They were perhaps the largest failures in Arzner's career. By "failure" I do not mean that the films were artistic failures, although in two cases this is true— *Nana* and *The Bride Wore Red* are less

Figure 35. Dorothy Arzner and friends, 1936. Arts Library—Special Collections, University Research Library, UCLA.

interesting than Arzner's other films. More important, these four films marked low points in Arzner's career, and all were failures commercially. While I think *First Comes Courage* is better than many critics (including Arzner herself) allow, it was Arzner's last film, and the project that precipitated her departure from Hollywood. The biggest commerical flop of Arzner's career was *Working Girls*, a film worthy of the kind of attention that *Dance, Girl, Dance* and *Christopher Strong* have received.

By grouping together four failed works, I am not necessarily suggesting that flops occurred whenever Arzner turned her attention to social class; attention to the intersections of class and gender is common in most of her films. In these four works, the working girl is portrayed through and against the conventions of romance, and the connection of "work" and "romance" is often awkward. As a result, the conventions of Hollywood romance are defamiliarized, even to the point of appearing downright silly. This foregrounding of the limitations of Hollywood romance may account for some of the perceived limitations of these films by the critics and audiences of the time.

Working Girls (1931)

Working Girls was the third of four films on which Arzner and screenwriter Zoë Akins collaborated. The film was, for all intents and purposes, shelved by Paramount; it never had a national release and received virtually no studio publicity. It never had a general release and is available only in archival prints to this day. This is unfortunate, since this film is one of Arzner's most significant achievements, and it is the most successful of her collaborations with Akins. Stylistically, it is daring and innovative.

Working Girls tells the tale of two sisters, May and June Thorpe, who come to New York City from Rockville, Indiana, determined to make careers for themselves as "working girls." The ambiguity of the film's title is never addressed directly in the film. But the double meaning of "working girl," in its innocent literal sense and in its acquired sense that women who worked outside the home were morally suspect (eventually the term "working girl" became a code for "prostitute"), is evident throughout. The two sisters must learn, simultaneously, the sexual politics of both work and romance. May and June move into the Rolfe House, a boardinghouse for single, working girls like themselves, i.e., women from rather poor backgrounds who have few available funds. The sisters go to work: they get jobs and boyfriends. As in all of Arzner's films featuring communities of women, strong bonds exist among the women who share the living quarters. Yet Arzner gently parodies such institutions. Miss Johnstone, the adminstrator of the home, is as busy shutting windows to keep out the sounds of music and partying across the way as she is taking care of business; one of the boarders remarks sarcastically that hearing music is supposed to be bad for their morals.

One of the most interesting developments in the film is the change that separates the two sisters as the film progresses. At the beginning of the film, they are virtually interchangeable, an effect emphasized by the similar coloring, makeup, and dress of the two actresses. The only significant difference is that May, the older of the two, seems a bit more mature and reasonable than her younger sister, June. As the film progresses, their dress changes considerably, with one sister becoming more frilly and feminine (and more irresponsible in her relationships with men), and the other more severe, butch, and businesslike (like Arzner herself, one is tempted to note), and much more astute in her relationships with men.

June interviews for a job as a research assistant to Von Schrader, a German scholar, and when he makes clear that he is looking for someone more educated, she calls her sister in, and May gets the job. June sets out to find herself a more frivolous job as a model, but she is snobbily rejected. June begins to pay more

Figure 36. Dorothy Hall (May) and Judith Wood (June) in *Working Girls,* 1931. MOMA Film Stills Archive.

attention to her dress and appearance, and she finds a job at a telegraph station in a hotel. Her first two customers become the romantic leads for June and her sister; one is a wealthy Harvard man (who sends a telegram to an ex-girlfriend), and the other is a saxophone player, who quickly invites June to have dinner with him.

Boyd Wheeler, the Harvard man, soon meets May in a shoe store. Unbeknownst to May, he is on the rebound (which June knows because of the telegram he sent); May and Boyd begin a romance. June is suspicious of the liaison precisely because of the class differences between them. Meanwhile, Kelly, the saxophone player, showers June with gifts. In the film's early scenes, June appears to be the more frivolous sister. Yet as the film progresses, she proves to be the wiser and more practical one. She is never swept off her feet by Kelly in the way that May is by Wheeler, and June's undisguised interest in material things makes her appear not so much naive and superficial as cunning and straightforward. Most important, June does not do what May does, namely, sleep with her boyfriend.

The question of premarital sex is presented in the film less as a moral issue than a practical one. May becomes pregnant, but in the meantime Wheeler has returned to Louise, his former sweetheart—a woman, none too coincidentally, of his own social background. June takes charge of the situation. First, she goes to May's employer, the German scholar, who had let May go when he became aware of his attraction to her and her lack of interest in him. June begs him to give May back her job, and he agrees. Shortly after May begins to work again, she accepts the marriage proposal he had made six months before, and he, confused and in a moment of weakness, agrees. When June discovers that her sister is pregnant with Wheeler's child, she is the one who breaks the news to the German scholar. June's job proves once again to be an asset, since she discovers through a telegram that Wheeler sends to sweetheart Louise that their engagement has ended, at her request. Once June has this information, she proceeds with her plan to force Wheeler to marry her sister.

One might expect that the intersecting working lives and romantic lives of the two sisters would conclude on this note—May with Wheeler in a curious but necessary cross-class marriage made possible mostly by June, who is more appropriately paired with Kelly, the musician. However, there is a twist to this symmetry; June and the German scholar fall in love, as if to suggest yet another cross-class fantasy, one involving education and learnedness as much as wealth (Wheeler may be a Harvard man, but he is never seen at work, and he is drunk most of the time).[1]

The changing fortunes of the two sisters are represented by their changes in appearance. As I've mentioned, the two women are dressed identically at the beginning of the film, and during the first few scenes it is difficult to tell them apart in terms of appearance. However, as the film progresses, June begins to dress in a less frilly, stereotypically "feminine" way, while May, who without her sister's direction would be virtually lost, becomes the more feminine dresser. The contrast in dress is made most strikingly in the decisive scene of the shift in power between the two sisters, when June tends to her ill sister in their room at Rolfe House. June wears a uniform that tends to be associated, in all of Arzner's films, with independence and autonomy (not to mention with Arzner's own style of dress): a suit and tie, with a beret. The difference between the two sisters, at this point, is not just one of clothing, for May's pregnancy becomes quite clear to her sister (and to the audience) during this scene.

A common preoccupation in Arzner's films is the contrast not only between individual women, but also between communities exclusively composed of women and mixed communities of men and women. In *Working Girls*, this contrast takes shape as a movement back and forth from Rolfe House, where men are permitted only in the reception area (and are gawked at by the residents), to the working world; the contrast is also evoked by the juxtaposition of Rolfe House and the unidentified, but supposedly dangerous, community that exists within earshot—from which music and dancing are heard. Interest-

Figure 37. Dorothy Hall (May) and Judith Wood (June) in *Working Girls*, 1931.
Arts Library—Special Collections, University Research Library, UCLA.

ingly, the working world from which Rolfe House provides a refuge is defined
from the outset more in terms of the male/female interactions that it enables
than in terms of work in any classic sense of the word. Indeed, the only really
traditional concept of a women's work force occurs during the credits of the
film, where we see women in silhouette at typewriters, and it is perhaps no
coincidence that this abstraction of women in the work force never really finds
a concrete match in the film. The work situations that May and June find for
themselves are unusual. May goes to work for the German scholar, whose office
and home are one, and June finds it odd that home and workplace should thus
be combined. June's job in the telegraph office is not a typical work environment, in that she has unusual autonomy—not to mention access to vital plot
information! In both cases, the women's jobs are immediately defined in terms
of their romantic lives—the scholar proposes to May, and June's first few minutes on the job introduce her to her sister's future husband and her own romantic companion for most of the film.

   Working Girls seems to establish contrasts (like romance/work) only to collapse them. Try as Mrs. Johnstone might to keep the noise and accompanying

festivities at bay by closing the windows, the inhabitants of Rolfe House none-theless create their own fun, whether by disobeying the rules of the house or by creating a female world of laughter and dance. Similarly, the worlds of home and paid labor, for women, are never separate. This intersection of seemingly opposing spheres finds, in *Working Girls*, a stunning representation in a scene that is among the most effective and gorgeous in any of Arzner's works. May and June have had a busy day of finding work and finding male companions. The doors of Rolfe House lock at midnight, and unless a girl has signed out for the night, missing the deadline means certain expulsion. June returns five minutes before midnight, in a taxi, from her evening spent with Kelly, who has showered her with presents. At three minutes until midnight, May arrives with Mr. Wheeler, the Harvard man, to whom she already affectionately refers as "Big Frog" (he calls her "Little Frog").

The elevator in Rolfe House shuts down at 11 P.M., so the two sisters must climb up several flights of stairs to their room. Virtually all communication in the film is observed by others, and this scene is no exception, as Loretta, the elevator operator, functions here (as she often does in the film) as a witness. After they have been let into the building by Loretta, the two sisters begin to mount the four flights of stairs to the room they share. From a long shot of the two women about to mount the stairs, the camera moves forward to frame them more closely, and follows their movements up the stairs. Striking effects of light and dark frame them as they climb, exhausted. Visually, the pair are in a state of suspension, their movement upwards at once an ironic reminder of both their aspirations and their limitations. They live in a home that forces the women to climb stairs after 11 P.M.; their fatigue is a reminder of the contrast between the taxi (June) and the personal automobile (May) that have brought them to the door and the institutional surroundings they call home. Yet they are moving upwards, mirroring their own desires to come to the big city and make their fortunes.

Although June and May are still dressed quite similarly, if not identically, their first full day in the city has already produced a significant difference be-tween them. June is loaded down with packages, gifts from Kelly—from candy and perfume to an umbrella and overshoes—while May has nothing. Although May is the older sister, this extended walk up the stairs marks the first shift in their relationship, wherein June is defined as the more astute and the more mature. Their conversation about men reveals an almost startling cynicism and wisdom on June's part and foreshadows how she will prove to be both more clever than her sister and her sister's protector.

June tells May that Mr. Kelly warned her that "a lot of these swell guys think any girl that works is fair game; and you're so darned soft. . . . " May is quick to point out that this Mr. Kelly is a new acquaintance as surely as Boyd Wheeler is, to which June replies: "Don't you worry about me not knowing how to say no. I even know how to say no and yes at the same time—which is something you'll never learn."[2] May insists that she doesn't want to learn such a thing, and the remainder of the film will demonstrate how saying "no and yes at the same time" is indeed what separates the two sisters. May is drawn to Wheeler's wealth and the fact that he is a Harvard man, but June points out that all she managed to get from him was a meal, whereas her saxophone player showered her with gifts.

The difference between the two sisters is identified specifically in terms of their understanding of class. June tells her sister that she doesn't want her "running around with somebody who thinks [she's] not in his class." When May suggests that she may well marry Boyd Wheeler some day, June exclaims, "Gosh, what a fool I've raised for a sister!"[3] May may well be the older sister, but June is quickly assuming the role of wiser, more experienced sibling.

May doesn't pay the price for her naiveté, since June ensures that the cross-class marriage her sister dreamed of occurs, even if not in quite the same terms May had imagined. But for June, there is a most curious pay-off. When she goes to Von Schrader to tell him that May is marrying someone else, he quickly falls in love with her. When June interviewed with Von Schrader for the job that eventually went to May, her lack of education and general knowledge was pointedly observed by the German scholar. Yet by the conclusion of the film, these two are paired. The pairing is suggested in a peculiar way, because Kelly enters the frame of June and Von Schrader just as she is telling the European that she needs a lot of petting. Kelly's exclamation is the last line of the film: "Why June, you always told me you didn't like petting!"[4] Framed between the two men, June seems to be demonstrating her ability to say "no and yes at the same time," as if to suggest that the "work" of managing relationships requires a precise and finely honed script. Indeed, June's role in *Working Girls* embodies both sharp observations on the complex nature of women's work and a fantasy of women's power to shape the world around them.

If June demonstrates the ability to say "no and yes at the same time," *Working Girls* also demonstrates Arzner's unique ability to say the same to the conventions of Hollywood cinema. *Working Girls* explores the stakes, for women, of binary opposites, ranging from home/workplace, to romance/work, to gender/class. It is impossible to neatly separate one term from the other in this film. The scene of May and June climbing the staircase in Rolfe House provides a stunning mise-en-scène of what might be called a threshold space, literally and figuratively. The vision of *Working Girls* is profoundly ambivalent, in that it is impossible to make clear and absolute distinctions between different realms, and also in the sense that the film both celebrates and critiques how women's work comprises so many complex variables. Arzner's own position as a working girl may have been vastly different from that of May or June, but her own relationship to the Hollywood cinema comprised complex variables as well.

Nana (1934)

I don't know if Lizzie Borden chose the title of her 1986 film *Working Girls* in conscious homage to Arzner's film, but there are some striking parallels between the two works. In both cases, however different the points of emphasis (Borden's film is about a group of prostitutes who work in a middle-class bordello), being a "working girl" means understanding economics in sexual as well as business terms. In addition, the bordello in Borden's film is presented in some of the same ways as Rolfe House in Arzner's film—a female community where women manage to create a utopian space despite the imposition of rules. Arzner had censorship problems with *Working Girls*, undoubtedly due in part to the direct approach to May's pregnancy and June's more savvy approach to the relationship between sex and money. The only film in which Arzner directly addresses prostitution is *Nana*, the film for which she was hired to replace another director, and which Samuel Goldwyn intended as a starring vehicle for Russian actress Anna Sten.[5]

I hesitate to make too much of the script adapting Émile Zola's novel to the screen (the final film departs so sharply from the novel that the credits read "suggested by Zola's novel"). Arzner's habit was to work closely with the writer, and to have a writer on the set at all times, and the conditions of production of *Nana* would appear to have made this difficult. However, in the case of *Dance, Girl, Dance*, where Arzner was similarly brought in to manage a project begun by someone else, Arzner's own changes to the already existing script resulted in what is perhaps her most successful and personal film. *Nana* is not one of Arzner's great successes, but some elements of the screenplay are suggestive of Arzner's preoccupations in other films. Most obviously, the relationship between Nana and Satin is foregrounded from the outset of the film. In Zola's novel, the relationship between the two women (first as fellow prostitutes, later as lesbian lovers) is important, but certainly not as central as in the film. Hence, in what is recognizable as a typical Arzner touch, Nana is defined from the outset as part of a community of women, and the friendship between her and Satin is a constant in the film.

Nana is a working girl in the tradition of the female leads of *Sarah and Son* and *Dance, Girl, Dance*; in these works the world of performance is intimately connected to that of sex. Nana's working life combines prostitution and the stage, and the two worlds are forever intertwined. Unlike the two other films in which women performers are central, here the central opposition is between "sex work" understood in two different ways: literally (as a prostitute) and figuratively (as a performer). Indeed, some of the most interesting moments in the film occur when there is deliberate ambiguity between performance and sexuality.

Figure 38. Anna Sten (Nana) and Mae Clark (Satin) in *Nana*, 1934. MOMA Film Stills Archive.

Nana is introduced in the film as a poor woman, scrubbing floors under the watchful eyes of a married couple; Nana's mother has just died and Nana cannot afford to buy a tombstone for her grave. To the man she exclaims: "It's men who make women whatever they are. I don't know what I'll be—but I won't be weak. And I won't be poor." Titles announce that a year has passed, and Nana enters a café in the company of Satin and Mimi, the three of them clearly coded as prostitutes (or "common women," as a man whom Nana eventually humiliates puts it).

Nana's display sparks the interest of Greiner, an impresario, and he sends a man to Nana who tells her that Greiner "has made more women . . . " Nana interrupts him: "Made them *what*?" "Made them famous," the man continues. "Oh," Nana replies, "now he interests me." Nana's humiliation of a potential client catches the impresario's eye, and the play on the word "made" suggests the interdependence, in the film, of Nana's work and her sexuality. To anyone familiar with Émile Zola's novel, this is hardly stunning news. But the film *Nana* functions in a more interesting way as a "reading" of Zola in Nana's relationships with other women. Zola's novel begins with theatre-goers—virtually all male—discussing the new discovery, Nana. Bordenave, the theatre manager, abruptly corrects anyone who refers to the space as a theatre—"You mean my brothel!" he interrupts, a virtual rhythmic cadence throughout the opening chapter. When Nana finally appears on stage, she is first laughed at and then recognized as a remarkable spectacle. The power of this "man-eater" (as Zola calls her) is measured by her hypnotic, mesmerizing effect on the male spectators. Hence, Zola's novel plays on absolute gender distinctions—male/female, onlooker/performer.[6]

In the film, however, and in keeping with the foregrounding of Nana's connection with Satin, Nana's appearances on stage are less absolutely defined in terms of a female performer versus a male onlooker. To be sure, attention is drawn in the film to the expectations of the male audience vis-à-vis Nana, but equal attention is drawn to two other spectators, Satin and Mimi. These two fellow prostitutes have visited the theatre regularly, trying to see their friend, but each time they are told that Nana doesn't want to see them. Meanwhile, Nana expresses concern about her two friends. When Nana finally comes on stage, the male members in the audience are appropriately dazzled by her performance (and a rather odd performance it is; despite the fact that Goldwyn wanted to make Sten a star in her own terms, her stage performance in *Nana* is like a bad imitation of Marlene Dietrich). They are not, however, the only spectators; Satin and Mimi have taken their seats in the balcony and impatiently (and angrily) await the arrival of the friend they think has betrayed them. ("When does our lady of the sewers come on?" one asks the other.) Mimi and Satin are moved to tears by Nana's performance, and shots of their reactions to their friend onstage provide an interesting counterpoint to the reactions of the male members of the audience.

Much attention has been paid, in feminist film theory, to the polarity of the gaze in classical cinema—where man is "bearer of the look," to use Laura Mulvey's phrase, and woman its object—and in particular to those situations, like Nana onstage, which epitomize the absolute division between woman as object and man as subject.[7] I have always found Zola's novel also to be a stunning demonstration of this process, and it is perhaps one of many non-coincidences that Zola's influence on the cinema has been noted by many filmmakers and theorists alike.[8] But in Arzner's *Nana*, there is no absolute polarity, no rigid opposition, between woman as performer and man as onlooker, since women in the audience are active spectators and impassioned onlookers. Indeed, reaction shots of the women are as fully a part of the continuity established in this scene as shots of the men are.

This is, I believe, one of the distinctive features of how "women's work" is presented in Arzner's films, particularly women's work onstage. There is no simplistic division between the male gaze and the female object, and women are active and complex subjects, regardless of what they are subject of or subjected to. It is significant in this context that the most famous scene in any of

Figure 39. Anna Sten as Nana. MOMA Film Stills Archive.

Arzner's films, Judy's speech to the audience in *Dance, Girl, Dance*, may address the audience as male, but the audience we actually see is not exclusively male. For in *Dance, Girl, Dance*, as in *Nana*, the working world of women is just that, and not a rarefied sphere where women exist only as victims or only as objects of male pleasure.

Unfortunately, however, this "reading" of Zola, and of some of the conventions of classical cinema, demonstrated in the foregrounding of the friendships among Nana, Mimi and Satin, and in the presentation of Nana's performance as one eagerly consumed by women as well as men, is not sustained in *Nana*. The film becomes centered on a conflict between two men, both of whom are supposedly ruined by their contact with Nana. In Zola's novel, Nana dies of smallpox, and she is surrounded by a circle of fellow prostitutes as she dies. Meanwhile, in the street, men are gathered, drawn both by her death and by the announcement of war. A rigid boundary line separates the world of men from the world of women in the novel; the men dare not enter the room, where Nana's death and disfigurement are described by Zola in stunningly repulsive detail. In the film, Nana dies by her own hand, clearly an easy, and not particularly satisfying, out. Instead of the sustained exploration of the intersections between gender, work, and performance that one might expect, given the beginning of the film and its representation of women in the theatre, the film moves towards a conclusion of tired clichés of the ruined woman who sacrifices herself. The spectacle of Nana's suicide cannot erase, however, the stunning mise-en-scène of the stage, where Nana's status as a working girl combines the pleasures and dangers of the look with the exploitation and delight of performance.

The Bride Wore Red (1937)

Even in a film that is ultimately disappointing, like *Nana*, there are elements suggestive of Arzner's unique touch and her ability to draw, even from material seemingly resistant to such inflections, complicated and complex portraits of women's lives. *The Bride Wore Red* was, for Arzner, an unsatisfying film. While the film echoes the preoccupations that are much more extensively developed in other films, *The Bride Wore Red* does focus, somewhat more explicitly than other films directed by Arzner, on the importance of costume and performance to any notion of female identity; and thus the notion of women's work, in this film, includes the realms of fashion and self-presentation.[9]

The plot of *The Bride Wore Red* is based on a practical joke. Two wealthy men are spending the evening gambling in a nightclub, and engage in a discussion about the evidence of class and good breeding. Using the image of a roulette wheel, one (Count Armalia) insists that chance decides who is rich and who is poor, while the other (Rudi Pal) insists that breeding accounts for absolute distinctions. In order to make his point, Armalia insists that the two men go to the seediest club they can find. Joan Crawford, playing Anni, a barmaid, becomes the concrete manifestation of Armalia's wager. Count Armalia, who argues in favor of the "performative" quality of social class, offers her a large sum of money and an all-expense-paid vacation if she will pose as a member of the aristocracy. She agrees and departs for Terrano, where she soon charms another wealthy man—none other than Rudi, the man with whom her benefactor made his original bet. Count Armalia's words to Rudi prove to be prophetic; describing Anni, he says, "Have her properly washed, dressed and coiffured, and you wouldn't be able to tell her from your fiancée."

With her new identity, Anni (now Anne Vivaldi) arrives at the train station and meets Giulio, the local postman and the film's embodiment of peasant purity. Indeed, the opposition of high class and low class is displaced, as the film progresses, by the opposition of city and country. As coincidence would have it, the maid assigned to Anni in the hotel is her old friend from the bar, Maria, who has found true happiness in the country. The film shows the poor—whether maids like Maria or postmen like Giulio—as more attuned to the values of the simple, nature-bound life. The process of the film will be to demonstrate to Anni that what she really desires is a life with Giulio, not with Rudi.

Her encounter with the wealthy at the resort may make her long for the riches that Rudi can offer, but it also makes her long for a life in closer touch with nature, neatly represented by Giulio.

Anni wins Rudi's affections away from Maddelena, his fiancée. In a twist typical of Arzner, Maddelena is one of the wealthy, but possesses none of their hypocrisy or arrogance, thus complicating the simple division between upper and lower classes. One of Arzner's preferred actresses, Billie Burke, plays the role of wife to Maddelena's father. As is typical for Burke, she is frilly and feminine, but there is a dry, almost acidic side to her portrayal of the suspicious and cynical woman of the world.

In order to make sure that Rudi proposes to her, Anni extends her stay at the hotel. In the meantime, Contessa di Meina (Burke) wires Armalia, supposedly a close friend of Anne Vivaldi's family, to inquire about Anne. His response—specifying the ruse and Anni's real status as a "cabaret girl"—gets lost when Giulio, carrying the telegram to the hotel, is met by Anni, and they kiss. But when Giulio discovers that Anni plans to marry Rudi, he threatens to deliver the copy of the telegram kept in the office. And this he does, during the farewell dinner for Anni and Rudi. Once her charade is discovered, Anni leaves the hotel and meets Giulio; having acknowledged her true feelings for him, Anni accepts his offer of marriage, and the film ends.

Performance is central to *The Bride Wore Red*, and even though the performance is not so literal or explicit as in *Nana*, the film nonetheless emphasizes from beginning to end the extent to which women's identities—sexual as well as class—depend upon performance. And women's social class also determines what kind of sexual performance is expected of them. Crawford's Anni is introduced through her performance of a song at the bar, and when she is introduced to the count she immediately assumes her status as an object to be consumed; indeed, she asks of the count if he has come to "stare at animals in the zoo." The central performance that she undertakes in the film, of course, is her attempt to act like a "lady." Two particular elements are significant here: her assumption of arrogant speech with servants, and her entrances in different types of clothing down the staircase of the hotel.

When Anni arrives at Terrano, Giulio offers to take her to the hotel in his cart, and she questions whether he should expect a lady to accept. When Anni arrives in her room, the maid enters and asks Anni if she would like her clothes unpacked. Just as Anni is basking in the luxury of being waited upon, she recognizes her old friend Maria. The assumption of wealth is equated with artifice, which comes as no surprise; but the film demonstrates the performative aspect of such speech by drawing on one of Arzner's preferred themes—female community and friendship. Indeed, even though Anni's relationship with Giulio is meant to be her passage to true self-discovery, she appears far more honest, frank, and direct with Maria. During one striking exchange between the two women, Maria wears one of Anni's costumes, making the "quotation" of artifice an important aspect of their relationship.

Similarly, Anni is assisted in her performance by one of the waiters, who subtly instructs her how to eat properly. Later, when she is about to depart with Rudi, she thanks the servant and tells him—in her best aristocratic tone—that a large check will be sent to him later. He informs her that this is not necessary, and that his cousin (virtually everyone in Terrano seems to be a cousin of Giulio) asked him to watch out for her. Still later, when Anni leaves the hotel in disgrace, only this servant continues to treat her like a "lady"—by opening the door for her after others refuse.

If the film contrasts Anni's "authentic" speech with her "performed" speech, in virtually every case the performed speech occurs in public places, while the authentic speech occurs either behind closed doors or in the expanses of forest that surround the hotel, but which are portrayed as quite distant from the social world the hotel represents. Similarly, the entrances Anni makes down the hotel staircase are public performances. Three such entrances occur. It is not surprising that dress is central to each entrance; what is interesting are the different and complex inflections that dress acquires. The title of the film refers to Anni's dream dress, a red, sequined evening gown, which is one of her first purchases once she is endowed by Count Armalia. But when she wants to wear it the first night at the hotel, Maria dissuades her, convinced that it is more appropriate to the seedy club where they knew each other when. Instead, Anni wears an outfit that is demure and excessive at the same time—a white dress with a veil, flowers in her hair, and a fan which she holds before her face. Anni receives the attentions of the crowd, presumably because she is distinctive, yet still one of them.

On the evening of her farewell dinner, once Anni has managed to get a marriage proposal from Rudi, she decides to wear her red dress. As she descends the stairs she once again is the object of attention (shades of Bette Davis wearing a red dress to the ball in *Jezebel!*). Maria advised her not to wear the dress when Anni arrived at the hotel. Now, however, Anni assumes that since she is about to become Rudi's wife, she no longer has to worry about following conventions; she can flaunt them. The dress does indeed provoke a reaction, as if to suggest that Anni always treads a fine line between being acceptable and outrageous, and in more general terms to suggest that the class identity she seeks is a function of appearance. The red dress signifies simultaneously Anni's desire for and her exclusion from the very values to which she aspires.

The complexity of "appearances" achieves yet another dimension when Anni comes down the stairs one final time to the notice of the crowd, at the film's conclusion, when her deception has been revealed. She wears a nondescript black cape—nondescript in the sense that it does not suggest one particular class affiliation; and it is indeed so nondescript that it could be worn by virtually anyone in the film, working-class or aristocratic. Once Anni and Giulio are reunited, she takes off the cloak to reveal a peasant costume that she wore to the "festa"—a carnivalesque celebration in which everyone dresses in supposed authentic peasant garb. Oddly, then, Anni adopts a costume from the most elaborate performance of the film to claim her authentic self. The film suggests not only that gender and class, for women, are equally a function of dress, of appearance; it also suggests, obliquely, that there is virtually no such thing as a female identity that does not rely on costume, staging, and performance. Whatever authentic identity Anni captures at the film's conclusion, it is an identity manufactured by the kind of women's work that keeps the illusions of performance alive.

First Comes Courage (1943)

Several times in the course of Arzner's career she was asked to finish films that others had begun. Her final film, *First Comes Courage*, marked the first time that another director had to finish a film she had started. Arzner became quite ill during the production of the film, and Charles Vidor finished it. As discussed earlier, for reasons having to do with more than her health, this was Arzner's last film as director.

First Comes Courage is set in Norway in 1942, and tells the story of Nicole Larsen (Merle Oberon), an Allied spy who receives her information by virtue of her romance with a German Nazi stationed in Norway, Major Paul Dichter (Carl Esmond). Dichter knows there is a leak somewhere, and a visiting Nazi has suspicions about Nicole. She passes on her information through bogus visits to an eye doctor, who then transmits her information by embedding it in eyeglass lenses. A message that suspicions are forming about Nicole reaches Allied officer Allan Lowell (Brian Aherne), who has been transferred to field service in order to assist the Norwegian underground by wiping out Nazi strongholds. Most of the film takes place as an alternation between Lowell, preparing for and executing his plans in the Norwegian town where Nicole lives, and Nicole, attempting to divert suspicion from herself while continuing to amass information. That a relationship exists between Lowell and Larsen is made evident through cross-cutting, although the specific nature of the relationship is made clear only when he is captured by the Nazis.

Allan has come to the Norwegian village to preside over a bomb attack and to eliminate a key Nazi. After he is captured, Nicole must develop a ruse in order to help him escape from the hospital where he recuperates after the shooting that killed his companion. She is advised by the eye doctor to take Rose Lindstrom, a nurse at the hospital, into her confidence. With some hesitation,

Nicole does so, and the two are able to move Lowell, dressed in a Nazi uniform, to Nicole's house.

Interestingly (and typically for Arzner), Rose's intervention occurs at just the moment when Nicole sees Allan for the first time and discovers that her comrade is also her lover from the past. The relationship that has been, throughout the film, the basis of spatial opposition, established only through cross-cutting, is now fully a part of the present tense of the film, a function of a single dramatic space. Nicole's alliance with Rose is significant for two reasons. First, Nicole must endanger her cover as a traitor in order to save Lowell, and second, this risk occurs in an alliance with another woman who functions, however briefly, as an indication of the strength of female bonding.

Indeed, for a brief moment, the highly anticipated reunion of Allan and Nicole is overshadowed by the alliance between the two women. Rose is blonde; she is a large, heavy-set woman, whose physical appearance contrasts markedly with the delicate brunette figure of Merle Oberon. The contrast between the two women plays on the butch (Rose)/femme (Nicole) imagery that appears frequently in portrayals of women in Arzner's films. Rose proves, as well, to be as unwavering in her strength as Nicole; when she is questioned by the Nazis, once she is suspected of having assisted in Lowell's escape, she refuses to break. Molly Haskell assesses the relationship between the two women: "True to Arzner, the most moving character in the film is a woman, a nurse, who assists Oberon and refuses to denounce her even when her own family is threatened. And the most moving scene is the one in which they embrace in a rapture of mutual understanding that transcends war, and that will nourish each of them in their lonely women's destinies in a way that romantic love never can."[10]

The bombing and assassination are to go ahead as planned, and as coincidence would have it, Dichter has planned for Nicole to become his bride on that very day. Dichter is increasingly uncomfortable with the suspicions cast his way about Nicole, and he feels his marriage to her will displace those suspicions. For Nicole, the marriage offers yet another opportunity to have more access to information. The wedding goes off as planned, and it is an odd ceremony, indeed—the couple march down an aisle of Nazis and wed beneath a Nazi flag, their hands joined over a copy of *Mein Kampf.* But Dichter has discovered the truth about Nicole; he passed false information about a munitions factory only to her, and it was bombed shortly after, thus proving her identity as a spy. He tells Nicole that she will die in a fake accident, but Allan appears on the scene to kill him before he can execute his plan.

Meanwhile, the raid is going off as planned, and both Dichter and Von Elser (the suspicious Nazi) are killed, while Allan and Nicole emerge unscathed. Allan tries to convince Nicole to return to England, but she insists that she must stay in Norway, particularly now that she has the additional status of widow of a Nazi officer. After a final kiss, Nicole disappears into the forest, while Allan rejoins the Allies, who are about to sail off. As he departs, a final series of match shots situates the two of them as they smile while the distance between them grows.

To be sure, Nicole Larsen is a different kind of working girl than May and June, Nana, or Anni; the profession of spying is hardly like those of research assistant or telegraph operator (*Working Girls*), prostitute (*Nana*), or cabaret singer (*The Bride Wore Red*). But Larsen's career as a spy is presented in ways remarkably similar to Arzner's other films preoccupied with women's work. Larsen's work involves a performance with her Nazi informer, where the typical activities of womanhood—companionship and dress, not to mention grace and charm under pressure—become, for her, strategic means to acquire information. The audience is informed of Nicole's true identity almost immediately in the film, since the first scene finds her walking down the town street to the friendly greeting of a Nazi and the bitter reprimand of a townswoman, only to enter the eye doctor's shop where, in the darkened room, he shines a light in her eyes and her true identity is revealed. Hence, from here on in, virtually all of Nicole's performance is recognized as a ruse, a disguise.

Where *First Comes Courage* differs from Arzner's other work is in the mythic heroism attributed to Nicole. Her work is that of a patriot, not just that of a woman trying to survive. But even here, *First Comes Courage* functions as an interesting grid through which to read other films about women and work. Nicole has two stirring speeches in the film, one in which she confronts the Nazi whom she marries out of her devotion to the cause, and another in which she tells Allan, her true love, that she cannot leave with him and forsake her activities in Norway. When Dichter tells Nicole that he knows she is a spy, she expresses contempt for him and denounces his weakness (all along he has been more concerned about his own safety than the principles he supposedly cares about); this revelation of her contempt makes her performances as a devoted companion even more impressive.

Nicole's most impassioned speech comes at the film's conclusion. Throughout the film there has been an interesting role reversal, to the extent that Nicole occupies fully and comfortably the position of "hero," with Allan in much more of a supporting role (although he kills Dichter, Nicole had previously saved Allan's life). After the success of the raid and the death of the Nazis, it is Allan who tries to convince Nicole that she should retreat to safety, and Nicole who insists upon the need to continue to fight.

There are curious echoes, in the final moments of the film, of a far more successful film released in the same year as *First Comes Courage—Casablanca*.[11] The final encounter between Rick (Humphrey Bogart) and Ilsa (Ingrid Bergman) is one of the best-known scenes in American film, from Rick's insistence that Ilsa depart with her husband, rather than stay with him, to his famous remark that "it doesn't take much to see that the problems of three little people don't amount to a hill of beans in this crazy world. Someday you'll understand that." At the conclusion of *First Comes Courage*, Allan says to Nicole that she has "done more than any woman could be expected to do." She tells him: "I'll quit when you quit." He insists that "we're not saying goodbye again ever." While the words may not be as classic as Bogart's "hill of beans," Nicole's reply to Allan rings familiar: "Oh but darling it isn't that kind of world any more. People don't dance and laugh and ski, as we once used to." I am not suggesting that any allusion to *Casablanca* is deliberate (the films were in production at approximately the same time), but rather that the mythic qualities associated with love and war, which find perhaps their most classic expression in *Casablanca*, are both cited and turned around in *First Comes Courage*. For in Arzner's film, Nicole expresses views that are more typically expressed by male heroes. Put another way, then, *First Comes Courage* twists the gender conventions of the war/spy genre, and in the process, celebrates women's work, not *as* love and romance, nor as a *substitute* for love and romance, but as what makes everything else possible.

6

Odd Couples

ALL OF ARZNER'S films contain romances of one kind or another. But I know of no Arzner film in which the requisite romance is played "straight" (so to speak). Virtually all of the pairings in Arzner's films contain elements that go against the grain of the clichés of Hollywood romance. Even the most apparently conventional couples—male/female and heterosexual—manage to be unconventional in subtle ways. In *Dance, Girl, Dance*, for instance, the romantic pairings between Jimmie Harris and a succession of women—Judy, Bubbles, and his wife—all play on a peculiar infantilization of the man. Judy's final pairing with impresario Steven Adams is odd in a different way, in that the Ralph Bellamy character works against the type of "leading man." In addition, Adams takes the place of Basilova as mentor to Judy, and Judy and Basilova form yet another odd couple, largely because of the play with butch and femme characteristics. In *Dance, Girl, Dance*, there are many types of couples that cross a wide range of boundaries, and that in itself is a distinctive feature of Arzner's work.

In *Working Girls*, the romantic intrigues in which the sisters become involved remain secondary to their relationship with each other, while *The Wild Party* insists simultaneously on the importance of heterosexual romantic love and female friendship. This wide range of coupledom is central to Arzner's work, and foregrounds the extent to which the male/female couple exists across a wide range of relationships. Now Dorothy Arzner is not the only filmmaker in Hollywood to put women center stage as the active agents of desire; the tradition of the "woman's film," for instance, is built upon women's desires—however defined—as primary movers of the narrative. But what is unique in Arzner's work is the extent to which desire, while apparently heterosexual in terms of women desiring men (and vice versa), is structured by female/female relationships.

I want to suggest that in those films directed by Arzner that are apparently most preoccupied with male/female couples, and in particular with the dissolution of those couples, there are distinct encounters between women that suggest the possibilities of other kinds of desire. In the two films discussed in this chapter, troubled heterosexual pairings—between Cynthia and Christopher in *Christopher Strong* (1933) and between Harriet and Walter Craig in *Craig's Wife*

Figure 40. Rosalind Russell and Dorothy Arzner on the set of *Craig's Wife*, 1936. Arts Library—Special Collections, University Research Library, UCLA.

(1936)—are crossed by various female/female relationships that emerge at key moments and occasion particularly striking visual and narrative formulations. In other words, men may well be objects of female desire in these films, but romances are complicated by the various female mediators who exist. The boundaries between desired object and mediator shift, and often far more screen attention is paid to the female/female interractions than is necessary to the plot.[1] In the language of 1970s film theory, Arzner may well "subvert" the boy-meets-girl formula of classical film; at the same time, this subversion does more than critique the dominant formula; it offers other possibilities of screen pleasure.

Thus, I am using the term "odd couples" to describe how the heterosexual couple is rendered strange, is defamiliarized. But I insist, simultaneously, on another, less heterosexual sense of the phrase "odd couples." I have noted in another context that publicity photographs of Arzner play consistently not only on her butch persona, but also on the play between butch and femme characteristics. Indeed, the longing gazes exchanged between Arzner and her numerous female leads provide one of the most curious and fascinating chapters in Hollywood's long history of picturing women. These publicity photographs echo how, in Arzner's films, relationships between women often take particular visual form, with oppositions (and attractions) formed around the competing terms of butch and femme characteristics. I have noted how, in *Working Girls*, the two sisters are virtually identical at the film's beginning; but as the film progresses the change in fortune is marked by the change in clothing, whereby the more butch of the two becomes more assertive. One of the most striking manifestations of butch and femme occurs in *Dance, Girl, Dance*, as we shall see in the next chapter.

Christopher Strong and *Craig's Wife* are two of the Arzner films seen most frequently today. Both films are concerned with the stakes of marriage, and alternatives to marriage, for women. Arzner's preoccupation with women's work becomes significant in these films too, since in both films the woman's work interferes with the relationship, even when, in the case of *Craig's Wife*, the work in question is precisely that of a homemaker. Most important, both of these films demonstrate the limitations of male-centered models of desire for women, as well as of simple reversals that assume the same terms—i.e., a female oedipal scenario wherein woman desires a man to replace her father. Women's desire in these films is certainly shaped by established conventions of heterosexual romance; but it is also structured and shaped by other women. In both films, the collapse of heterosexual relationships is accompanied by a play on differences among women, wherein attraction between women becomes a powerful source of visual pleasure.

Christopher Strong (1933)

Christopher Strong traces the doomed relationship between Cynthia Darrington, an aviatrix, and Christopher Strong, a distinguished gentleman and member of Parliament. The film opens with a treasure hunt that claims the attentions of Monica Strong, Christopher's somewhat wild and rebellious daughter, and Harry, her (married) boyfriend. The guests are challenged to find a man who has been married more than five years and has remained faithful to his wife. Monica brings Christopher in as the trophy. The female counterpart to Christopher Strong—a woman over the age of twenty-one who has never had a love affair—is Cynthia Darrington, whom Harry meets when her car runs him off the road. Cynthia and Christopher meet, in other words, as the odd "men" out in the aristocratic world of parties and pleasure.

From the outset, Christopher's relationship to Cynthia is fatherly, both figuratively (he is old enough to be her father; she and his daughter become friends) and literally (the only mention of Cynthia's parents occurs in this opening scene; Christopher knew Cynthia's father). But any resemblance to

Figure 41. Billie Burke and Dorothy Arzner on the set of *Christopher Strong*, 1933. MOMA Film Stills Archive.

standard oedipal fare is immediately complicated by the relationship between Cynthia and Monica, for that friendship becomes the pretext for meetings between Cynthia and Christopher. With considerable hesitation, the two—Christopher and Cynthia, that is—become lovers; Lady Strong becomes suspicious, but keeps up a stoic front. Largely through Cynthia's interventions, Monica and Harry, who are forced apart at the insistence of Monica's parents that she not see a married man, are able to reunite and marry, with her parents' eventual blessing. But they discover Cynthia and Christopher's affair, and at precisely the moment when two other significant and parallel events have occurred— both Monica and Cynthia are pregnant. Realizing that Christopher would obtain a divorce and marry her out of a sense of duty, and realizing that his primary commitment is to his official family, Cynthia commits suicide.[2]

Cynthia Darrington's initial appearance at the party is one of Arzner's most exquisite stagings of the relationship between butch and femme. Hepburn swaggers among the assembled guests, and her clothing—tailored jacket, jodhpurs, beanie—signifies both her distinction and her marginality. Hepburn's role in the film as Cynthia Darrington, an independent woman and a woman in love, is fabulous. Many of the attributes later considered so central to the Hepburn persona—independence, athleticism, androgyny, butch flirtatiousness—are amply on display in the film. Cynthia Darrington resembles neither the men nor the women at the party; rather, her style borrows from both masculine and feminine attire, and is highly evocative of Arzner's own style of dress. Indeed, Cynthia's uniqueness at the party may be because she is a virgin, but virgin could easily be read as a euphemism for lesbian, especially when Cynthia exclaims to the guests that she has never been married . . . "in any sense of the term."

Christopher Strong is no exception to the tendency in Arzner's work for subplots to be far more intricately connected to the main narratives of the films than is usually the case in classical film narrative.[3] Monica and Harry's attendance at the party is the pretext for the initial meeting of Cynthia and Christopher. Harry is married, and both Christopher and Lady Strong are horrified that Monica is seeing a married man. As Christopher's attraction to Cynthia grows, so does his willingness to be more open to his daughter's rebellious ways, thus creating disagreement and discord with his wife. The most significant collision of the plot and the subplot occurs during a vacation in Cannes, where Cynthia joins the Strong family in their villa. At a party, Monica, whose relationship with Harry has ended at her parents' insistence, flirts with a man named Carlo. Lady Strong has left the party early, and when Carlo wants to take Monica home, Christopher agrees. It requires no imagination to realize that his lapse in judgment is due to his own desire to be left alone with Cynthia.

In other words, then, the subplot of Monica and Harry's fortunes not only highlights the development of Cynthia and Christopher's relationship, but it is intricately connected to it. Similarly, the character of Lady Strong, played by Billie Burke, acquires a function far more complex than that of the wife betrayed and abandoned for a younger woman. Indeed, when Cynthia makes her decision to kill herself rather than face the consequences of her pregnancy, Lady Strong's benefit seems to be far more a factor than Christopher's (who, by the conclusion of the film, seems to me little more than a prig). Cynthia's suicide mission occurs after Christopher has—unconsciously—made the choice of his own "official" family over his relationship with Cynthia; the fact that Monica and Cynthia discover their pregnancies at the same time is obviously significant. But just as important, the mission occurs after an unusual discussion between Cynthia and Lady Strong, during which Lady Strong thanks Cynthia for bringing Monica back to the family fold, and indirectly acknowledges Cynthia's affair with Christopher. This discussion seems to me less important as a staging of the ultimate victory of conventional marriage than as a staging of an encounter between two women that ultimately has more powerful ramifications than does heterosexual romance.[4]

Christopher Strong demonstrates one of the most striking aspects of the

Figure 42. Katharine Hepburn as Cynthia Darrington in *Christopher Strong*, 1933. MOMA Film Stills Archive.

important collaborative process with the writer that was as crucial, if not more so, to Arzner's work as her status as "star-maker." As mentioned earlier, Arzner valued the writer's input, and whenever possible she kept the writer on the set. Despite the fact that Zoë Akins was indisposed for much of the preparation of *Christopher Strong*, her script demonstrates one of the most significant aspects of her and Arzner's collaboration—the critical and subversive revision and re-reading of "original" sources, in this case, a novel by Gilbert Frankau. Although Arzner once insisted in an interview that British aviatrix Amy Johnson, rather than American Amelia Earhart, was the model for Cynthia Darrington, Gilbert Frankau's British novel is not about an aviatrix at all, but about a race car driver.[5] Hence the change in profession obviously taps the reputations of both women, the British setting tending to emphasize Johnson; the American distribution, Earhart.

One of the scenes in the film that has received critical acclaim—even by those who otherwise dismiss the film—occurs when Christopher and Cynthia make love for the first time.[6] The entire scene focusses on Cynthia's extended arm, with the lovers' voices offscreen; Chris has given her a bracelet, and he asks her to give up flying. The scene consists of one extended shot, with Cynthia's arm extending into the frame to turn on the bedside lamp. We see only her arm and a clock on the table. Cynthia wears a bracelet on her wrist, as well as a large ring. In voice-over she says: "I love my beautiful bracelet. And I've never cared a button for jewels before. Now I'm shackled." Christopher inquires about her ring, which bears the Darrington family crest and, in Latin, the words "courage conquers death." Cynthia adds, "but not love," and Christopher asks Cynthia to give up her altitude flight—"for me."

What bitter irony, that this supposed moment of afterglow becomes the staging of Christopher's authority. For Cynthia agrees to give up flying. This scene accomplishes what no other scene in the film has—the conquest, so to speak, of Cynthia by Christopher. Now what I find particularly interesting here is that this image is one of the most distanced and abstracted images in the entire film. In none of the other, more typically Hollywood, portrayals of Cynthia and Christopher is he able to assert with such finality or authority his power. What an interesting twist this is, since the suggestion is made that Cynthia Darrington's image so exceeds and problematizes the notion of woman as man's property that she must be, quite literally, banished from the frame in order for this summary statement of possession to occur.

That Cynthia refers to herself as "shackled" contains more than a touch of irony. Consider the equivalent scene in Frankau's novel: Felicity (the character who becomes Cynthia in the film) and Christopher go away together to a country cottage in Ohio, and after the fact, once Christopher is on his way back to England, the scene is recalled: "So adorable, those hands. So adorable, that head, tousled after some sweet surrender. So adorable, her frank youth, her courageous acceptance of his love, her gay companionship."[7] The description continues: " . . . they had found more to say. And always, mind exploring mind had discovered some new treasure. For of such texture—mental woof threading physical warp—had been the mantle cast over them by the fine weaver, Love."[8] The language used to describe their first sexual encounter could be described in a variety of ways—excessive, melodramatic, flowery, sentimental—but definitely *not* as ironic. Akins and Arzner transform a maudlin description of sexual love into an ironic comment, and at the same time, they use the close-up of Hepburn's arm to sustain and enhance the irony of the entire scene.

For contemporary feminist audiences, *Christopher Strong* stands as one of the best examples of Arzner's irony, and the image of Cynthia's extended arm is one of the most stunning examples of Arzner's ironic subversion of the norms of classical cinema. I believe the scene is also significant in two other ways—as a subtle reference to Sir Christopher's relationship with his wife, and as a condensation of many of the conflicts and tensions that are played out in the film. Immediately after the bracelet scene, we see Monica and Harry in a car, going to pick up Christopher. Then we see Lady Strong in her boudoir, obviously distressed that her husband has not yet arrived home. She sits down at her vanity and proceeds to remove her jewelry—including several bracelets. The point is made, subtly and effectively: Cynthia's lone bracelet leads, symbolically and otherwise, to a life of waiting, to a display of shackles. Now the two images of heterosexual union are quite different. The isolated shot of Cynthia's extended arm with disembodied voices over is a peculiarly abstracted and distanced image, while the image of Lady Strong in her boudoir is much more traditional, moving from a long shot of her contained within the accoutrements of femininity, to a close-up of her before her vanity mirror as she removes her jewelry. Yet the distinctly different images of the women in Christopher's life are connected by the common motif of shackles.

Similarly, throughout *Christopher Strong*, subtle connections are drawn between seemingly opposing pairs. I have noted that when Cynthia and Christopher meet at the treasure hunt, they are both outsiders to the world of excessive frivolity and partying. But throughout the film, attention is drawn to the problematic and constantly shifting relationship of margin and center, of "abnormal" and "normal." Key conversations in the film turn on the inflections of morally loaded terms like "bad" or "nice." At the treasure hunt, when Harry and Monica hear the request to find the man married for five years and the virginal woman over twenty-one, they tease each other about how distinctly unqualified they are for those descriptions. "Bad, bad . . . " Monica says to Harry; and he responds that "I wish I were—or that you were—*really* bad." At the very least, Harry and Monica fall into ambiguous territory insofar as "badness" is concerned, but immediately Monica invokes the standard of her father. "I know a man who isn't bad," she says, and she leaves the party to find him.

The nature of transgression is picked up immediately in the next scene, at the Strong household, where Christopher is working in his study and Lady Strong paces, worried about her daughter. Lady Strong muses that "sometimes I think you and I are the only nice people still left in the world." But the notion of "niceness" is just as ambiguously defined as "badness" was in the preceding scene; Lady Strong goes on to voice her fears that Monica sees her parents as "stuffy and old-fashioned." "Bad" and "nice" do not make for a clearly defined opposition, since the terms are defined so ambiguously. But this is, of course, precisely the point—the film is preoccupied with the ambiguous definitions of opposing pairs. At the treasure hunt, Monica describes her taste for a wild social life by telling Cynthia that she too likes to "fly," but in a different sense than Cynthia does. The play on the word "fly" makes for a succint representation of the dilemma explored in the film: Do Monica and Cynthia, indeed, "fly" in totally opposing ways? And is Cynthia's profession of flying totally incompatible with the kind of flying Monica has in mind?

The most interesting manifestations of this preoccupation with ambiguous opposition and the subsequent subversion of dualisms occur in the various pairings of individuals and juxtapositions of scenes. Cynthia and Christopher's first meeting, at the treasure hunt, occupies a somewhat curious "space." Carrie, the hostess of the party (and Christopher's sister) introduces them, and we see Carrie, Monica, Christopher, and Cynthia, with party guests milling about, in a medium shot. The camera then isolates Cynthia and Christopher in a closer shot—the kind of isolating movement one expects to signify a forthcoming romance. Interestingly, however, what motivates the closer shot is the mention of Cynthia's father, and the fact that Christopher knew him and sent her a lovely note when he died. In other words, then, yet another ambiguity characterizes the initiation of Christopher and Cynthia's relationship, a question as to whether their relationship is primarily a romantic one, or primarily a substitute for the father–daughter one. But this question does not remain in a conventional oedipal frame for long, for the triangle of Cynthia, Christopher, and Cynthia's father is immediately resituated as the triangle of Cynthia, Monica, and Christopher. Indeed, the friendship that develops between Monica and Cynthia emphasizes yet another kind of ambiguity—i.e., does Christopher mediate Monica's and Cynthia's relationship, or is it Monica who mediates between Cynthia and Christopher? Significantly, Cynthia's father is never mentioned again, and I can think of few examples of Hollywood plots where the place of the father is evacuated so quickly in order to permit a woman—Monica—to step into his place.

Cynthia and Christopher form, then, a very odd couple. The oddest configuration of their relationship occurs when Christopher comes to Cynthia's apartment, presumably to discuss his worries about Monica. Cynthia is preparing to attend a dress ball as a moth, and she wears a shimmery, tight dress and a headdress complete with antennae. At no other moment in the film is Cynthia so obviously in costume (and so incredibly silly-looking), and this is precisely the moment that Christopher's attraction to Cynthia is announced. There is no small irony in the fact that the two scenes that comprise the most visible declaration of heterosexual love—this one, in which she looks like a cybernetic insect, and the "bracelet scene"—are the most ironic and parodic scenes in the film.

Indeed, whenever Christopher and Cynthia are portrayed together, there is a curious visual quality. Although Christopher never changes and the changes in Cynthia are never so drastic as the contrast between her riding outfit and her moth costume, there is a movement in the film traced by her changing relationship to clothing. Cynthia is never quite as frilly and classically feminine as Monica and Lady Strong are (and at least once during the film, Monica favors the kind of clothing worn by Cynthia), but her visual presentation in the film moves back and forth from femme to butch. One of the most striking juxta-

Figure 43. Katharine Hepburn and Colin Clive in *Christopher Strong*, 1933. MOMA Film Stills Archive.

positions in this respect occurs when Cynthia, in Cannes with the Strong family, kisses Christopher on the veranda, while Lady Strong watches, distraught, from her bedroom. Cynthia wears an evening gown not unlike the kind of attire favored by Monica and Lady Strong. Immediately following this scene, we see Cynthia with two men, at a diner counter, planning a flight, and Cynthia now wears the familiar outfit of jodhpurs and beanie in which we first saw her. The juxtaposition is striking; Cynthia exists quite literally in two different worlds.

Given Cynthia's first appearance in the film, so comfortable in her trademark clothing and equally comfortable about how different her looks are from those who surround her, the butch persona tends to be associated with Cynthia's profession, and the more "feminine" clothing she wears with the romance with Christopher. Yet the division of butch/career and femme/romance is never so clear-cut. Occasionally Cynthia's more feminine attire bears the influence of her flying outfits. The most striking example of this is seen when Cynthia and Christopher share a meal in a tavern, and unbeknownst to them, they are seen by Monica and Harry, who are appropriately shocked. Cynthia's conversation with Christopher makes clear the extent to which she is bored with a life in which her primary profession is as his mistress. Cynthia's clothing in this scene is a bit more severe and tailored than what she has worn in previous scenes with Christopher, and she wears a little hat that is modeled after the beanie so jauntily sported by her with her jodhpurs and trenchcoat. The subtle change in clothing suggests a feminine style that cannot quite resist the infiltration of other codes, other styles.

Christopher and Cynthia are an "odd couple" not only in that the relationship simply cannot survive, but also in that their pairing becomes the pretext for a series of other couplings, odd and otherwise. By the conclusion of the film, Monica and Harry are united, as are Christopher and Lady Strong. Cynthia fits nowhere in the neat pairings that she has enabled. Ultimately, Cynthia Darrington's sacrifice is that she willingly and consciously adopts the role of mediator—initially, between Harry and Monica, and finally, between Christopher and his wife. Cynthia's death allows Lady Strong and Christopher to remain together. This ending certainly can be read as a restoration of the couple and the family at the expense of Cynthia's life. But underneath that pat conclusion there is yet another odd coupling, whereby Cynthia choses Lady Strong's happiness over her own.

Craig's Wife (1936)

Like *Christopher Strong*, *Craig's Wife* tells the tale of a woman left alone. To be sure, the two films are different in many ways—Harriet Craig may be isolated, but she does not die; and whereas Cynthia cannot reconcile the worlds of love and career, for Harriet those worlds are painfully identical. But in both cases, the heroines find themselves confronted with the reality of a patriarchal universe in which Cynthia's claims to career and love simultaneously, and Harriet's claims to autonomy, are rendered impossible. Put another way, those claims result in tragedy, not in happiness.

Craig's Wife is based on the play by George Kelly, who was not pleased with Arzner's version.[9] The film adopts an ironic note not present in the play, and thus exemplifies a process we have seen in several of Arzner's films, including *Christopher Strong*—a revision of the original source, both to problematize some of the conventions and to highlight women's points of view. The film, like the Kelly play, tells the story of a woman obsessively devoted to her home at the expense of all human contact, especially that with her husband, Walter (played by John Boles). She is manic about the objects that surround her and suspicious of everyone, including a widowed neighbor, Mrs. Frazier, played by

Billie Burke. In the course of the film, Harriet loses virtually everything: her maid, her husband, her sister, and her niece's devotion.

At the conclusion, she has one last chance at connection with another human being, when Mrs. Frazier comes to visit, but Mrs. Frazier leaves, and Harriet is left alone. The characterization of Mrs. Frazier and the film's ending are quite different from Kelly's play. In the play, Mrs. Frazier is portrayed as a pathetic human being, lonely and desolate, and by the play's conclusion, Harriet is seen as having become like Mrs. Frazier, but even lonelier. In the film, however, Mrs. Frazier is not drawn so stereotypically or so negatively, and the film's ending suggests, rather, that Harriet has one final opportunity to connect with another human being. Billie Burke's role as Mrs. Frazier is her second in an Arzner film, and here, as in earlier films, Arzner plays upon the contrast between two women, one severe and dark, the other frilly and blonde. As I have noted, Burke was one of Arzner's preferred actresses, and after Arzner left Hollywood she produced several plays in which Burke starred.

Burke's role in *Craig's Wife*, as the widow next door who tends her rose garden, seems quite different than her part in *Christopher Strong*, in which she plays the title character's proper, betrayed wife. But in both films, Burke embodies a sweet femininity that could easily drift off into either pathos or parody, but does not. In *Christopher Strong* and *Craig's Wife*, Burke's characters are initially foils for Cynthia and Harriet, respectively. But as both films progress, it becomes clear that there will be no easy relegation of either Burke's extremely feminine, or Hepburn's/Russell's more butch persona, to secondary status. Burke's presence in these two films is crucial to a reconfiguring of women's relationships that celebrates butch and femme simultaneously.

Craig's Wife echoes *Christopher Strong* for its revisionist approach to the original source; in this case, the screenplay was adapted from Kelly's play by Mary McCall. If Rosalind Russell appears as a complex entity in the role of Harriet Craig, it is due not only to her performance, but also to the subtle changes wrought by McCall and Arzner to Kelly's script. In the play, Harriet Craig is a one-note failure, a woman doomed to a life of bitter loneliness, just like the widowed Mrs. Frazier across the way. Again, Mrs. Frazier represents Harriet's one last chance for human community, and the film reads less as an indictment of a willful woman than as a critique of the culture in which so few choices are available to women like Harriet. Indeed, one of the distinguishing features of *Craig's Wife* is its critique of the institution of marriage. To be sure, few of Arzner's previous works portray heterosexual couples in a utopian or even attractive light, but *Craig's Wife* makes even more explicit what is suggested in other films.

In Kelly's play, Harriet's argument for marriage as a business contract and a home as capital is presented as a caricature of feminism, whereas no such intimation is made in Arzner's film. Certainly, Harriet Craig, as portrayed by Russell, embodies many clichés of the domineering wife; but Mrs. Craig's position (in the film) is defined fully within patriarchy—not as a critique of it. Any critique present in the film belongs to the film, not to Harriet Craig. This is not to suggest that Arzner presents Harriet as a victim; rather, she presents her as a woman with a limited number of choices, whose obsession about her house is in many ways an extension of what is considered a more "normal" preoccupation for women.

Craig's Wife may be most succinctly described as a series of departures. Harriet Craig's obsession with her house and with propriety is so strong that eventually everyone leaves. And virtually everyone leaves in couples—Ethel (Harriet's niece) and her boyfriend, an instructor in Romance Languages; Mazie and her boyfriend, after he makes an unexpected visit to the house; and Aunt Austen and Mrs. Harold, in what I find one of the most delightful couplings of the film—the two women, one wealthy and one a servant, leave to travel around the world. While only the coupling of Aunt Austen and Mrs. Harold is distinctly not heterosexual, there is nonetheless no small irony in the fact that the middle-class home of the Craig's is so inhospitable to heterosexuality. Outside of the Craig home, another departure of a different kind occurs: Fergus Passmore, a friend of Walter, kills his wife and himself. The only solo departure is Walter's, suggesting somewhat ironically that the best way he can "become a man" is simply to leave, by himself. When Harriet is left alone in her house at the end of the film, yet another potential coupling occurs, when Mrs. Frazier brings her some roses.

For all the preoccupation in the film with the couplings (and recouplings) of its cast of characters, another dimension—visual as well as narrative— emerges to establish different kinds of couples as they are viewed by individuals within the film. At key moments in the film, interactions between individuals are accompanied by the presence of a witness. Often, this witness is Harriet herself. Visually, then, *Craig's Wife* configures triangulated relations of looking.

Our introduction to Harriet occurs when we see her in her sister's hospital room; Ethel, Harriet's niece, is seated next to her mother, while Harriet sits stiffly on a chair at the opposite end of the room. The closeness and the strong emotional bond between mother and daughter are completely alien to Harriet. When Harriet moves toward the bed, the three women are framed in a literal triangle, with Harriet looming over the two women. Harriet's first action in the film—and thus the introduction to her as a character—is to symbolically break the bond between mother and daughter. Harriet insists that Ethel accompany Harriet to the Craig home, ostensibly so that Harriet's sister can recover in peace. It does not require much imagination to see in this insistence upon isolation a projection of Harriet's simultaneous desire for autonomy and her

Figure 44. Harriet Craig (Rosalind Russell) looks on in the hospital room with her sister and her niece Ethel in *Craig's Wife*, 1936. MOMA Film Stills Archive.

distrust of any strong emotional bonds. At the same time, Harriet's insistence affords a representation of one of Arzner's preferred strategies for the representation of women—contrast in costume. When Harriet speaks to a nurse in the hall about the possibly detrimental effects of visitors, the two women make for a striking contrast of black (Harriet) and white (the nurse), as well as of two different versions of severity—Harriet's rather fussily severe suit, and the nurse's uniform.

There is an emphasis throughout *Craig's Wife* on theatrical presentation. The Craig living room is presented as if it were a stage, and the opening shots of the film set the dramatic tone. Two servants are seen in close-up as one admonishes the other to be careful with the objects on the mantel, and a subsequent cut to a long shot of the living room both dwarfs the individual women and demonstrates the overwhelming sense of space that dominates the film. The house is not only a setting, and it is even more than a character in its own right; it is also a threatening presence vis-à-vis the individuals who move through it. Virtually every character who enters the living room treads carefully, knowing that this is sacred space. They play parts that are uncomfortable to them. Ironically, Harriet is perhaps the most uncomfortable player of all, since sooner or later events transpire that she cannot control with the same authority she exercises as set decorator and stage director.

The emphasis on staging, on theatricality, complements the emphasis placed on Harriet's function as both witness and outsider. In one very striking example of the mise-en-scène of Harriet's role, Harriet is framed as both part of the domestic space and as excluded from it. After Harriet has returned home, she is shocked and distressed to see her husband, Aunt Austen, Mrs. Frazier, and Mrs. Frazier's grandson Timothy, standing outside the house together. The group is framed by the door, emphasizing even more strongly the theatrical effect. Harriet is quite literally excluded from what appears to be a happy family portrait of several generations. Harriet's distressed look is shown inside the house, and the irony of her situation is captured perfectly in this juxtaposition. She is the ultimate creature of domesticity, yet she is excluded from the simulated family portrait.

A series of mirror shots in the film also foreground the function of witnessing, with the sense of one couple intruded upon by another, as well as the framing effect. But in these instances, the couple does not comprise two different individuals, but rather Harriet and her own reflection. Three times we see Harriet carry on a conversation with another woman via the mirror, and in each case—with Mrs. Harold, with Aunt Austen, and with Ethel—the primary exchange seems to be between Harriet and her own reflection in the mirror, with the interlocuter functioning more as an intrusion. In these instances, Harriet is not the witness; the other women are. Nonetheless, Harriet's own distance from any conversation is marked.

The most striking embodiment of this combination of theatricality and witnessing occurs early in the film when Harriet and Ethel are returning, on a train, to Harriet's home. During the ride, Harriet expounds upon her philosophy of marriage to a somewhat shocked Ethel. Harriet explains that she married as a way to be independent. At this moment, Arzner's film departs quite sharply from Kelly's play, which depicts Harriet as far more villainous and far more calculating. Harriet explains to Ethel her desire for independence, and in Kelly's version, tells her:

I'm simply exacting my share of a bargain. Mr. Craig wanted a wife and a home; and he has them. And he can be perfectly sure of them, because the wife that he got happens to be one of the kind that regards her husband and home as more or less ultimate conditions. And my share of the bargain was the security and protection that those conditions imply. And I have *them*. But, unlike Mr. Craig, I can't be absolutely sure of them; because I know that, to a very great extent, they are at the mercy of the *mood* of a *man*. [She smiles knowingly.] And I suppose I'm too practical-minded to accept that as a sufficient guarantee of their permanence. So I must secure their permanence for myself.[10]

When Ethel asks how Harriet plans to do so, Harriet replies: "By securing into my own hands the control of the man upon which they are founded."[11] Julia Lesage has noted how Kelly utilizes feminist language to depict Harriet in villainous terms. Lesage notes, "Kelly's pejorative use of the word *independence*, repeated various times, indicates that his dialogue stands as an ideological reaction to women's gaining the right to vote in the U.S. in 1920."[12] In Arzner's film, however, this key speech is reduced to a much tamer discussion, in which Harriet does indeed stress independence, but in a way that avoids the pathology of Kelly's account. On the train, Harriet tells Ethel, "The only road to independence for me was through the man I married. I married to be independent." Contemporary feminist commentators on *Craig's Wife* suggest that Arzner creates sympathy and understanding for Harriet Craig, thus preventing the audience from vilifying her. Lesage notes that the "dilemma of love in marriage . . . is laid out with all its sides sympathetically presented," while Melissa Sue Kort says that the film changes Harriet "from villain to victim. While we cannot absolve her from her fanaticism concerning the house or her dishonesty with her husband, we do sympathize."[13]

Arzner's film may well indeed create a more sympathetic portrait of Harriet than does Kelly's play. I think it is just as important to stress, however, that in this scene, in which Harriet delivers her philosophy of life and in which Arzner definitively alters the image of Harriet presented in Kelly's play, there is a very striking and somewhat peculiar mise-en-scène. The discussion between Ethel and Harriet consists primarily of a conventional shot reverse/shot structure, with each woman portrayed in her train seat, facing the audience, while in the background we see the windows of the train and scenery rushing by. The images of each woman, alone, are interrupted occasionally by two-shots of them, giving a larger sense of the space of the train. Yet whenever these two-shots occur, something happens in the background. At precisely the moment that Ethel announces (in close-up) that she and her boyfriend—the instructor of Romance Languages—are engaged, there is a cut to the two women as a man enters the frame and sits down in the background, facing the train window, and busies himself with writing. In the ensuing shot reverse shot of Ethel and Harriet, this unidentified man forms the background of Ethel's space. In other words, then, during the entire conversation, one is made aware, however unconsciously, of a man occupying the background.

Figure 45. Harriet Craig (Rosalind Russell) and Ethel (Dorothy Wilson) discuss marriage in *Craig's Wife*, 1936. From the Collection of Jenni Olson.

Similarly, approximately halfway through the scene, the two-shot of Ethel and Harriet occurs from a different angle, and now another man seated behind the two women quite literally occupies not just the background, but also the space between the two women. The cut to this two-shot occurs after Ethel, in isolated close-up, has responded to Harriet's claim that she married to be independent with a query: "Independent of your husband, too?" Harriet's reply— "independent of everybody"—is uttered with the cut to the two women, now framed in such a way that a faceless man comes between them. And what is Harriet actually doing when she claims her desire to be independent of everyone? Powdering her nose. In fact, while Harriet's attention is surely given to her words and the dialogue with her niece in this scene, she nonetheless is quite occupied with the accoutrements of femininity—powdering her nose, removing her gloves.

In other words, then, all the while that Harriet claims her desire for independence, everything in the frame suggests that even as simple a matter as a conversation between two women cannot occur "independently." While Har-

Figure 46. Mrs. Frazier (Billie Burke) and Harriet Craig (Rosalind Russell) at the conclusion of *Craig's Wife*, 1936. MOMA Film Stills Archive.

riet and Ethel speak, men take up space as the world races by outside. Particularly in the second half of the scene, where the man in the background quite literally comes between Ethel and Harriet, the man's presence is both abstract and looming, suggesting that this nameless character is also a potential eavesdropper. True, the man is a part of the scenery, but this is precisely the point— he has a certain authority simply by virtue of being there. This power is not available to Harriet, despite her speech about marriage for independence, and despite her function as stage manager in her own home.

Even though Ethel is shocked at her aunt's philosophy, I find the conversation between two women to be precisely what *Craig's Wife* imagines as a utopian possibility. One could certainly regard the conclusion of the film as Harriet's tragic end. But consider what has happened: All of the men, whether abstract figures like the man in the train or familiar ones like Walter, have disappeared. Harriet is left with her empty stage, until Mrs. Frazier—seemingly opposed to her in every way—comes in. Once the Craig home is finally desecrated with cigarettes and a broken vase (Walter's parting acts of rebellion), it

Figures 47 and 48. On the set of *Craig's Wife*, John Boles and Rosalind Russell pose (Figure 47), and their pose is imitated by Boles and Arzner (Figure 48). MOMA Film Stills Archive.

is ironically swept clean and made ready for something else. Whatever else one might say about the conclusion of the film, when virtually everyone except Harriet and Mrs. Frazier have been evacuated from the house, one thing remains true—the chance to sustain and extend a conversation among women has finally been made possible.

7

Dance, Girls, Dance

COMMUNITIES OF WOMEN function, in Arzner's career as well as in her films, as perhaps the most consistent and important feature. In this chapter I turn to the two films which epitomize the cinematic implications of those communities. The title of this chapter is taken from what is undoubtedly Arzner's best-known film, *Dance, Girl, Dance*. I chose this title not only because the 1940 film is so important to any discussion of the female world central to Arzner's work, but also because of the importance of dance in Arzner's work. It is no coincidence that the two films that explore in detail the complexities of female communities are also those in which dance acquires crucial symbolic and narrative significance.

To be sure, dance functions quite differently in the two films. In *The Wild Party*, social dancing and festivities define the changing dimensions of the relationships of the women to each other, to men, and to the world at large. *Dance, Girl, Dance*, of course, is more explicitly concerned with dance as a profession, as it traces the divergent and intersecting careers of two different dancers with different aspirations. Nonetheless, both films share a preoccupation with dance as it embodies the relationship between the private and the public spheres, and as it combines women's desires for artistic expression and community.

In addition, the two films are preoccupied with what I will call heterosocial and homosocial worlds, that is, with the shifts from modes of interaction and community based on opposite-sex, versus same-sex, relationships. I have noted that, frequently in Arzner's films, the development of heterosexual romance intrudes upon all-female worlds, and that while the films often conclude with the requisite happy couple, such conclusions seem somewhat fragile in regard to the amount of time and energy devoted, screen-wise, to the female worlds. *The Wild Party* and *Dance, Girl, Dance* are the boldest demonstrations of this process.

The relationship between homosocial and heterosocial worlds is not just a thematic preoccupation with stylistic effects in Arzner's work. One of the most interesting historical shifts in twentieth-century America was the change, for women, from a public sphere organized largely in homosocial terms to one dependent on heterosocial interaction.[1] Additionally, this shift was crucial to the lives of women whose emotional and affective lives were spent in the company of other women. If, in nineteenth-century America, romantic friendships between women were an accepted fact of life, with the passage of time such relationships would be classified as pathological, as detrimental to so-called normal heterosexual development. Throughout the early decades of the twentieth century the term "lesbian" was used increasingly as a mark of illness, of disease.[2] Neither of the two films under consideration here are concerned, explicitly, with lesbianism (although one character in *Dance, Girl, Dance* is the most obvious butch in Arzner's work). However, both films negotiate the complex implications, visual and narrative as well as thematic and emotional, of women together.

The Wild Party (1929)

Arzner's work with Clara Bow was one of the most successful collaborations of her career. While Bow was one of the most gifted performers of the 1920s, her films with Arzner (*Get Your Man* [1927] and *The Wild Party* [1929] showcase her abilities remarkably well. The actress was nervous about the coming of sound film, and there are some moments in *The Wild Party* when her Brooklyn accent overpowers her; but, on the whole, her transition to talking pictures was a success.

The Wild Party takes a community of women as its explicit starting point: the film opens in 1930 in a Winston College dormitory room, with Stella Ames (Bow) and a group of girlfriends giggling and chatting about their club—the Hard Boiled Maidens. The women are uniformly attractive, slender, and fashionable, but a gradual contrast is introduced in two ways—with the arrival of Helen, Stella's best friend, who is studious and serious (suggested by her glasses and her sensible bathrobe); and later, with the appearance of James "Gil" Gilmore, a new professor of anthropology.

Stella tells her girlfriends of how, when she and Helen were sharing a sleeping berth on the train returning to Winston College, she got up at night for a drink and returned to the berth, chilly, and suggested to Helen that they sleep "spoon fashion" to keep warm. A male voice asks her who invited her in, and Stella is shocked to discover that she has entered the wrong compartment. The next morning, when Stella and Helen go to the dining car, Stella finds a spoon with a note from the man, reminding her of the dangers of spooning. As "coincidence" would have it, the man is, of course, the new professor, and the film traces the predictable yet somewhat unusual courtship of Stella and Gil.

The predictability of their pairing is undercut by the emphasis on Stella's friendship with Helen. The budding relationship between Gil and Stella is by no means the only narrative development in *The Wild Party*. The principal subplot of the film concerns the coveted alumnae scholarship, for which Helen is

Figure 49. Helen (Shirley O'Hara) and Stella (Clara Bow) in *The Wild Party*, 1929. MOMA Film Stills Archive.

a candidate. Under Stella's tutelage, Helen begins to socialize more, and she eventually meets George, a young man to whom she is attracted. At a party, Helen spends the night on the beach with her new love, thus breaking college rules. If this transgression is discovered, she risks losing the scholarship. Unfortunately, Helen writes to George and alludes to the night on the beach. The letter is found by a snoopy coed who passes it along to the college authorities. Pretending to be the author of the letter, Stella takes the blame on Helen's behalf, and her loyalty to her friend coexists in the film with her developing romance with Gil. The scene in which Stella finds Helen in George's arms is striking for the emphasis, visual as well as narrative, on the bond between the two women. Andrea Weiss, commenting on the "subtextual lesbian dynamic" of the film, describes the scene as follows: "George tries to reassure Stella that he loves Helen and would not take advantage of her, but he misunderstands the cause of Stella's alarm. She starts to cry and responds, 'I'm jealous, you see, I love Helen too!' In this shot Helen moves from George's to Stella's arms, and the camera moves to exile George from the frame while the two women romantically embrace."[3]

If the hard-boiled maidens are largely and notoriously interchangeable, Stella and Helen's friendship is founded upon their differences. Stella—true to the Clara Bow persona—is bubbly and energetic, while Helen is shy and reserved; Stella is not a serious student, but Helen is regarded as the best student at the college. The female bond to which principal attention is drawn in the film is a bond based on difference as much as similarity. In this respect, the developing relationship between Gil, the serious scholar, and Stella takes as its model the friendship we have already seen between the two young women.

The Wild Party develops according to a series of oppositions—fun versus seriousness, frivolity versus intellect, laughter versus severity. To some extent, the most extreme opposition in the film is between Gil and Stella, which is, obviously, a gender opposition as well. But the oppositions are also embodied in Stella and Helen's friendship, and as a result the gender opposition is never so absolute, and the relegation of the friendship subplot to secondary status never so total, as one might expect.

Indeed, it is not even entirely appropriate to describe the friendship between the young women as a "subplot" to *The Wild Party*, since the female friendship and the heterosexual romance are completely intertwined. Stella is willing to give up everything, her romance with Gil in particular, in order to save Helen's chances of winning the scholarship. Thus, loyalty to her friend comes before romance. Ironically—and predictably—it is just this decision which sparks the professor's decision to follow Stella when she is suspended for the previously mentioned transgression. Not only does her loyalty demonstrate that she is far more mature than he had acknowledged, but also and especially it makes him realize that he doesn't really want to be in a university setting; rather, he wants to do fieldwork. Hence, at the conclusion of the film, Stella and Gil are preparing for a future "in the jungle."

The Wild Party never seems to be quite certain whether the college setting is a utopian or a claustrophobic environment, particularly given Gil's final words about the frustration of teaching students who aren't interested in the material. One senses that Gil's change of heart is necessary for the requisite happy ending, since earlier in the film he had made an impassioned speech to Stella about the sacrifices made by women of earlier generations so that women of her generation could go to college. In general, then, the way the college environment is presented throughout the film leans far more toward a utopian view, for the college provides the support and encouragement of a female community.

As noted, dramatic opposition does not require male/female difference in the film, as one usually expects in classical Hollywood films. Stella and Helen's friendship is nurtured as much by their differences as by their similarities. And when the film does portray male/female difference, it is less a function of the typical (for Hollywood, that is) man as subject/woman as object dichotomy. For example, the professor's first meeting with a classroom full of coeds is presented in a hilarious shot, in which the crossed legs of the women in the class-room form a virtual wall framing his entry. The effect is as much mockery of his stodginess as their frivolity.

Another kind of opposition between two different kinds of display occurs when Stella and three of her friends are forbidden to enter the "costume," a dance which is similar, the film's titles inform us, to a male stag party. A shot of the ballroom shows a sea of women's legs, adorned in a variety of different costumes—male as well as female, contemporary as well as historical. The effect is carnivalesque, a utopian topsy-turvy world where gender and identity are performed, engaged with in playful terms. Yet Stella and her friends disrupt the event. They are dressed as chorines, and after they take off their identical fur coats to reveal skimpy (and identical) costumes, with their bare legs exposed, their attempt to enter the ballroom as a makeshift chorus line is thwarted by one of their classmates—who is dressed as a shepherdess. The forbidden entry functions in two different ways. First, their clothing is too revealing and their costumes too provocative, thus connoting a censorship of anything so explic-itly sexual. But second, this scene, in combination with the scene that follows, suggests that in this all female world, there is, rather, no place for the classical representation of women as objects of the male gaze. It is possible to read the forbidden entry, in other words, in two opposing ways—as a repression of sexu-ality, or, conversely, as a refusal of stereotypical associations of women with sexual objectification.

Once the girlfriends are forced to leave, they go to a road-house. Here, their playfulness and costume meet with a very different kind of response: a group of male customers who take their appearances all too literally, forcing their attentions on the girls. At the costume, the costumes of Stella and her friends stood in contrast to those of the other women, and that contrast was underscored humorously by Little Bo Peep telling Stella and her pals to leave. There is little humor in the roadhouse scene. It is shot in the familiar terms of shot reverse shot, where the men leer and the women are leered at. What was playful in the previous scene here becomes dangerous. Stella attempts once again to perform—in this case, to pretend that she is genuinely interested in one of the men, so as to give her friends room to leave—but the act works only to a point. She manages to get her girlfriends out of the bar, but the men persist, a fight breaks out, and Stella is left behind, forced into a car with three men. Gil, out for an evening stroll, saves the day, protecting Stella and fighting off the three drunken men. Their romance begins with a passionate kiss, after Gil has warded off the danger of the "wild party."

Helen is conspicuously absent from these scenes, but Stella takes her along to another dance which stands in sharp contrast to the earlier costume. Whereas the guests at the previous dance were all women, this is a dance for both men and women. The men dress alike and the women dress alike in the uniforms of formal attire. Here, then, a symmetry of identical opposites occurs, unlike the costume, where a more frenzied anarchic atmosphere prevailed. There is a kind of boring predictability to the dance, broken only when an obnoxious drunken man makes unwanted advances to Helen. Interestingly, Stella and her friends are here entirely successful in "performing" him away; they feign interest in him, and then spin him furiously until he veers, out of control, away from the ballroom. In this space of heterosexual coupling, in other words, the women exercise far more control than they did in the roadhouse. The confines of the college offer the women control over the rituals of heterosexual courtship, a control not available to them once they leave the safe space of the college for the roadhouse.

This dance marks an obvious change in Helen, who for once is portrayed without her eyeglasses and in a dress quite similar to those worn by the other women. This is also the fateful night when she falls in love with George and, without realizing it, they spend the entire night talking on the beach. Stella's discovery of them plays upon the changing dimensions of the two women's relationship, because she immediately assumes a protective role vis-à-vis Helen, just as Gil did vis-à-vis her during the roadhouse incident, a role that climaxes with Stella's decision to put her friendship with Helen before her romance with Gil. Initially, Stella is shocked when she discovers Helen and George, and she immediately assumes the worst—an assumption echoed by George, who tells Stella that she is right to assume the worst of men most of the time, just not this time.

In the end, Stella gets her man but not college, which Gil assures her will not offer educational opportunities to equal those of the jungle, while Helen gets her alumnae award and presumably keeps George as well. In the process, the film enacts a fantasy whereby the realms of female friendship and heterosexual romance are not only compatible, but necessarily intertwined. The importance of such a dynamic co-existence cannot be overemphasized, particularly since in this respect the film departs sharply from the novel, *Unforbidden Fruit*, by Warner Fabian, upon which it was based. Fabian was a popular writer in the 1920s, and his novel *Flaming Youth* (also made into a successful film featuring Colleen Moore) was considered the quintessential flapper novel.

In many ways E. Lloyd Sheldon's adaptation of the novel for the screen is literal; large chunks of dialogue are lifted directly from the novel, for instance. But where the film and the novel differ is in the treatment of the relationship between "romantic friendships" among women and heterosexual romance. Fabian's novel, published in 1928, is a stunning example of the supposed "dangers" of romantic friendship, functioning as a warning of what communities of women can create. In his preface to the novel, Fabian remarks upon the "peculiar atmosphere of compressed femininity which produces an intellectual and social reaction not unlike the prison psychosis of our penal institutions."[4]

The book covers a fairly wide range of the "psychoses" produced by an all-female environment, virtually all of them having to do with sex. As in Arzner's film, there is variation among the women, but the variation is decidedly downplayed by the fact that they all have distorted attitudes toward and excessive preoccupations with sex. For the most part, the sex in question concerns sex with men. A notable exception occurs in the minor character of Olga, who is introduced early in the novel, only to disappear for the bulk of it and reappear quickly at the conclusion. Olga has a crush on Verity, a freshman, who is soon taken under the wing of the college girls who belong to the group, called the "Hard-Boiled Virgins" (rather than maidens, as in the film).[5] Verity is innocent, and a significant development of the novel is her introduction to romance via the tutelage of her fellow "virgins." She has been asked to room with Olga; she is uncomfortable with her, but she doesn't understand why. Sylvia ("Stella" in the film) and Starr, the hard-boiled virgins, do. When Verity says of Olga's invitation to room with her, "I almost feel as if I'd been asked to room with a man," the "two older girls exchanged looks."[6]

Olga persists in her pursuit of Verity, sending her flowers and inviting her to her family's home for vacation. Sylvia makes explicit the difference between Olga and themselves: "It ill beseems a hard-boiled virgin . . . to go in for schoolgirl crush stuff. You're in college now, kid."[7] Once the hard-boiled virgins have thus dismissed Olga and her supposed "school-girl crush" syndrome, the novel abandons her as well, only to have her reappear briefly at the conclusion, which takes place a year later at the beginning of a new fall term. Olga has spread a rumor that Verity will not return to school, and Starr reacts in a voice "fiery with scorn." As if to make absolutely explicit the pathology of one like Olga, she says: "You know how that kind are when they turn on any one."[8]

One of the most obvious aims of *Unforbidden Fruit* is to titillate the reader with tales of female sexual independence run amok. While the novel focusses largely on illicit heterosexual behavior, the "schoolgirl crush" of Olga obviously is also, if more briefly, pathologized. To be sure, the young women in the novel are not presented as particularly glowing advertisements for heterosexuality, but it is not heterosexuality which comes in for scorn (as lesbianism does), but rather female autonomy and independence. In the concluding pages of the novel, Fabian has one of his heroines wonder about the "disrupting, commanding impulse which had swept her companions before it like a conquering wave"; and two causal possibilities are offered, the "superfeminized environment" of the women's college, or the tendency of post-adolescent girls to develop "a sort of mob-psychology of self-recognition and self-realization."[9]

To be sure, there are many more characters and many more plots and subplots in Fabian's novel than in Arzner's film, but in most cases the different characters of the novel are condensed into filmic characters.[10] Olga is banished from the film, as are any accompanying tendencies to portray intense female friendships as perverse or resolutely opposed to "normal" femininity. In addition, *The Wild Party* takes a decidedly different view of Stella's friendship with Helen and her motivation for presenting Stella's letters to George as her own. In the novel, Sylvia certainly wants to protect her friend, but throughout the novel any sense of morality is a function of men—the professor, in particular; hence, after Sylvia leaves, she wants the professor to tell her she did the right thing. In other words, her protection of her friend is as much a function of her attachment to the professor as to her girlfriend.

The film establishes no such rigid demarcations. While the film ends, as one might expect, on a more cheerful note than the novel (in which the women are pretty much condemned to sterile lives), I see this as less the legendary need of Hollywood to sentimentalize its stories than one more sign of the profound revision of Fabian's novel that occurs in the film. Ultimately, *Unforbidden Fruit* portrays all female friendship as pathological. By establishing a rigid line between homosocial and heterosocial worlds, by vilifying female autonomy, and by singling out "romantic friendships" for particular scorn, the novel serves an ideological function common in early-twentieth-century popular literature.[11] The film, on the other hand, not only refuses any such rigid line between normal and pathological behavior, but also celebrates the female world of love and ritual.[12]

The screen persona of Clara Bow is also significant in the rereading of Fabian's novel. Bow was Paramount's most successful commodity, and she was regarded as the quintessential woman of the decade—modern, sexually independent, and sexually available. The combination of Warner Fabian and Clara Bow seemed a perfect match, because Fabian's earlier novel, *Flaming Youth*, had been the basis for what was then the ultimate flapper film, and one of Bow's most successful screen incarnations was as the "It" girl in *It*. "It" referred to sex appeal, specifically to a kind of animal magnetism to attract the opposite sex, and the film *It* makes the point, indirectly but obviously, that those with "it" are resolutely heterosexual (for example, a man coded as gay wonders why he doesn't have "it"). Clara Bow's well-publicized affairs offscreen also contributed to her role as a sex symbol (eventually the affairs caused serious damage to her career).[13] *The Wild Party* certainly plays on Bow's status as the "It" girl, but it also redefines "it" as a quality informed by close bonds between women. If "it" (as heterosexual sex appeal) was the inspiration behind *It*, then "it" also propels the plot in *The Wild Party*, but redefined as the erotic component in friendships between women, specifically the magnetic attraction between Stella and Helen.

Someone once suggested to Arzner that the friendship between Stella and Helen in the film had "lesbian undertones." Arzner reacted very negatively to the suggestion and said that lesbianism was a ridiculous tag to put on a friendship.[14] I believe that the easiest way to interpret her reaction is through the ubiquitous closet, i.e., through the assumption that Arzner separated her life from her films, and that to read lesbianism wherever two women share closeness and intimacy is to violate that separation. While this may well be the case, when one reads *The Wild Party* in relationship to Fabian's novel, another response to Arzner's denial emerges. In eliminating the lesbian character, *The Wild Party* eliminated the pathologizing view of lesbianism present in the novel. The world of female friendship that is celebrated in the film may deny any explicit lesbian content, but it also denies any representation of lesbianism as a disease. I am not trying to defend the closet here, but rather to suggest that the kinds of subversions that Arzner performed during her career need to be seen in specific contexts. In the present example, Arzner's film may not equate female friendship with lesbianism, but it does refuse to validate the view, increasingly popular (as Fabian's novel makes clear) during her lifetime, that there is anything unhealthy, immoral, or otherwise lacking in intense female bonds.

Dance, Girl, Dance (1940)

Two forms of dance are contrasted in *The Wild Party*—one, the "costume," where the women create a carnivalesque atmosphere, which is disrupted by the stereotypically sexualized chorus girls played by Stella and her pals; the second, the formal dance of rigid gender dichotomy, also disrupted by Stella and her friends' dismissal of a drunken guest. Certainly, this contrast conveys a sense of opposite worlds, that is, an all-female world versus a coupled world of men and women. But Stella and the "hardboiled maidens" are never totally at ease in either world, and dance functions in the film to suggest that gender is performed as much as it is assumed "naturally." In *Dance, Girl, Dance*, it performs a much more explicit function. Here, radically different kinds of dance are juxtaposed to suggest the different relationships between women and performance.

Dance, Girl, Dance is, today, the best-known of Arzner's films, and it has become something of a classic in feminist film studies.[15] Since 1970s film theory developed an analysis of cinema based on the way in which the look functioned as the quintessence of power—cinematic and narrative, as well as sexual—the scene which has drawn the most attention in the film occurs when a female performer turns to her audience and tells them how she sees them.[16] This scene in Arzner's film functioned both as a summary of the limitations of the classical Hollywood cinema (where woman was the object of the male look) and an indication of what would be unique and specific to women's cinema (a "return" of the look, and an attendant critique of the assumptions of classical film narrative).

It does not require too much imagination to see why the "look" would be so important to the analysis of the cinema, since film is primarily a visual medium that relies upon the engagement of the look of the spectator. What was particular to 1970s film theory was the understanding of the look as a form of authority and power, and what was particular to 1970s feminist film theory was the insistence upon the gendered quality of the authority and power of the look. For feminist film theorists, the classical Hollywood cinema offered a range of scenarios with man as the subject of the look, woman as its object. For example, shot reverse shot structures of dialogues between men and women may subtly establish the woman as the object of the gaze by portraying her in more extreme close-ups, or with the male's voice given more screen time. Literal performances staged within films more often than not define men as onlookers and women as performers.[17] *Dance, Girl, Dance* was considered unique for its demonstration of the process, naturalized in other films, whereby women are made objects of the male gaze, as well as for its critique of this objectification.

While many of Arzner's films do indeed revise and challenge the assumptions of classical film, I think it is a mistake to focus exclusively on the "return of the look," particularly since such an approach focusses necessarily on the relationship between male voyeur and female object of the look. Where Arzner's films are most challenging is not in a reversal of the male subject/female object dichotomy, but in bracketing the dichotomy itself and therefore extending the look beyond the power of the male. We have seen an explicit representation of this process in *Nana*, where Nana's performance is shaped by reaction shots from both men and women. This is not to say that the look is not important in Arzner's work, but rather that it functions in a wide range of ways that do not always neatly fit the parameters of contemporary film theory.

The plot of *Dance, Girl, Dance* concerns the differing paths to success for Bubbles (Lucille Ball) and Judy (Maureen O'Hara), both members of a dance troupe led by Madame Basilova (Maria Ouspenskaya). The dance troupe performs vaudeville-style numbers in bars and nightclubs, much to the chagrin of Basilova (who bemoans her status as a "flesh peddler"). Bubbles has "oomph," a kind of dancer's version of "it," and eventually she leaves the troupe and enthusiastically pursues a career as "Tiger Lily White." Judy, in contrast, is a serious student of ballet, and the protégée of Basilova. However, it is Bubbles who gets the jobs, and she arranges for Judy to be hired as her "stooge," i.e., as a classical dancer who performs in the middle of Bubbles's act, and thus primes the audience to demand more of Bubbles.

Hence two radically different modes of performance—burlesque and ballet—and two radically different approaches to one's career—exploitation versus artistic self-expression—are juxtaposed in the film. One of the achievements of the film is the fact that while Bubbles and Judy embody different poles

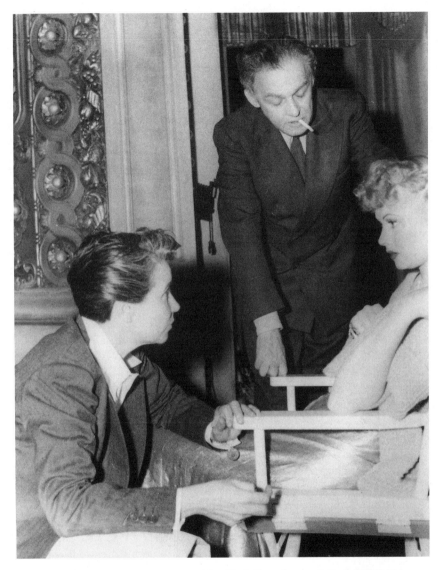

Figure 50. Dorothy Arzner and Lucille Ball on the set of *Dance, Girl, Dance*
(1940). Arts Library—Special Collections, University Research Library, UCLA.

of the opposition, neither woman is villainized in the process, surprising in
terms of Bubbles. The contrast between the two women is even more striking
than that between Stella and Helen in *The Wild Party*, and once again, the
contrast is an element of the bond between them, not an obstacle.

As I have argued at various points throughout this book, the attention paid to Arzner's sensitivity to gender tends to obscure how many of her films are concerned with social class, and particularly with social class as it shapes women's aspirations in different ways. *Dance, Girl, Dance* is no exception. Bubbles may become rich through her career, but she is definitely from a less than privileged background. A montage sequence approximately halfway through the film details her rise to fame; she is referred to in newspapers and magazines as a "burlesque" queen who takes Broadway by storm, and ticket prices go up accordingly.[18] In her musical numbers, especially "Jitterbug Bite," Bubbles explicitly confronts "class" (in the sense of upper-class values and pretensions) in order to dissociate herself from it, and in a striking scene early in the film, she promises a showman that she does not possess an ounce of class. Certainly, class (and the lack of it) here is meant to function primarily in terms of sexual appeal, but the point is that "class," for Arzner's heroines, is always simultaneously a function of social class and sexuality.

Judy is a poor, struggling dancer too, but her artistic aspirations suggest the kind of "class" consistently mocked by Bubbles. Particularly interesting in this respect is the rehearsal of the American Ballet Company that Judy watches. The performance begins with a traditional ballet performance (by a woman who bears a remarkable resemblance to Lucille Ball), and at one point the curtains behind her open to reveal a strikingly different kind of performance. Judy's face registers shock and surprise, then interest. The dance that follows is ballet, but ballet inflected by urban sights and sounds—dancers dressed as workers, street vendors, and office workers (and, in an unfortunate stereotype, in blackface as a Harlem couple). *This* kind of dance challenges the rigid boundaries between "high" art and "low" art, between vaudeville and ballet, and between Bubbles and Judy.

If this "hybrid" form of dance breaks down the opposition between the kinds of dance favored by Bubbles and Judy respectively, then the awe-struck look bestowed upon the Bubbles look-alike by Judy as she watches her perform also suggests a more complicated and ambiguous relationship between the two of them than that of the stereotypical good girl/bad girl rivals and enemies. Bubbles bumps and grinds her way up the economic ladder, while Judy simultaneously pirouettes up the path of artistry. This scene also reminds the viewer that another thing both women share is a desire to climb out of the class into which they were born. The heterosexual intrigues that pair Judy and Bubbles with Jimmie Harris at various points, and Judy with Steven Adams at the film's conclusion, are significant less as pure romances than for the possibilities they offer of class mobility. For the male romantic leads live in an entirely different world, class-wise, than the women in the film. Like the working girls of the films discussed in chapter 5, Bubbles and Judy live in a world where social class and gender always intersect. And even though the dance troupe may not occupy a space as clearly delineated as Rolfe House in *Working Girls*, the community of women is central throughout *Dance, Girl, Dance*. Indeed, the heterosexual intrigues of *Dance, Girl, Dance* are not only functions of class difference; they also mediate relationships between women. Jimmie Harris is, ultimately, a mediator in the relationship between Bubbles and Judy, while Steven Adams assumes the role previously held by Madame Basilova in Judy's life.

Relationships between women are foregrounded in *Dance, Girl, Dance* through the representation of dance as a form in which different desires intersect. This complex representation of dance and a community of women can be seen as significant on another level, for the type of modern dance embodied by Adams's company is evocative of the way in which, several decades previous to *Dance, Girl, Dance*, women choreographers like Marion Morgan, Arzner's long-time companion, developed a new approach, which became known as modern dance. Morgan did not work officially on Arzner's films after *Manhattan Cocktail*, but her influence echoes in a variety of ways, none more strongly than in *Dance, Girl, Dance*. I am not suggesting a direct, unmediated relationship between Morgan and this film, but I am suggesting that the values attributed to dance as both an expressive medium and a means to convey the complexities of the relationships between women make sense in light of Arzner's forty-plus years in the company of Morgan.

Arzner was brought in as director of *Dance, Girl, Dance* as a replacement for another director, and she immediately made changes in the script, which had been adapted by Tess Slesinger and Frank Davis from a story by novelist Vicki Baum (best known in Hollywood circles as the author of the novel *Grand Hotel*). The most significant change made by Arzner was to transform the head of the dance troupe from a man to a woman, from "Basiloff" to "Basilova." In the Slesinger/Davis script, he is called "Pops" by the dancers; his name is Vladimir Basiloff, "Formerly Imp. Russ. Ballet," as the sign on his studio announces.[19] Arzner preserves the role of "Pops," but the crucial change in gender refocusses the entire film. In the original screenplay, Steven Adams becomes a substitute for Basiloff, with paternal authority passed from one man to another, in a conventional female oedipal drama par excellence. In the original script, with Basiloff in charge of Judy's destiny, the relationship between dancer and manager is entirely paternalistic, and the major movement is the change in Judy from one kind of tutelage (Russian, classical) to another (American, modern). The paternalistic effect remains a constant from one "master" to another, and the script presents a female oedipal drama, in which the romantic figure replaces the father figure. In Arzner's version, the female oedipal element is subverted; Basilova may be a nurturing figure vis-à-vis Judy, but she is hardly maternal in the same stereotypical way that Basiloff is paternal. To be sure, Basilova is supportive and encouraging of her dancers; but with her slicked-back hair, necktie, and overall butch appearance, she confuses gender expectations. In particular, Basilova gazes longingly at Judy when she practices a new dance, thus appropriating the desire that traditionally and stereotypically in Hollywood films is reserved for men.

Most significantly, this is yet another example of how, in the film, relations between and among women are every bit—if not more—important than the entry of the female characters into the world of "coupledom" and heterosexual romance. And in the process, a figure from Arzner's own past is suggested—the name "Basilova" is surprisingly evocative of "Nazimova," both of them Russian, both of them emigrés, both of them dancers.[20] Although I know of few explicit biographical references in Arzner's work (even the references to dance in *Dance, Girl, Dance* that are suggestive of the influence of Marion Morgan are general, and not identified via a specific person), Basilova seems to be a strongly condensed figure of Nazimova, of Marion Morgan, and of Arzner herself. Indeed, when Basilova is pictured with Judy, the effect is strikingly similar to the numerous publicity photographs of Arzner pictured with female stars. Not only do Arzner and Basilova dress alike; they both exchange looks of desire and longing with their more "femme" companions.

Hence, the change from Basiloff to Basilova brings relationships between women center stage, and takes away much of the metaphoric baggage of Judy's budding relationship with Steven Adams. The addition of Basilova is interesting in other ways, as well. As the most explicitly butch female character in any of Arzner's films, it is easy to see a parallel between the dance mistress and Arzner herself, not only in terms of their "looks," as mentioned above, but also as supposedly "masculinized" figures, attempting to function in a world made to the measure of fleshpeddlers. Throughout Arzner's work, contrasts between and among women, whether butch or femme, function productively, not in terms of absolute oppositions.

While the change from "Basiloff" to "Basilova" is the most striking change from the original script, Arzner's particular touch is also present in the different ways a minor supporting character is changed. Arzner wanted to make the relationship between Bubbles and Judy the center of the film, and so the role of Sally, another member of the dance troupe, is reduced. In the script (as in the film), Sally lives with Judy and Bubbles. A subplot in the script pairs Sally with a baker who lives in the same building, and who offers Judy a job as his assistant. When Judy takes the job as Bubbles's stooge, the job goes to Sally, and Sally and the baker become romantically involved. Sally remains in Arzner's film, but her primary function is to mediate the relationship between Bubbles and Judy. Sally pokes fun at Bubbles in the opening scene of the film when Jimmie Harris prefers Judy's company, and Sally is giving Judy homemade soup when Bubbles arrives with her offer of employment. The last time we see Sally, she is asleep in the room when Judy returns from a date with Jimmie, and, figuratively, Sally remains asleep during the rest of the film. In the original script, Sally was another woman paired with a man; in the film, she is a woman who serves to highlight the pairing of two women. Interestingly, once the heterosexual intrigues are set into motion, Sally virtually disappears from the film. Yet her very presence is a tantalizing reminder of the bonds that connect women.

Ultimately, of course, the significance of *Dance, Girl, Dance* cannot be measured in the literal terms of biography. Yet at the same time, I find it no coincidence that the most successful of Arzner's films is, at once, her most personal—personal in the sense that the world of performance, as represented in the film, is broad enough to include Bubbles and Judy and Basilova. Additionally, the film suggests the costs and risks of feminine performance, for when Basilova dons a frilly hat to accompany Judy to her audition with the ballet company, she is immediately killed when she steps out into the street and is hit by a car. In other words, as soon as she assumes a feminine attribute, presumably in order to be more "presentable," she dies. In *Christopher Strong*, heterosexuality is lethal; in *Dance, Girl, Dance*, femininity is lethal, at least for Basilova.

Consider, in this light, the famous scene of Judy's rebuke to her audience that occurs near the conclusion of the film. Judy prepares to play the now-familiar role of stooge, but something in her snaps. Instead of accepting her role, she defiantly moves to the front of the stage, crosses her arms in front of her, and confronts her audience. Her speech is a stunning demonstration of the intersection of class and sexual politics, for Judy's critique is not just of men who take women as sexual objects, but also of "dress suits" who take their pleasure in the spectacle of vaudeville:

> Go ahead and stare. I'm not ashamed. Go on. Laugh! Get your money's worth. Nobody's going to hurt you. I know you want me to tear my clothes off so's you can look your fifty cents worth. Fifty cents for the privilege of staring at a girl the way your wives won't let you. What do you suppose we think of you up here—with your silly smirks your mothers would be ashamed of? And we know it's the thing of the moment for the dress suits to come and laugh at us too. We'd laugh right back at the lot of you, only we're paid to let you sit there and roll your eyes and make your screamingly clever remarks. What's it for? So's you can go home when the show's over and strut before your wives and sweethearts and play at being the stronger sex for a minute? I'm sure they see through you just like we do.

I see Judy's confrontation less as a challenge to the very notion of woman as object of spectacle than as the creation of another kind of performance. Oftentimes the scene is discussed as if the audience were exclusively male, which it is not, even though Judy addresses men in her speech. When the camera pans

Figure 51. Judy (Maureen O'Hara) and Basilova (Maria Ouspenskaya) in *Dance, Girl, Dance*, 1940. MOMA Film Stills Archive.

the reactions of the audience to Judy's speech, the responses of women are quite clearly visible. Women squirm uncomfortably in their seats just as surely as men do, and when release occurs in the form of applause, it is a woman—Steven Adams's trusty secretary—who initiates it. Arzner's view of performance and her view of the relationship between subject and object were never absolute; women may be objectified through performance, but they are also empowered; men may consume women through the look, but women also watch and take pleasure in the spectacle of other women's performance.

After Judy makes her speech, after the applause, Bubbles emerges from behind the stage curtains to pick a fight with Judy onstage, much to the delight of the audience (indeed, the laughter which the fight provokes seems yet another cathartic response to Judy's confrontation of her audience).[21] For 1970s feminist film theory, the applause and subsequent catfight were demonstrations of the limits of Arzner's subversion of the classical Hollywood cinema. As Claire Johnston puts it, describing Judy's confrontation and what follows:

> This return of scrutiny in what is assumed within the film to be a one-way process, a spectacle to be consumed by men, constitutes a direct assult on the audience *within* the film and the audience *of* the film, directly challenging the entire notion of spectacle as such. This break, a *tour-de-force* in terms of Arzner's work, is nevertheless directly recuperated by the enthusiastic applause which follows, and the discourse of the woman, although it appears momentarily supreme, is returned to the arena of the spectacle.[22]

In the context of 1970s film theory, this kind of assessment of Arzner's work and of the feminist project in film was enormously important. Looking back on that decade, it is as if the primary task was to claim the sexual politics of the look as crucial to any understanding of the classical Hollywood cinema and its alternatives. With the privilege of hindsight, as interpretations of this scene suggest, the understandings of 1970s feminist film theory seem momentously important, yet limited by two assumptions: of heterosexuality as a master code of meaning and representation, and of visual pleasure as a bad object. What I find remarkable about Arzner's films in general, and about *Dance, Girl, Dance* in particular, is that they suggest both the importance of the theoretical claims of 1970s film theory and their limitations. In its celebration of women and performance, of female friendship, and of a diversity of female representation, *Dance, Girl, Dance* reminds us, always, that there are women on *both* sides of the stage, and that they take pleasure in looking at each other.

PART III

Girl Director Sets
New Standards of Beauty

HOLLYWOOD—New standards of feminine perfection have been set
here—and by a girl! The old idea that it took a man to choose a perfect girl, has
gone overboard.

— "Girl Film Director Sets New Standards of Beauty,"
Los Angeles Record, Feb. 10, 1927

8

Looking for Dorothy

DOROTHY ARZNER HAD a unique career in Hollywood as the only woman director who endured. Throughout that career, Arzner was written about in newspapers, trade journals, fan magazines, and the popular press. Particularly during the first several years after Arzner signed her directing contract with Paramount, articles about her were numerous, focussing on her unique status as the only "femme megger" (*Variety*'s term) in Hollywood. Stories of her ascent to the role of director were common, and one of the more popular fictions of her success cast her in the role of a female Horatio Alger. Indeed, the fact that Arzner had worked her way up the rungs of Hollywood production provided a ready-made tale for her success.

A 1927 story, "Dorothy Arzner, Horatio Alger Heroine, Shows Way for Ambitious Girls in Films," describes Arzner's path, from typist to director, from "lowliest to most exalted."[1] A story appearing in 1930 takes the Horatio Alger theme a step further, suggesting that Arzner's own success is worthy of a motion picture plot: "Miss Arzner's climb into the front rank of picturedom would supply the plot for a feminine Horatio Alger story that might well be entitled 'From Typist to Movie Director, or How One Girl Took a Job and Grew Up with It.'"[2] It makes a certain amount of sense that any explanation of Arzner's career would draw upon the myths and institutions of the industry in which she worked. Horatio Alger tales thus offer the possibility of a simple reversal—of a female success story in place of a male one.

The subject of this chapter is how Dorothy Arzner was both dealt with and created in the popular press. But my concern is with what exceeds and goes beyond the possibilities of what one might call the Horatio Alger syndrome, i.e., the assumption that Arzner's Hollywood career could be explained by substituting "female" for "male" in the typical success story. Previous chapters have detailed how Arzner's career was charted, particularly in reviews of her films, from her status as "star-maker" to the simultaneous compatibility and incompatibility of her films with established notions of the "woman's film." I have also noted how Arzner's career tended to be explained in terms of certain myths of her childhood destiny, as if the very fact of being daughter to a Hollywood restaurateur who catered to film folks instilled in her a desire to become a director. More crucially, of course, these myths "explained" Arzner in relationship to men—to her father, and later, the director James Cruze, who in some stories was credited (incorrectly) with getting Dorothy's first director's contract for her. The Horatio Alger syndrome also explains Arzner in relationship to men, although in a different way, by assuming that her career can be understood and interpreted according to the same stories and myths that explain men's careers.

I have titled this chapter "Looking for Dorothy" in homage to Isaac Julien's celebrated film on Langston Hughes, *Looking for Langston* (1989). The film is subtitled "A Meditation," and Julien has described how his search for the intersections of Black and gay identities in Hughes's life necessitated a focus on the "looking." Hence, *Looking for Langston* is, for Julien, "about Black gay desire; it's an imaginary search for a Black gay identity."[3] The imaginary search undertaken in the film underscores the extent to which "looking" from the vantage point of Black gay desire involves piecing together fragments and questioning assumptions. To be sure, there is no simple equivalence between Julien's focus on the "looking" and my own; there are worlds of difference between Hughes and Arzner, between Julien and myself. But what *Looking for Langston* undertakes, passionately, is a meditation on the visual myths and icons surrounding a specific legend and the attendant repression of homosexuality, and it is to that simultaneous focus on specificity and repression that this chapter is indebted. In my own research on and search for Dorothy Arzner, I found the Horatio Alger syndrome to be consistently blocked and disrupted, for Arzner did not always fit so readily into available myths and conventions. When articles about Arzner engage with her status as a woman, and in particular with her status as an image, it is no longer possible to plot her success by substituting "woman" for "man." Arzner may have worn "masculine" clothes, but she was never easily assimilable to a male vantage point. Some feminist critics have assumed—naively and incorrectly, in my view—that Arzner wore "masculine" clothes simply in order to "pass," so to speak. I have learned, however, that when Arzner's appearance enters the scene of writing—as it inevitably did—far more complicated and peculiar twists and turns occur.

So much about Arzner contradicted established notions of what a woman should look like. While some articles did not mention what Dorothy looked like, these were the exceptions and definitely not the rule; indeed, one of the most striking aspects of the Arzner archive is the extent to which commentators felt compelled to comment on her appearance. As a director, Arzner was not really expected to "look like" anything or anyone; there were few established codes for what a director looks like, except of course for the expectation that he be male. As a woman, however, Arzner was inevitably compared, subtly or explicitly, with the standards of female beauty and identity for which Hollywood has been so renowned—or notorious, depending upon your point of view. In other words, the very presence of a woman director stirred up some cherished and unexamined notions of identity. In Arzner's case, what was stirred up was not only her identity as a woman, but her identity as a woman in whom the codes of gender and of sexuality were anything but conventional.

Consider, for example, a 1927 newspaper story which appeared accompanied by a large portrait of Arzner (figure 52). "Girl Film Director Sets New Standards of Beauty," the title reads, and under Dorothy's photograph one finds this caption: "She has just set new standards for 'the perfect girl.' " One would assume, given the prominence of the photograph of Arzner in the story, that the "new standards of beauty" are those set by Arzner's looks. And in many ways, the portrait of Arzner is just the kind of picture one would expect to illustrate such a claim, particularly given the large size of the photograph and its placement as the literal center of the story. Then there are the details that don't quite fit—her short hair, her thick eyebrows, her direct and forthright gaze. Are these the elements that consitute the "new standards"? Only in reading the article does one discover what is truly meant by the "new standards": Arzner, as director, has definite ideas about the kind of woman who will appear onscreen as the feminine ideal. "New standards of feminine perfection have been set here—and by a girl!" the article begins. But the standards in question are not embodied in Arzner; they have evolved, the article continues, from an argument between her and Clara Bow, in preparation for *The Wild Party*. "Miss Arzner needed eight girls. She wanted them 'typically Wellesley graduates,' conforming to the measurements of a recent graduation class. Miss Bow held out for Follies types." Supposedly the director and the actress compromised, and the desired measurements for the eight young women are reported.[4]

This news story captures the representational dilemma that Arzner embodied: as a woman in Hollywood, she had to have looks, but as an unconventional woman, as a woman whose image signified a butch persona, her looks threatened to challenge the common standards of female beauty. Now in some ways, Arzner's appearance conforms to some aspects of the "New Woman," who became an increasingly visible type in the 1920s and to whom, indirectly, the "new standards of beauty" in the newspaper story alludes. The New Woman was associated with the flapper, that is, with specific images of womanhood made popular in advertising and in motion pictures.[5] In more general terms, the New Woman embodied independence and autonomy and, in terms of her appearance, a somewhat androgynous look. Hence, when a large photograph of Arzner appears with the phrase "new standards of beauty," there is an immediate context that comes to mind. Yet however much Arzner evoked new standards of beauty, there was always an edge in her appearance, a much more distinct lesbian persona than what was permissible within the confines of popularized images of the New Woman. Yet lesbianism was always associated, however indistinctly, with the New Woman.[6]

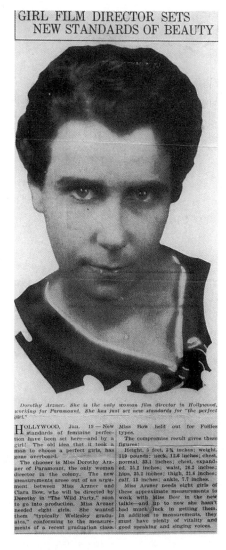

GIRL FILM DIRECTOR SETS
NEW STANDARDS OF BEAUTY

Dorothy Arzner. She is the only woman film director in Hollywood, working for Paramount. She has just set new standards for "the perfect girl."

HOLLYWOOD, Jan. 19 — New standards of feminine perfection have been set here—and by a girl! The old idea that it took a man to choose a perfect girls, has gone overboard.

The chooser is Miss Dorothy Arzner of Paramount, the only woman director in the colony. The new measurements arose out of an argument between Miss Arzner and Clara Bow, who will be directed by Dorothy in "The Wild Party," soon to go into production. Miss Arzner needed eight girls. She wanted them "typically Wellesley graduates," conforming to the measurements of a recent graduation class. Miss Bow held out for Follies types.

The compromise result gives these figures:

Height, 5 feet, 3¾ inches; weight, 119 pounds; neck, 12.6 inches; chest, normal, 33.1 inches; chest, expanded, 35.2 inches; waist, 26.2 inches; hips, 35.2 inches; thigh, 21.6 inches; calf, 13 inches; ankle, 7.7 inches.

Miss Arzner needs eight girls of these approximate measurements to work with Miss Bow in the new talkie—and up to now she hasn't had much luck in getting them. In addition to measurements, they must have plenty of vitality and good speaking and singing voices.

Figure 52. "Girl Film Director Sets New Standards of Beauty," *The Los Angeles Record*, Feb. 10, 1927. Arts Library—Special Collections, University Research Library, UCLA.

Indeed, one of the influences on the New Woman, acknowledged or not, was the increasing visibility of lesbians, and it can be argued that the New Woman was one of many styles that played with lesbian visibility.[7] In other words, the New Woman represented a complex response to the new visibility of lesbians. On the one hand, lesbian identity and lesbian style were mainstreamed. On the other hand, the New Woman also represented panic about lesbianism, and the attendant desire to protect heterosexuality. Hence, the appropriation of lesbian style, from short haircuts to man-tailored suits, became a way of purging the "lesbian" from the New Woman. The popularization of styles and looks associated with lesbianism ironically displaced the threats that lesbianism might represent to heterosexual norms. But the displacement was never absolute. The New Woman is at the very least a contradictory figure who both summons up and represses lesbian possibilities.

Hence, the story that accompanies the photograph of Arzner in "Girl Film Director Sets New Standards of Beauty" might be seen as a way of "managing" the butch image. The photograph itself is contradictory, in that Arzner's face is offset somewhat by the traditionally feminine dress collar she is wearing. The very placement of the photograph makes the woman as image (regardless of what *kind* of image she embodies) the center of attention. In the story proper, its somewhat misleading title is explained in terms of role reversal: "The old idea that it took a man to choose a perfect girls [sic], has gone overboard." So, initially, the story corrects its title by placing Arzner not as the personification of the new standards of beauty, but as a woman who has usurped man's traditional place as judge of female beauty. Such a role reversal feeds into stereotypical definitions of lesbians as male wanna-bes. The story then changes direction by contrasting Arzner and Clara Bow in terms of social class: Arzner wanted a "college girl" type, while Bow preferred a more vaudevillian look. I am not certain how the measurements of college women and "Follies types" would differ, but ultimately the article is significant less for any information it provides about Arzner's career than for its demonstration of how markedly different Arzner was from the women usually pictured in Hollywood.

The picture of Arzner can be read as provoking a certain anxiety: How to describe how she looks, in both senses of the term? In this particular article, the dilemma is solved by describing in detail the measurements of the women Arzner is looking for. This is not to say that comments on Arzner's own physical appearance were avoided in stories about her. One of the most peculiar symptoms of the dilemma represented by Arzner's image is that certain presumably incontrovertible facts of her appearance become subject to interpretation. Consider this representative sample, four descriptions of Arzner (the first is from 1927; the second, from 1930; and the last two, from 1936):

> Sometimes, during the direction of a scene, she speaks so softly that it is necessary for her assistant to echo her orders in his chesty baritone. For the most part, she dresses in sport clothes and flat heels and eye-shading felt hats. There is something about her that commands immediate attention—and respect.
>
> It is an open secret on the Paramount lot that Miss Arzner's company is the best disciplined in the studio—and that it is self-disciplined.[8]

The only woman director in the 'movies' pondered gravely before answering. She sat quietly—a slight, almost frail figure. Black, short hair, with here and there a thread of gray, was brushed smoothly back from her wide, thoughtful forehead, and blue eyes under heavy brows looked at one steadily and directly. The face mobile and sensitive, harbored a strength and power for some reason rather surprising.[9]

Hers is a very satisfying face, brilliantly alive; her skin is clear and healthy, without aid of cosmetics; her eyes are a deep, violet-blue, shadowed with long lashes, and I should hate to be the one to double-cross or try to fool those eyes.

. . . she wears a severely tailored tweed suit, with mannish shirt and tie, when working. She orders her shirts by the dozen from a New York firm and says she feels this is the only sort of costume suited to her job.[10]

The case of Dorothy Arzner, Hollywood's lone woman director, illustrates two tenets of present-day industry. The first is that an intelligent woman can do pretty much any kind of work she sets her mind on doing, and the second is that she need not sacrifice her femininity in doing it.

. . . Hollywood's maverick woman megaphone wielder has dark brown hair brushed back from a high forehead in a short bob, and gray-blue eyes. She wears tailored suits on the set and all her clothes, tailored or evening, are in combinations of black and white or gray. . . . [11]

These four descriptions of Arzner are drawn from sources as diverse as *The New York Times* and fan magazines, thus suggesting that regardless of the publication, a quintessential portrait of Arzner took shape as her directing career developed. Much of the language in the profiles of Arzner suggests an enigma that needs to be solved, particularly in terms of masculinity and femininity. Phrases like "open secret" suggest—very indirectly—one solution to the enigma. But more commonly, writers employ various turns of phrase to suggest that Dorothy's appearance is not easily readable, and that her character is not easily decipherable. Notice how, in these descriptions, details of Arzner's appearance are noted, accompanied by attempts to describe her personality. She dresses in "sport clothes and flat heels and eye-shading felt hats" and "something about her . . . commands attention and respect." She has "black, short hair" and "blue eyes under heavy brows," and her face harbors surprising "strength and power." Her skin is "clear and healthy, without aid of cosmetics," her eyes are "deep, violet-blue," and the writer would hate to "double-cross or try fool those eyes." Arzner is "intelligent" and has not "sacrifice[d] her femininity," but the description that follows mentions only masculine features. It may be too much to say that Dorothy Arzner had a mesmerizing effect on those who profiled her for the popular press, but their powers of description seem to become suddenly vague and imprecise when it comes to drawing conclusions from the physical presence.

In these four descriptions, Arzner's appearance is described largely in terms of masculinity. In other contexts, signifiers of masculinity and femininity circulate, often in confusing fashion. Or perhaps more to the point, there is a need to remark upon Arzner's masculine clothing, and then immediately to search desperately for some feminine attribute; her soft voice and small figure are conveniently present to temper the butch persona. A 1927 fan magazine article describes her as "slim and blue-eyed and black-haired. That hair is cropped as close as a boy's. There is an amazingly level gaze under her unplucked eyebrows. Her voice is soft and gentle—an excellent thing in a woman, even a woman director."[12] The voice is clearly an important factor, suggesting feminine attributes that might otherwise be hard to find. A 1928 profile notes: "Miss Arzner . . . has a soft, melodious voice, which, however, is so distinct, she never has to raise it. She was a symphony in tan, which, somehow seemed to accentuate her beautiful dark brown eyes and hair, her tan suit with white shirt, brown four-in-hand, and felt hat, looking decidedly business-like, yet feminine as well."[13]

The voice, then, provides a way of remarking on a feminine trait in the sea of supposed masculinity signified by Arzner's clothing, hair, and face. Arzner's eyes are signficant in this context as well. The eyes seem to function as a safety zone, as if in a visual descent from the "short bob" to the "heavy brows," they provide a resting place that is neither masculine nor feminine. One of the more interesting descriptions of Arzner's physical appearance appeared in 1927, and—unusually for such profiles of Arzner—no photograph of the director accompanied the piece.

> The director of "Fashions For Women" and "Ten Modern Commandments" is one of these magnetic women, who isn't really pretty, but who looks pretty,—which is so much better, really, than being pretty if you don't look pretty. All women will know what I mean, and a few men. She has sparkling, intelligent gray eyes and straight eyebrows, and unremarkable mouth, nose and chin and a good skin, with dark, close-cropped hair. Her beauty lies in her radiant charm, her animated intelligence. She has a keen level outlook on life, loves to analyze situations and people and is a splendid talker. Altogether, you could easily be fooled into thinking that Dorothy Arzner is beautiful.[14]

This rather convoluted explanation of Dorothy's looks contains some of the details that we have seen—the short hair, the heavy eyebrows, and the peculiar attempt to describe her as pretty, but not really pretty. The eyes—here, of "sparkling, intelligent gray"—receive special attention. Now consider how the same author, Grace Kingsley, described Arzner in a piece published two years later. After noting the Arzner is not married and doesn't intend to marry, Kingsley continues:

> Probably you have imagined the Only Woman Director a deep-chested, broad-shouldered lady, large and aggressive, but you are again due for a surprise.
>
> Instead there greeted me a slim little lady with a slim little face, short hair, very black brushed back in a boyish bob, and lovely sapphire blue eyes, heavily fringed, under rather strongly marked brows, while her smile revealed small white teeth.
>
> She had a little-girl shyness about her too, which, paradoxically combined with a quiet poise, made her a most piquant personality.
>
> I couldn't help thinking as I looked at her of that writer who recently declared that in order to succeed at anything, one must have wistfulness. Dorothy Arzner, for all her will power and her poise and her fine determination, has great wistfulness.[15]

Subtle gradations from gray to blue (sapphire blue, no less) notwithstanding, it is perplexing that the same journalist should see, in the space of two years, a different set of eyes. Indeed, if one were to believe the descriptions written about those eyes, they changed colors numerous times in the space of a few years. Writers usually agree that Dorothy's eyes are remarkable, but how odd that they cannot agree on their color. How to explain this? Variations from blue to gray are understandable, since the two colors often shade one into the other, but Kingsley's shift from gray to sapphire blue is abrupt. When those remarkable eyes range so widely in color one begins to wonder just what is going on here. If the eyes are so striking, why can't the writers agree on their color? Is it possible that these descriptions of Dorothy's eyes have far less to do with the eyes, and far more to do with a physical presence that simply does not lend itself to easy coding or representation within available means of description? Is it possible, in other words, that the apparent neutrality of the eyes, in terms of masculinity or femininity, is illusory, and that the changing colors record the confusion that Dorothy's presence registered on those who wrote about her?

Aside from the attention drawn to Dorothy's eyes, Kingsley's 1929 profile also introduces another important element in the picturing of Dorothy: her marital status. Kingsley's segue from Dorothy's unmarried status to what one might expect from a single lady—a "deep-chested, broad-shouldered lady, large and aggressive"—summons the spectre of the Amazon, the invert, the lesbian. The ensuing characteristics that are enumerated—the small white teeth, the shyness, the poise, the wistfulness—all seem selected to be marshalled against the image of Dorothy as the "mythic mannish lesbian."[16] We have already seen how the circulation of masculine and feminine traits both summons and represses the image of the lesbian. One writer even referred indirectly to the notion of the "third sex," which was one of many popularized explanations for lesbian and gay identities. The author of a 1936 profile notes: "Her clothes, like the rest of her, are a compromise between the motion picture director who is neither man nor woman but sentient sexless machine."[17] While one might wonder just what a "sentient sexless machine" entails, the phrase "neither man nor woman" manages to be precise and vague at the same time.

When Arzner's marital status is mentioned, it is most often as a kind of troubling symptom, almost as if the sparkling eyes and small white teeth and soft voice can only go so far—the woman still is unmarried. Consider this description of Arzner, which appeared in *Time*, accompanying a review of *Craig's Wife*: "Dorothy Arzner is short, stocky, with a quiet executive manner, a boyish bob and an interest in medicine and sunsets. . . . She has never married, goes out little, is now making *Mother Carey's Chickens* for RKO."[18] In the same year, a newspaper story described her as follows: "She rides and walks strenuously, priding herself on being in hard trim always. She weighs 115 pounds and is five feet, four inches tall and becomingly tanned. She is not married."[19] In both of these cases, the fact that Arzner is not married is tied to her dedication to her career and her "hard trim," as if to reinforce the notion of a woman devoted solely to her Hollywood career, but, even more than that, a "sensible" woman for whom marriage would represent a kind of frivolity.

A feature on Arzner in a 1934 issue of *Family Circle* situates Arzner's marital status in the context of a philosophy of life:

> In appearance she is tall and slender, with a slight hunch to her shoulders. She dresses in a not too extreme tailored fashion, wearing generally a jaunty crush hat with a gay feather or ornament on it. Despite some obvious masculine touches in her attire, she is feminine, having an almost pre-war (or ultra-modern) distaste for loud and vulgar women. This can be attributed not to prudery but to an innate fineness and sensitivity, feminine at its source. No shouting feminist, she believes that woman's place is shoulder to shoulder with man, each giving to the other what the other needs (in marriage as well as in other relationships). She is not married.[20]

Now by noting that Arzner believes in a certain kind of equality between men and women "in marriage as well as in other relationships," her unmarried status is mitigated somewhat. The implication is that she believes in marriage, she just isn't married herself. In other respects, the *Family Circle* piece follows the trends we have seen in other descriptions of Arzner's appearance. Observations on what is masculine about her appearance are immediately followed up—and tempered—by suggestions of what is feminine about her. (In this case, her "distaste for loud and vulgar women" seems a stretch even by the standards set by many of the articles written about Arzner.) In terms of Arzner's physical appearance, this article introduces yet another point of interpretation: her physique. Here she is described as tall and slender; elsewhere, as we have seen, she is described as petite.

The confusion about whether Arzner is large or small is not unlike the range of different colors her eyes acquire. For in both cases, the physical attrib-

utes acquire qualities that have more to do with her sexual and gendered identity than with the physique itself. Now this in itself is not exactly surprising
news—the very point of objectifying the female body is to dematerialize that
body. But again, what is striking in Arzner's case is the wide range of responses
her body evokes. Some writers get quite specific about her body, dispensing with
adjectives like "slim" to give actual measurements: "Miss Arzner is just two
inches taller than 5 feet and weighs only 118 pounds, and, in boots, breeches
and flannel shirt, looks boyish; but when she speaks in her well-modulated voice,
stars, featured players, bit people, extras, electricians, carpenters, property men
and photographers jump to their tasks."[21]

And here is another specification, written after Arzner was named associate
producer at Columbia:

> Miss Arzner, small and unassuming, carries her new responsibilities jauntily
> on her well-tailored shoulders. If a knotty problem confronts her she runs her
> fingers through her sleek bob but she makes no temperamental fuss about it.
>
> While studying a script, Miss Arzner curls up on her easy chair and might
> easily be mistaken for a school girl going over tomorrow's lessons instead of
> an important executive doing her work. She is 5 feet 4 inches tall, weighs 115
> pounds, brushes her hair straight back and plays a thumping good game of
> golf.[22]

Now 5′4″ and 115 pounds, or 5′2″ and 118 pounds, would justify the adjective
"slim," as would virtually all photographs of Arzner. But the *Time* profile mentioned previously described her as "short and stocky."[23] And even when
Dorothy's slimness is acknowledged, peculiar comparisons create a very strange
physical image indeed. During the time Arzner was working on *Sarah and Son*,
for instance, a brief newspaper notice compared her to Napoleon!

> To share even one characteristic with the great Napoleon is often the aim of
> men, but it is the real privilege of one woman in Hollywood, namely Dorothy
> Arzner, only woman director for Paramount. She resembles the great Corsican
> in her posture—that of standing with her hands clasped behind her back. In
> all other respects she is feminine and dainty.[24]

The comparison of Dorothy to Napoleon is about as campy a reference to her
butch persona as one can imagine, even if the ostensible point of comparison
is the posture they presumably share. I've suggested that the physical descriptions of Arzner waver between an acknowledgment and a denial of her butch
persona, particularly insofar as the juxtaposition of her "masculine" and "feminine" characteristics are concerned. While I think that Arzner's image was most
immediately "readable" in terms of codes and conventions associated with lesbianism, it is also true, as noted above, that aspects of her persona could be
"read" in relationship to the fashions of her era. Consider, then, the following

descriptions of Dorothy from 1929 and 1928, respectively, which situate her as more "typical" of her era:

> Despite a certain reservation, a becoming dignity, this slender girl creates the impression of extreme youth. Modern youth. She has enthusiasm. Her interesting blue eyes are alight with eagerness which radiates from beneath level black brows. Close-cut dark hair is swept back from a broad forehead that denotes intelligence, just as her firm, small chin and the well defined line of her jaw signify strength of character and determination.
>
> The graceful lines and gentle curves of her slender figure would excite the envy of many a model. And the admiration of many a man. She wears her clothes with a boyish ease; and despite an apparent distaste for the usual frills and frothy furbelows of femininity, there is a softness in the very severity of her apparel, which is very appealing.[25]

> Five minutes talk with this young woman director will tell you why she is successful. In fact, you don't have to talk to her at all. To look at her is sufficient. If you could have seen her the day I interviewed her at Paramount Studios swinging down the concrete walk of the big lot, planting her tan oxfords firmly with each step, shoulders and head up, cool gray eyes alert, you would have recognized the sure-fire qualities that make for success.
>
> She stepped into the publicity office where I had been delayed, shot a keen glance at me, and came forward with a strong grip of the hand. At once I thought here's a woman who could run the studio if she had a mind to!
>
> Not that there is anything aggressive about Dorothy Arzner's manner. She isn't masculine. Neither is she especially feminine. Just one of those modern college girl types, with a certain air of boyishness and an awful lot of confidence.
>
> Her black hair was cut in a boyish bob and brushed straight back from a strong forehead. She wore a slip-on sweater and skirt of tan; a soft silk blouse with Buster Brown collar. If I remember rightly, a gay striped scarf was twisted about her neck.[26]

In both of these descriptions, Arzner's appearance is described as stylish, first and foremost. The operative adjective here is "boyish," according to the styles of the day—the *garçonne* look, i.e., the diffusion of boundaries between "boy" and "girl," that was popular in the 1920s.[27] The specific fashion type evoked, the "modern college girl," is not unlike the characters in some of Arzner's own films. Now there is no question that a boyish, androgynous look was indeed popular during the era when Arzner began her film career; but from the outset, Arzner took a popular look to an extreme that could only marginally signify "fashion" in the most mainstream—and heterosexual—sense of the term. Nonetheless, these portraits of Dorothy reflect an existing discourse of fashion that could be conveniently tapped to represent her in more conventional ways. Put another way, the appeal to fashion—to the college girl type, to her boyish sense of style—is a way of negotiating the Arzner persona.

In reading Dorothy as a "fashionable," rather than as a "marginal" image, we come back to a frame of reference that was always present, implicitly or explicitly, in representations of her—that of the standard of Hollywood beauty, alluded to and yet contradicted in the news story discussed at the beginning of this chapter. The difference in looks between Dorothy and her female stars was often noted, albeit in indirect or subtle ways.

Consider (figure 53) this 1930 story on the making of *Sarah and Son*, which features photographs of Arzner, writer Zoë Akins, and star Ruth Chatterton. Arzner has a full figure photograph, while Akins and Chatterton are portrayed in head shots. Arzner is not in full butch regalia, as she often is in photographs; nonetheless, her difference from the other women—even from Akins, who does not match Hollywood standards of beauty, either—is striking:

> In appearance Dorothy is the very antithesis of Ruth. Where the actress is lovely with all the aids known to beauty experts, the director is plain and sturdy, with a slightly retroussé nose that to all appearances has never known a powder puff. Dorothy wears her hair in a short boyish bob and slips her slender little body into strictly tailored woolen suits while Ruth luxuriates in silks and satins.[28]

The layout of the photographs of the three principal female participants in *Sarah and Son* both reinforces and undercuts the image of Dorothy as the "direct opposite" of Chatterton. Only Dorothy appears in a full body shot, and the photograph in question emphasizes her butch persona less than many others do. In fact, the suit Arzner wears may be "tailored," but not "strictly" so, and she is wearing a skirt. The face that is singled out for commentary in the text is overshadowed by the full body shot; and not surprisingly, Chatterton's face looms largest over the article. Arzner's image in this article foregrounds the extent to which she both fit and did not fit into the conventions of representation of the female form; she was simultaneously fashionable and marginal. She "fit" to the extent that she was described, constantly, in visual terms; and she did not "fit" in far more obvious ways, in that discrepancies always existed between how she looked and how female bodies are conventionally described. Ultimately, no amount of description of Arzner could reconcile what "fit" with what did not.

An interesting strategy in this context is a different representation of Arzner's physical presence: the cartoon. A full page feature on Arzner appeared in a St. Louis newspaper in 1929, and included a photograph of Arzner framed by pen and ink renditions of various stages of her career (figure 54).[29] The woman in the drawings bears no resemblance to Arzner, but even more significantly, the first three images, showing Arzner as a typist, as an author, and as an editor, eliminate her face from view altogether! Only when Arzner is

Figure 53. "All-Women Film Breeds Nary a Scrap," *Sunday News,* June 19, 1930. Arts Library—Special Collections, University Research Library, UCLA.

portrayed as a director is a full body view allowed, now in a pose that resembles Arzner only because it is clearly modelled after publicity photographs of her and her assistant on the set. The photograph of Arzner here—the same one that appears in the "Girl Film Director Sets New Standards of Beauty" story—is distinctly unlike the drawings that supposedly represent her. As already noted,

Figure 54. "A Woman Picture Director," *The St. Louis Post-Dispatch Daily Magazine,* 1929. Arts Library—Special Collections, University Research Library, UCLA.

this photograph is contradictory in that the collar of the dress worn by Arzner is distinctly feminine. But if the illustrations were meant to feminize Arzner by comparing her to popular images of women of the day, they have the opposite effect, by making Arzner seem at odds with those images. The contrast in this layout makes Arzner appear more butch, not more femme.

Other cartoon renditions of Arzner were far more direct in caricaturing her butch persona. In a 1938 cartoon (figure 55), the photograph of Arzner in profile performs the unusual (for stories about Arzner, that is) function of toning down the extreme implications of the caricature, in which Arzner's face is reduced to a butch haircut and a pair of eyebrows. Here the parody is heightened by the contrast between what Arzner wears in the photograph (a suit and tie) and what she wears in the cartoons (dresses and high heels). A drag effect is created, although it isn't clear which rendition of Arzner is supposed to be in drag. Arzner is caricatured in yet another way in a 1936 cartoon accompanying a story about the production of *Craig's Wife* (figure 56). After noting that the "crew on the set are under the spell of Miss Arzner," and that the "actors are affected, too," the writer describes the following scene:

> Miss Russell, in a clinging white evening gown, is standing with her back to a mantel. She listens carefully as the woman in the gray, mannish-cut suit tells her how to act the scene. When she replies, her voice drops to the same inaudible murmur.[30]

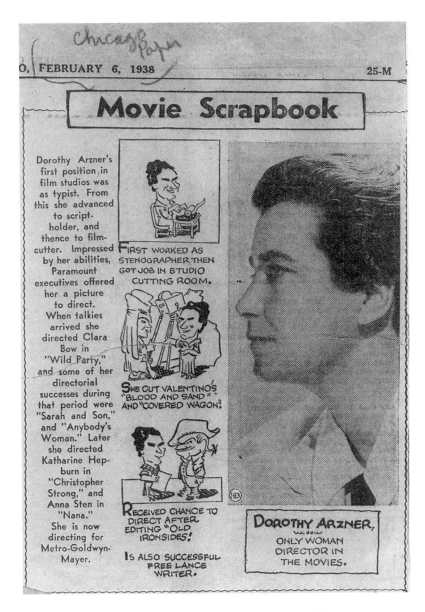

Figure 55. A Chicago newspaper caricatures Arzner, February 6, 1938.
Arts Library—Special Collections, University Research Library, UCLA.

Figure 56. A cartoon depicting Dorothy Arzner and Rosalind Russell on the set of *Craig's Wife*. MOMA Film Stills Archive.

Something interesting has occurred between 1929 and 1936. If, in the late 1920s, it was possible to imagine Arzner in relationship to the prevailing styles of the era—collegiate or boyish—this was no longer the case by 1936.[31] To be sure, these cartoon renditions of Arzner cannot stand in for an entire history of fashion, but they foreground the changing relationship of an obviously butch woman like Arzner to the prevailing styles of the era. It was possible in 1929 to suggest some resemblance between Arzner and the androgynous, boyish fashions of the time; but in the later cartoons, Arzner is portrayed as a parody, as a mockery of femininity. Most significantly, the types to which she is likened are less fashionable than clichéd—a battle-ax and a priggish schoolmarm.

The final type of portrayal of Arzner to which I turn is the supposed first-person account. Arzner was interviewed often, and while some of the information conveyed in those interviews chimes with statements she herself made about her career, other information clearly had more to do with myths of the sole female director. I've already mentioned how Arzner objected to the notion that she chose a career in film direction because of her father's catering to Hollywood personalities in his restaurant. My point is not to be able to distinguish absolutely between genuine and false interview quotations, but rather to see Arzner's supposed "own words" as elements that contribute to a construction of her persona.

It comes as no surprise that Arzner's opinions were solicited not only on matters pertaining directly to the film industry, but also on current women's issues. In a 1929 article, for instance, Arzner is quoted as stating that "the next war will be won by the side possessing the largest number of feminine fighters."[32] More typically—especially as her directing career proved to be long-lasting—Arzner was quoted in order to explain her approach to the cinema. Her collaborative approach was indeed significant in its own right; it also provided a means of identifying her status as a woman in terms that departed somewhat from the norm of autonomy associated with male directors. Arzner's strong belief in the collaborative nature of motion pictures provided a way of qualifying her particularly "masculine" attributes. The point is made succinctly in an article about her career in which Arzner says: "Every picture, of course, is the product of the combined efforts of a group of artists, but, I believe, it should be even more so. I believe that in the industry everyone from a prop boy to producer should be privileged to offer any ideas at any appropriate time."[33] The title of the article: "A Woman's Touch."

One of the most curious reportings of Arzner's opinions is found in a 1929 newspaper piece on the types of male stars preferred by female moviegoers. The title of the piece is "Do Ladies Prefer Brunettes?" (figure 57). The photo layout plays upon a most bizarre ambiguity. A photograph of Arzner—the same one featured in "Girl Film Director Sets New Standards of Beauty"—appears next to a descending trio of photographs of male, brunette actors. Directly beneath Arzner's photograph is a photograph of George Meeker, distinctly blonde and distinctly unlike the others—including Arzner. Not only is Meeker blonde, he strikes a far more effeminate pose than any of the other figures. Now I am certain that the title of the piece is meant to be quite straightforward, and that the "brunettes" are understood to be actors; in other words, the meaning is, presumably, entirely heterosexual. But when one first sees the article, the effect of the photo layout is potentially jarring. Indeed, one is tempted to ask, *which* attractive brunette pictured on the page might ladies prefer?

The ambiguity is only reinforced by the text of the article, although in quite a different way. Arzner is quoted as an expert on what women audiences prefer in the way of actors:

Women admire virility in their screen heroes more than anything else . . .
They want a dash of devilry [*sic*] in their men—the kind, you know, that

Figure 57. "Do Ladies Prefer Brunettes?" *The Sunday Post*, October 20, 1928. Arts Library—Special Collections, University Research Library, UCLA.

turns out all right in the eighth reel. There is only one way they can get this, from the virile, vital men, best exemplified in the brunette type.

. . . I think people will change their choice pretty soon, as entertainment becomes more aesthetic—I mean away from the body angle—mental romance will replace or overshadow physical passion. Then another type of player will attract the picture-goer into the golden palaces. This new type of hero will be blonder and perhaps slightly effeminate—and as a contrast, a somewhat masculine type of woman will play against him. But remember I am not talking about the present time.

. . . It comes down to symbolism. [. . . .] Sunshine, that is—lightness has always suggested the spiritual, the effeminate. The night, that is the dark, suggests the material-man.[34]

Arzner's authority to speak on women's desires in relation to actors seems to be a function of her roles as director and as potential moviegoer (although her prediction about the future heroes for which the world is not yet ready seems to evolve from an identity other than director or moviegoer). Most curiously, she evaluates the differences between brunette and blonde leading men in some of the same kind of language that one associates more typically with the classification of women in the movies. Yet this reversal doesn't quite work, largely because any simple opposition between blonde and brunette men is undone by that striking photograph of a brunette woman who displaces any opposition between masculinity and femininity.

Arzner's decision to leave Hollywood in 1943 meant that, for a period of three decades, she was virtually invisible to the public eye. But when interest in Arzner's unique career was sparked in the 1970s, and especially after the Directors Guild of America tribute to her in 1975, articles once again began to appear. The notion of a woman director was no longer quite so anomalous, even if women directors were still—and are still—exceptions that prove the rule in Hollywood. While the interest in Arzner's looks and her image was not as strong as it was during the first decade of her career, some familiar contours emerge in these more contemporary profiles, which most often are illustrated with photographs from Arzner's past. One of the most thoughtful pieces on Arzner, written by Mary Murphy and published in the *Los Angeles Times* in 1975, the day before the Directors Guild tribute, begins: "A tiny woman in a white pantsuit and soft white shoes which look like baby booties opens the door. Her hair is slicked back into a ducktail, exactly as it has been since she was 15, but now the vibrant brown color has been shaded honey blonde and the roots are graying."[35]

The passage of time, it appears, brings yet another layer to the Arzner image. The ever-present hairdo is now a "ducktail," still signifying a butch image.

But it is a personal quirk, a stylistic flourish that she has worn throughout the years, as if to suggest a kind of stubborn eccentricity. The hair is a perfect image of the career. And just as supposedly "masculine" details were immediately countered with feminine ones in articles that appeared during Arzner's career, the hair is described as dyed, with some gray roots showing, so as to emphasize that, ducktail notwithstanding, Arzner still shares in the feminine rituals of preoccupation with hair color. I find it somewhat remarkable that three decades after Arzner left her directing career, some things, like the preoccupation with her hair, never change. (Not to mention the shoes like baby booties—one of the more extreme images of diminutive size in the Arzner archive.)

Murphy's profile refers to some of the images of Arzner that circulated during her Hollywood career. She notes that Arzner was compared to Napoleon, and that she battled with the giants of the film industry. Interestingly, Murphy challenges these images by following precisely the pattern we have seen in earlier accounts of Arzner. "What is missing from these descriptions," Murphy writes, "is any hint of Arzner's warmth or vision, any sense of the fiery enthusiasm beneath the stern manner. The face that looks so harsh in setside photographs is soft and likable in person."[36] The article is illustrated with a 1927 photograph of Arzner on the set with her cameraman, and a 1943 photograph of her and Merle Oberon on the set of *First Comes Courage* (figures 58, 59). Whatever else one might say about these photographs, I don't think "harsh" is quite the look they convey. The search for euphemisms for "butch lesbian" is seemingly never-ending.

Murphy's article is popular journalism, which is usually assumed to be radically different from academic scholarship. Yet there is at least one similarity between Murphy's article and the feminist analyses of Arzner that began to appear at about the same time. As coincidence would have it, the two pictures of Dorothy Arzner that are used to illustrate Murphy's piece reflect how, in feminist discussions of Arzner, the "accompanying illustrations" of Arzner tended to be of two types. Arzner is either shown amidst the vast machinery of the classical Hollywood cinema, or she is shown in the company of a distinctly more "feminine" star. If the first type of image foregrounds one of the major preoccupations of feminist film theory—the difficult relationship between women and the apparatus of the cinema—the second type foregrounds what tended to be repressed in feminist film theory. For the dominant trope of 1970s film theory was "sexual difference," understood in the exclusive and narrow terms of heterosexuality. Pictures of Arzner foreground both what feminist film theory articulated—the relationship between woman and the apparatus of the cinema—and what it did not—relationships between women.

I have suggested elsewhere that the feminist engagement with Arzner was both critical and symptomatic. Part of *The Woman at the Keyhole* examines lesbian authorship in film and the curious ways in which Dorothy Arzner has been

Figure 58. Dorothy Arzner and cameraman Al Gilks, 1927. Arts Library—Special Collections, University Research Library, UCLA.

fetishized in feminist film theory—literally present as an image, while the unmistakable lesbian implications of that image are denied and repressed. The rediscovery of Arzner in the context of feminist film theory was consistently illustrated, and the deployment of pictures of Arzner went far beyond what was necessary simply to "show" who the director was.

Consider how Arzner makes an appearance on the covers of several books devoted to feminist film studies. Karyn Kay and Gerald Peary's anthology *Women and the Cinema* features four women on its cover in various permutations of female identity—Jane Fonda in *Klute*, Arzner in the late 1920s with her megaphone, Marlene Dietrich, and Brigitte Bardot in a wedding dress. For each of the actresses, the image in question situates their personae in terms of shifting boundaries—*Klute* was one of the most important films in Fonda's career shift from sex kitten to serious actress, while the image of Bardot in a wedding dress also plays on her standard role as sex kitten. Of these four women, only Dietrich stares directly at the reader, soliciting her gaze, and Dietrich is shown here in one of her famously seductive poses. But what of Arzner,

Figure 59. Dorothy Arzner and Merle Oberon on the set of *First Comes Courage*, 1943. Arts Library—Special Collections, University Research Library, UCLA.

standing with her personalized megaphone? If the actresses represent both sexualized images and their discontents, Arzner articulates rather a different kind of shifting boundary, that between "masculinity" (the hair, the pose) and "femininity" (the lace collar), as well as that between the stance behind the camera, rather than in front of it. But Arzner's appearance here, among these actresses, foregrounds one of the dilemmas of feminist film criticism—the problem of representing women as anything but objects of the cinematic gaze. Put another way, Arzner's image upsets some of the easy dichotomies of subject/object, masculine/feminine.

Perhaps the most strikingly symptomatic depiction of Arzner is the cover of the British Film Institute pamphlet that appeared in 1975 (figure 60).[37] It shows Arzner seated next to a large camera, with a male assistant seated next to her, and they look toward what initially appears to be an unidentified field of vision—in the language of the cinema, to an unspecified reverse angle. But when the pamphlet is opened, the reader/viewer sees that the photograph continues on the back cover, and that in that continuation of the photograph, two women—the two sisters of *Working Girls*—are looking at each other. (The

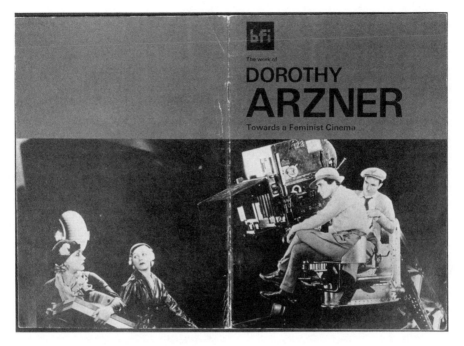

Figure 60. The cover of *The Work of Dorothy Arzner: Towards a Feminist Cinema*, British Film Institute, 1975.

scene in question is the staircase conversation detailed in chapter 5.) The two women not only supply the field of vision that appears initially to be absent from the cover, but they also reflect, symmetrically, the positions of Arzner and her assistant. Now Arzner's male assistant projects the kind of look that has been central to feminist film theory—a voyeuristic gaze that situates the two actresses as objects. But Arzner's look has another function; it both upsets any simple relationship between the male subject and the female object of the look and eroticizes the exchange between the two women on the set. Echoes of this erotic exchange are found in numerous publicity photographs of Arzner on the set with actresses.

The Woman at the Keyhole is concerned primarily with how feminist film theory has (or has not) addressed Arzner, and with how her "rediscovery" by feminist film critics in the 1970s involved a curious mixture of factors. Despite the relatively academic boundaries of feminist film theory, I see the circulation of Arzner's image in feminist film theory as symptomatic of other preoccupations that speak fundamentally to questions of the visibility of women—including lesbians—in Hollywood. Consider, for example, the citation and appropriation of Arzner's image that occurred in 1991 when Jodie Foster appeared on the cover of *Interview* magazine at the time of her directorial debut in *Little Man Tate*.[38] A series of images depict Foster in Arzneresque costumes and poses. As if to suggest Foster's movement from one side of the camera to the other, the story also includes photographs more typical of an actress. We have seen how publicity photographs of Arzner on the set depict her in friendly and flirtatious poses with actresses. In the story on Foster, the roles of director and actress are divided into separate photographs, as if to suggest both Foster's dual role and the inevitable quality of performance associated both with acting and directing. If Foster strikes Arzneresque poses in her director images, she adopts the personae of different actresses—Lauren Bacall, Greta Garbo—in her actress images. Now Foster's "appropriation" of Arzner is precisely that, an adaptation; Foster wears the makeup that Arzner did not, and wears her hair in a mid-length bob. One could argue that this appropriation of Arzner's image is a kind of "de-dyking" of the Arzner persona, while it simultaneously conjures up the ambiguity associated with both Arzner and Foster. Thus, this appropriation serves as a useful reminder that the Arzner persona was also a performance, a style, and an attitude.

I've attempted to emphasize, in this chapter, how the "picturing" of Arzner during her career reveals what a challenge she presented to established codes of femininity and female behavior, particularly insofar as her butch persona was concerned. Yet it is inaccurate to say that Arzner's image was erased. Rather, it was interpreted and negotiated. To be sure, it was also denied—but denial and erasure are not the same thing. All of these needs and desires to explain the Arzner persona attest to how powerfully the image of this "femme megger" resisted conventional definitions of masculinity and femininity. Contemporary reinterpretations of the Arzner image, whether in feminist film theory or in photographs of Jodie Foster, suggest how powerfully this image continues to fascinate us.

Conclusion

Lesbian Detection

OCCASIONALLY WHEN I have presented my work on Arzner, questions have been raised concerning the "necessary" connections between a butch persona and lesbianism. I have come to be quite suspicious of the term "androgyny" in this context, since it so often functions as a code for "not necessarily lesbian," which in turn functions as a code for "heterosexual until proven otherwise." Indeed, there are photographs of Arzner where her look might quite appropriately be described as "androgynous," and the term "androgyny" is not necessarily homophobic—witness the current circulation of the term as signifying a type of lesbian style.[1] What strikes me, more specifically, is a resistance to using the term "lesbian" in any kind of historical or effective sense.

Jennifer Terry, describing what she calls "deviant historiography," takes from Michel Foucault the notion of "effective history": "Effective history exposes not the events and actors elided by traditional history, but instead lays bare the *processes* and *operations* by which these elisions occurred."[2] The previous chapter was devoted to such a "laying bare" of how Arzner's butch persona was both summoned and repressed in popular accounts of her career. In this conclusion, I turn to how, in lesbian representation of the last ten years or so, Arzner's persona has been reappropriated. What happens when the lesbian persona is negotiated not as a symptom that threatens to upset sexist and heterosexist assumptions, but rather as a part of a validative, affirmative project in relationship to lesbian history and lesbian identity? How, in other words, have contemporary lesbian artists and writers developed effective history?

I suggested in *The Woman at the Keyhole* that, in general, it seems that there have been two Arzners—a textual one and a pictured one. In reductionist terms, feminist film theorists have largely been interested in Arzner's films (the "textual" Arzner), while lesbians have been primarily interested in Arzner's persona (the "pictured" Arzner). This is not a rigid opposition; the fascination with photographs of Arzner on the part of feminist film theorists speaks to a fascination with the persona, and lesbians are among the greatest fans of Arzner's films. Nonetheless, the interest in Arzner has been characterized by a divide between her work and her image.

In Tee Corinne's collection of images of lesbians, *Women Who Loved Women*, two pictures of Dorothy Arzner appear, with some interesting alterations.[3] One image is based on a photograph of Arzner and Joan Crawford, but

Figure 61. Dorothy Arzner, ca. 1937. Arts Library—Special Collections, University Research Library, UCLA.

with Crawford erased; the other image takes a portrait of Arzner, posing amidst the cumbersome machinery of cameras, and erases the cameras. In both images, Arzner's body fills the frame, unlike many other images in the collection which feature close-ups of women's faces. The butch image which was discussed in such convoluted detail during Arzner's career becomes here a different kind of signifier, one requiring a very different kind of commentary. The butch image of Arzner is situated among various representations of lesbianism, some based on a butch look (Radclyffe Hall, Gladys Bentley) and others based on the reputations of the women that precede them (Colette, Virginia Woolf). While Corinne's images "read" lesbian identity out of the Arzner image, the collection as a whole provides a kaleidoscopic view of the varieties of lesbian visibility—i.e., not all lesbians look alike, and butch is not the only measure of a lesbian image. In Arzner's case, though, the butch persona provides the most obvious "proof" of lesbian identity.

Corinne's appropriation of Arzner's image suggests, most obviously, that what was repressed and negotiated in Arzner's time becomes a clear, straightforward image of lesbian identity in the context of a new historical era. When I read Corinne's introduction to the volume, however, I am curiously reminded of the accounts of Arzner discussed in the previous chapter. Corinne has this to say about Arzner: "Quiet, closeted women like film director Dorothy Arzner worked in Hollywood near flamboyant and equally closeted bisexuals like Garbo and Dietrich."[4] The purpose may be different, but Arzner is still contrasted with actresses of her era. During her lifetime, Arzner's quiet voice was marshalled as a feminine trait among the disturbing masculine ones; here, Arzner's quiet character is a symptom of something different, yet equally in need of negotiation: the Hollywood closet. My point here is *not* that there is "no difference" between Corinne's appropriation of Arzner in the name of a proud and affirmative lesbian identity and the convoluted accounts of Arzner's image during her lifetime. What I do want to stress is that there is no appropriation without negotiation, and that for contemporary lesbian representation, the closet has been one of the most vexed and complicated institutions of lesbian history.

Corinne's volume embodies what one might call a process of lesbian detection—an effort to rethink and reconstruct the various images and gaps and silences of the past. More specific and literal contours of that process of lesbian detection vis-à-vis Arzner appear in another recent text. Arzner appears briefly but significantly in an example of what may well be the prototypical lesbian cultural text of the 1980s—the Naiad novel. Katherine V. Forrest is the author of a series of novels published by Naiad, and she is particularly well known among gays and lesbians for the Kate Delafield mysteries. In the 1989 mystery novel *The Beverly Malibu*, Delafield becomes involved in the investigation of the murder of Owen Sinclair, former Hollywood director who was a friendly witness before HUAC. Sinclair lived in an apartment building inhabited by other veterans of the film industry, including Paula Grant, a woman in her 50s, who discovered the murdered man and for whom Delafield discovers a growing attraction. When Delafield enters Paula Grant's apartment to question her, here is what she sees:

Three sling chairs made of good leather faced a gray tweed sofa. Another sling chair, this one of wood and canvas, appeared to be an authentic director's chair: the name DOROTHY ARZNER was stencilled across its back. This chair was not to be sat upon; it reposed in a place of honor below a black-framed poster of Joan Crawford in a film Kate had never heard of, *The Bride Wore Red.*[5]

Kate may be unfamiliar with Arzner and *The Bride Wore Red*, but she soon discovers more familiar sights on Grant's walls:

> More than a dozen similarly framed posters and movie photo montages adorned the walls. Kate's glance sped in surprised recognition: Shirley Maclaine and Audrey Hepburn in *The Children's Hour.* Candice Bergen as Lakey in *The Group.* Susan Sarandon and Catherine Deneuve in *The Hunger.* Garbo, in sculptured black and white androgyny, in *Queen Christina.* Mariel Hemingway and Patrice Donnelly soaring over a track hurdle in *Personal Best.* A bar scene with the two female stars of *Lianna.* And on the dining room wall, Helen Shaver looking bemusedly into the distance as Patricia Charbonneau leaned back confidently against a Chevy convertible in *Desert Hearts* (18–19).

In a room populated with images of what might be called the lesbian cinematic canon, only Arzner functions as an unfamiliar name and an absent image. While Kate immediately is drawn to the images she recognizes, her male heterosexual partner becomes "fixated" (p. 19) on the image of Joan Crawford. Paula Grant supplies the information that Arzner directed Crawford in *The Bride Wore Red* in 1937, when Grant was fourteen and her mother, who worked in the MGM costume department, was assigned to the picture. Kate Delafield immediately recognizes from Grant's "evident adulation" of Arzner that this was her first sexual attraction to another woman.

Hence, in a closet scenario par excellence, Dorothy Arzner becomes a link between the lesbian present and past of Hollywood and between three different generations of lesbians, even though her lesbianism is never explicitly stated. Forrest pays lesbian homage to Arzner, but in a more subtle way than Tee Corinne does in her graphic inclusion of Arzner among famous lesbians. Yet in Forrest's novel, the absence of any image of Arzner functions as a sign of the invisibility of lesbians in Hollywood, an invisibility to which *The Beverly Malibu* addresses itself by attempting to puncture that myth. The director's chair with Arzner's name on it, sealed off from the rest of the room as a shrine, resembles the contours of the ubiquitous closet itself, albeit a closet with permeable and quite seductive boundaries. If there is an epistemology of the closet, as Eve Sedgwick (and others) have argued, there is also a romance of the closet, whereby the lesbian researcher, like the lesbian detective, thrills in the circulation of ostensibly secret knowledge.[6] Yet "secrecy" is not quite the right term here, since also at stake—particularly insofar as the closet is concerned for *women*—is a challenge to conventional boundaries between the private and the public spheres.

Indeed, in Forrest's novel the invasion of Paula Grant's home by the forces of the law opens a precarious threshold between private and public space, and the fact that one of those forces of the law is a woman upsets the conventional parallels between the private sphere of women and the public sphere of men. The recognition of shared lesbian identity occurs on that threshold between private and public space. The closet, as a figure of the precarious boundary between privacy and publicity, can submerge or repress lesbian possibilities, but can also enhance them. In Forrest's novel, the romance of the closet depends upon the different relationship of women to the private and the public.

Hollywood, as much as any twentieth-century institution, has reconfigured the boundaries between the private and the public, as well as within each term. The capacity of Hollywood to manufacture a "private sphere" for public consumption puts into question the very sanctity and secrecy of said privacy. Yet, however much Hollywood may have played upon the tenuous and usually gendered boundaries between the private and the public, it maintained a rigid gender distinction between those who controlled film production—virtually always male—and those who were controlled by them. In that painfully obvious and crucial sense, Arzner's relationship to the Hollywood closet has to do with the *simultaneity* of gender and sexuality.

The supposed safety of the closet has to be questioned in Arzner's case, since she flaunted an identity that signified "butch lesbian." If the closet has served as the primary metaphor for the particular quality of the oppression of homosexuals—don't ask, don't tell, in the words of the most current deployment of crises of homosexual visibility—the image of the butch exists at a curious juncture between visibility and invisibility. For always implicit when visibility is raised as a question is another question—visible to whom? Just as the closet represents a complex point of negotiation for the appropriation of Arzner, so the question of spectatorship—of how images are consumed, read, and interpreted—has been crucial in the process of lesbian detection.

Dry Kisses Only is a video by Kaucyila Brooke and Jane Cottis that explores lesbianism and the cinema through the question of spectatorship, and specifically through an examination of how presumably heterosexual films are consistently read "against the grain" by lesbian viewers. Arzner is indirectly referred to in *Dry Kisses Only* through one of her films, *Christopher Strong*, which is read for its lesbian subtext. *Dry Kisses Only* performs a variety of readings on films that range from Hollywood classics that foreground female friendship and/or rivalry (*The Great Lie, All about Eve*), to films with butch characters (Joan Crawford in *Johnny Guitar, The Killing of Sister George*), to films with lesbian characters and/or scenes (*The Haunting, The Hunger, The Killing of Sister George*). The readings are performed in a variety of ways, from the showing of scenes drawn intact from the films, but isolated from the heterosexual contextualization (*The Great Lie* lends itself particularly well to this technique), to a com-

Figure 62. Dorothy Arzner at home, ca. 1940. Arts Library—Special Collections, University Research Library, UCLA.

plete re-editing of the scene in *All about Eve* when Eve introduces herself to Margo Channing, with an explicitly lesbian Eve substituting for Anne Baxter's Eve. *Christopher Strong* is cited in the video for two reasons—Katharine Hepburn's butch image, and the relationship between Monica and Cynthia. Hepburn's entry into the party early in *Christopher Strong* is shown "intact," as it were; and the relationship between Monica and Cynthia is highlighted in a scene where Monica visits Cynthia's home, angry that she has been ignored.

The scene is repeated in the video, with specific moments repeated several times—particularly Cynthia's embrace of Monica.

Nowhere in the video is Arzner even mentioned. Unlike *The Beverly Malibu*, *Dry Kisses Only* displays an interest only in Arzner's films, not in her. The case made for lesbian spectatorship in *Dry Kisses Only* concerns the relationship between text and viewer, and a variety of spectator positions are elicited in the tape, from a hilarious academic lecture, to lesbian-in-the-street (or on-the-beach) interviews, to a gossip column report. *Dry Kisses Only* theorizes lesbian spectatorship as having to do with creative and subversive reception, with the appropriation of existing texts, rather than with who creates those texts in the first place.[7] One could say that *Dry Kisses Only* brings lesbian spectatorship out of the closet.

I see, in my own work on Arzner, echoes of the kind of lesbian detection outlined in both *The Beverly Malibu* and *Dry Kisses Only*, i.e., an interest in both text/film and persona/image. Arzner is associated with mystery, with the hidden gay and lesbian past (and present) of Hollywood, and with the different manifestations of the coming-out process shown in Forrest's novel. The image of a director's chair with the name "Dorothy Arzner" written on it suggests both a tantalizing presence and a sad absence. The romance of the closet that characterizes *The Beverly Malibu* is certainly not only a fictional construct, for virtually any exploration of lesbian history involves a complex negotiation of visibility, secrecy, codes, and knowledge. Although *Dry Kisses Only* offers another kind of lesbian detection, one that turns away from that mysterious director's chair in Paula Grant's apartment to focus on the images on the wall, the same complex negotiations are necessary to produce these readings. While I am convinced that Arzner's films are of enormous interest in terms of their "lesbian subtexts," I cannot define lesbian spectatorship purely in terms of her films. I have tried to include both the chair and the images in my field of vision.

Notes

Introduction

1. I am using the term "butch" in terms of style and visual presentation. Recent lesbian writings have explored the wide and complex range of meanings associated with "butch," as with "femme," not to mention "lesbian." See in particular Joan Nestle, *A Restricted Country* (Ithaca, New York: Firebrand Books, 1987); Joan Nestle, ed., *The Persistent Desire: A Femme-Butch Reader* (Boston: Alyson Publications, 1992); Elizabeth Lapovsky Kennedy and Madeline D. Davis, *Boots of Leather, Slippers of Gold: The History of a Lesbian Community* (New York and London: Routledge, 1993); and Leslie Feinberg, *Stone Butch Blues* (Ithaca: Firebrand Books, 1993).

2. Edward Baron Turk, "Speaking of Sex," *Civitas* 1 (Spring 1992): p. 4.

3. Charles Higham and Roy Moseley, *Princess Merle: The Romantic Life of Merle Oberon* (New York: Coward-McCann, Inc., 1983), p. 152.

4. Charles Higham, *Lucy: The Real Life of Lucille Ball* (New York: St. Martin's Press, 1984), p. 52.

5. Jane Gaines, "Costume and Narrative: How Dress Tells the Woman's Story," in Jane Gaines and Charlotte Herzog, eds., *Fabrications: Costume and the Female Body* (New York and London: Routledge, 1990), 180–211. Gaines has also explored the importance of costume and costume design in Arzner's work; see "Dorothy Arzner's Trousers," *Jump Cut*, no. 37 (1992): 88–98.

6. See Claire Johnston, ed., *The Work of Dorothy Arzner: Towards a Feminist Cinema* (London: British Film Institute, 1975).

7. Judith Butler, *Gender Trouble: Feminism and the Subversion of Identity* (New York and London: Routledge, 1990), p. 140.

8. Blanche Wiesen Cook, *Eleanor Roosevelt*, vol. 1 (New York: Viking Penguin, 1992), p. 14.

1. Apprenticeship

1. *Behind the Makeup* (1930) and *Charming Sinners* (1930), both Paramount productions, were initially co-directed by Arzner and Robert Milton; Milton received official credit. Arzner also completed *The Last of Mrs. Cheyney* (MGM, 1937) for Richard Boleslavsky, who received screen credit.

2. Douglas Gomery, *The Hollywood Studio System* (London: Macmillan, 1986), p. 28.

3. Florabel Muir, "All-Women Film Breeds Nary a Scrap," *Sunday News*, January 19, 1930. Arzner scrapbook, Dorothy Arzner Collection, University of California, Los Angeles, Arts Library—Special Collections. Subsequent citations to material from the Dorothy Arzner collection will be abbreviated "Arzner Collection, UCLA." Some citations, particularly to clippings in Arzner's scrapbook, are incomplete: I provide as much information as is available.

4. Interview with Dorothy Arzner (1), Oral History Project, University of California, Los Angeles, Department of Special Collections. Subsequent citations to material from these collections will be abbreviated "UCLA Special Collections."

5. Interview with Dorothy Arzner (1), Oral History Project, UCLA Special Collections.

6. Ruth M. Tildesley, "Dorothy Arzner, Director," *The Woman's Journal*, 1927, p. 25. Arzner scrapbook, Arzner Collection, UCLA.

7. Interview with Dorothy Arzner (1), Oral History Project, UCLA Special Collections.

8. Mary Murphy, "Film Director Dorothy Arzner: Tribute to an Unsung Pioneer," *Los Angeles Times*, January 24, 1975.

9. Noting that "there was more to her departure than illness," Mary Murphy reports that during a discussion of Charles Chaplin, Arzner said, "Yes, it was so unfortunate that he was blackballed but then we were all blackballed at some time." Murphy explains: "Eventually her vision of women and how they should be portrayed on screen and treated in the studio clashed with the dictates of Louis B. Mayer, whom she calls 'the great dictator.' " See ibid.

10. Interview with Dorothy Arzner (1), Oral History Project, UCLA Special Collections.

11. "First Woman Director of the Directors Guild: Dorothy Arzner," *Westlake Magazine*, Spring 1982, p. 12. Arzner Collection, UCLA.

12. In an interview with Karyn Kay and Gerald Peary, Arzner refers to the film by another title, *The Secret Doctor of Gaya*. *Stronger Than Death* was the official release title of the film. See "Interview with Dorothy Arzner," in Claire Johnston, ed., *The Work of Dorothy Arzner: Towards a Feminist Cinema* (London: British Film Institute, 1975), p. 23.

13. Maeve Druesne describes Nazimova as "an aggressive businesswoman" who "owned her own production company, overseeing virtually every phase of production herself: scripting, titling, editing, casting and acting." See "Nazimova: Her Silent Films," part 1, *Films in Review* 36 (June-July 1985): p. 323.

14. See Kenneth Anger, *Hollywood Babylon* (New York: Dell Publishing, 1975), p. 113.

15. Michael Morris, in *Madam Valentino: The Many Lives of Natacha Rambova* (New York and London: Abbeville Press, 1991), insists that, while Nazimova's lesbian affairs are a matter of record, Rambova was definitely not a lesbian nor was she involved romantically with Nazimova.

16. See Rider McDowell, "Allah Be Praised," *Première* 5 (April 1992), 72–76.

17. Cited in Maeve Druesne, "Nazimova: Her Silent Films," part 2, *Films in Review* 36 (August-September 1985): 407.

18. Herbert Cruikshank, "Director Dorothy Arzner: The One Woman behind the Stars," *Motion Picture Classic*, September 1929, p. 76. Arzner Collection, UCLA.

19. Interview with Dorothy Arzner (2), Oral History Project, UCLA Special Collections.

20. Boze Hadleigh, interview with George Cukor, *Conversations with My Elders* (New York: St. Martin's Press, 1986), p. 170.

21. Adrienne Rich, "Compulsory Heterosexuality and Lesbian Existence," *Signs* 5 (Summer 1980): 631–60.

22. Dorothy Arzner, quoted in Kevin Brownlow, *The Parade's Gone By . . .* (New York: Alfred A. Knopf, 1968), p. 286.

23. See Denise Hartsough, "Cutting Film: Women's Work" (unpublished manuscript, 1983), p. 10: "Some accounts treat the terms 'cutter' and 'editor' as synonyms . . . but more often 'cutting' refers to preliminary, manual work performed by subordinates, while 'editing' refers to final decisions by supervisors."

24. Brownlow, *The Parade's Gone By*, p. 286.

25. Ibid., p. 283.

26. Interview with Dorothy Arzner (1), Oral History Project, UCLA Special Collections.

27. Ibid.

28. Ibid.

29. Kay and Peary, "Interview with Dorothy Arzner," p. 21.

30. Grace Kingsley, "Leave Sex Out, Says Director," *Los Angeles Times*, September 18, 1927. Arzner scrapbook, Arzner Collection, UCLA.

31. Jesse L. Lasky with Don Weldon, *I Blow My Own Horn* (Garden City, New York: Doubleday 1957), p. 180.

32. Richard Koszarski, *An Evening's Entertainment: The Age of the Silent Feature Picture, 1915–1928* (New York: Charles Scribner's Sons, 1990), p. 248.

33. "San Francisco Girl Earns Big Salary in Movie Post," *San Francisco Call & Post*, June 25, 1927. Arzner scrapbook, Arzner Collection, UCLA.

34. I am using the phrase "visual pleasure," of course, to refer to Laura Mulvey's famous argument about the nature of cinematic identification in the classical Hollywood cinema, whereby man has the authority of the look and woman becomes its object. See Laura Mulvey, "Visual Pleasure and Narrative Cinema," *Screen* 16 (1975), 6–18. For assessments of how important Mulvey's argument has been to feminist film studies, see Janet Bergstrom and Mary Ann Doane, eds., *Camera Obscura*, special issue on "The Spectatrix," (1989) pp. 20–21. The visual pleasure inspired by these photographs of Arzner on location is more akin to that theorized by Marjorie Garber as represented by cross-dressing, which "offers a challenge to easy notions of binarity, putting into question the categories of 'female' and 'male,' whether they are considered essential or constructed, biological or cultural." See *Vested Interests: Cross-Dressing and Cultural Anxiety* (New York and London: Routledge, 1992), p. 10.

35. Richard Henshaw notes that Arzner made an impact in film editing, "considerably more of a one than as a director." See "Women Directors: 150 Filmographies," *Film Comment* 8 (November–December 1972): p. 34. Kevin Brownlow also suggests that Arzner's renown was due more to her editing skills than her directing skills: "It was her association with *The Covered Wagon* that brought Miss Arzner's name into the film history books—the only editor from the entire silent period to be officially remembered." See Brownlow, *The Parade's Gone By*, p. 287.

36. The other scandals were Fatty Arbuckle's trial for the attempted rape of a young actress who later died, and the murder of William Desmond Taylor.

37. For a discussion of *The Red Kimono*, see Kevin Brownlow, *Behind the Mask of Innocence* (New York: Alfred A. Knopf, 1990), 89–93.

38. Kay and Peary, "Interview with Dorothy Arzner," p. 22.

2. Successes and Failures

1. *Chicago Evening American*, April 19, 1927; Donald Burney, review of *Fashions for Women*, n.d.; Dorothy Arzner scrapbook, Dorothy Arzner Collection, UCLA Arts Library—Special Collections. Subsequent citations to material from the Dorothy Arzner Collection will be abbreviated "Arzner Collection, UCLA." Some citations, particularly to clippings in Arzner's scrapbook, are incomplete; I provide as much information as is available.

2. Whitney Williams, "*Fashions for Women*: Triumph for Director and Star," *Los Angeles Sunday Times*, April 17, 1927. Arzner scrapbook, Arzner Collection, UCLA.

3. Grace Kingsley, "Woman Director's Contract," *Los Angeles Times*, April 12, 1927. Arzner scrapbook, Arzner Collection, UCLA.

4. Review of *Ten Modern Commandments*, *New York News*, July 11, 1927. Arzner scrapbook, Arzner Collection, UCLA.

5. Review of *Ten Modern Commandments*, *Variety* (New York), July 15, 1927. Arzner scrapbook, Arzner Collection, UCLA.

6. Fleet Smith, "Paramount's First Woman Director Puts Men to Shame," *The Portland Oregonian*, July 31, 1927. Arzner scrapbook, Arzner Collection, UCLA.

7. Esther Ralston, *Some Day We'll Laugh: An Autobiography* (Metuchen, New Jersey: Scarecrow Press, 1985), p. 107.

8. Ibid.

9. Ibid., p. 108.

10. "Close-ups," *The Boston Herald*, July 13, 1927. Arzner scrapbook, Arzner Collection, UCLA.

11. Harry T. Brundidge, "Dorothy Arzner, Woman Director, Tells of 'Faces on the Cutting Room Floor,' " *The St. Louis Star*, May 4, 1929. Arzner scrapbook, Arzner Collection, UCLA.

12. Review of the Marion Morgan Dancers, *The Wisconsin News*, April 1, 1919. The Dance Collection of the New York Public Library at Lincoln Center.

13. Flyer for the Marion Morgan School of Dance. The Dance Collection of the New York Public Library at Lincoln Center.

14. Elizabeth Kendall, *Where She Danced: The Birth of American Art-Dance* (New York: Knopf, 1979; reprint, Berkeley and Los Angeles: University of California Press, 1984), p. 135. Marion Morgan is a part of the history of modern dance analyzed and documented by Kendall, and I am indebted to her study for its valuable contextualization of Morgan's career.

15. Katherine Lipke, "Dancing? Everybody's Doing It Now!" *Los Angeles Sunday Times*, May 2, 1926. The Dance Collection of the New York Public Library at Lincoln Center.

16. Advertisements for the Marion Morgan Screen Dancers, "Producing Spectacles, Dances and Originalities in Film Productions," *Standard Casting Directory*, September 1926, November 1926, April 1927. The Dance Collection of the New York Public Library at Lincoln Center.

17. Interview with William Kaplan by Francine Parker, Directors Guild of America Oral History Project, DGA Archives, Los Angeles.

18. Numerous postcards from Morgan to Arzner during Morgan's European travels express gratitude for making the trips possible. Arzner Collection, UCLA.

19. Review of *Get Your Man*, *Variety*, December 7, 1927, p. 20.

20. *Photoplay Magazine*, June 1929, p. 54; Katharine Zimmermann, "Clara Bow's First Oral Film Causes No Wild Cry for More," *New York Telegram*, April 4, 1929. Arzner scrapbook, Arzner Collection, UCLA.

21. *Sound Waves* 2 (April 1, 1929), p. 11. Arzner scrapbook, Arzner Collection, UCLA.

22. Gordon Bietry, "Clara Bow at Paramount," *Los Angeles Record*, April 5, 1929. Arzner scrapbook, Arzner Collection, UCLA.

23. See, for example, Beverle Houston, "Missing in Action: Notes on Dorothy Arzner," *Wide Angle* 6, no. 3 (1984): 24–31.

24. See Esther Ralston, *Some Day We'll Laugh*; and David Stenn, *Clara Bow: Runnin' Wild* (New York: Doubleday, 1988), especially chapter 1.

25. Clara Bow was not only exploited by men around her; she was shocked to discover that her personal secretary, Daisy Devoe, stole from her.

26. Interview with Dorothy Arzner (1), Oral History Project, UCLA Special Collections.

27. Information on Zoë Akins is drawn from Anthony Slide's entry in Robert E. Morsberger, Stephen O. Lesser, and Randall Clark, eds., *American Screenwriters. Dictionary of Literary Biography*, vol. 26 (Detroit: Gale Research, 1984).

28. Akins was also close to Willa Cather; for a discussion of their friendship and mentorship, see Sharon O'Brien, *Willa Cather: The Emerging Voice* (New York: Oxford University Press, 1987; reprint, New York: Ballantine, 1988), especially pp. 359–60.

29. Regina Crewe, "Preview Reveals Picture to Hold All Enthralled," *New York American*, March 13, 1930. Arzner scrapbook, Arzner Collection, UCLA.

30. *Variety*, March 19, 1930.

31. Review of *Sarah and Son, Kansas City Star*, March 16, 1930. Arzner scrapbook, Arzner Collection, UCLA.

32. Pierre de Rohan, "See *Sarah and Son*," *New York Telegraph*, March 15, 1930. Arzner scrapbook, Arzner Collection, UCLA. Andrew Sarris, "The Ladies Auxiliary, 1976," in Karyn Kay and Gerald Peary (eds.), *Women and the Cinema* (New York: Dutton, 1977), p. 387.

33. Ye Ed, "The Movies," *Beverly Hills Script*, April 26, 1930. Arzner scrapbook, Arzner Collection, UCLA.

34. Karyn Kay and Gerald Peary, "Interview with Dorothy Arzner," in Claire Johnston, ed., *The Work of Dorothy Arzner: Towards a Feminist Cinema* (London: British Film Institute, 1975), p. 24.

35. Interview with Dorothy Arzner (1), Oral History Project, UCLA Special Collections.

36. George C. Warren, "Chatterton Film Wins at Paramount," *San Francisco Chronicle*, August 22, 1930. Arzner scrapbook, Arzner Collection, UCLA.

37. Review of *Honor among Lovers, Variety*, March 4, 1931, p. 14.

38. Claire Johnston describes the conclusion of the film as follows: " . . . this ironic, even pathological, gesture of substituting the lover for the dead child facilitates the 'happy ending,' but this regression also represents the mark of Joan's desire on the final images of the film text." See "Dorothy Arzner: Critical Strategies," in Johnston, *The Work of Dorothy Arzner*, p. 7. Pam Cook says of the conclusion that the "image of reconciliation, unity, plenitude is shot through with connotations of death, loss and absence. The entire text of the film is cracked open as the workings of ideology in the construction of female desires are exposed." See "Approaching the Work of Dorothy Arzner," in Johnston, *The Work of Dorothy Arzner*, p. 15.

39. Kate Cameron, "March-Sidney Team Bolsters Weak Plot," *New York News*, June 11, 1932. Arzner scrapbook, Arzner Collection, UCLA.

40. Review of *Merrily We Go to Hell, Kansas City Journal Post*, June 3, 1932. Arzner scrapbook, Arzner Collection, UCLA.

41. Review of *Merrily We Go to Hell, Kansas City Star*, June 5, 1932. Arzner scrapbook, Arzner Collection, UCLA.

42. See *Variety*, March 18, 1931; and June 21, 1932.

3. The Independent

1. Sheridan Morley, *Katharine Hepburn* (London: Pavilion, 1989), p. 39.

2. Anne Edwards, *A Remarkable Woman: A Biography of Katharine Hepburn* (New York: Morrow, 1985; reprint, New York: Simon and Schuster, 1986), p. 96.

3. Gary Carey, *Katharine Hepburn: A Biography* (New York: Pocket Books, 1975), p. 55.

4. Michael Freedland, *Katharine Hepburn* (London: W. H. Allen & Co., 1984), p. 31. Freedland quotes Pandro Berman, who took over production of the film from David O. Selznick, that Hepburn was "not at all easy to work with. . . . She was a sweet and fine girl. But she had a little bit of a chip on her shoulder about Hollywood—until she became part of it."

5. Charles Higham, *Kate: The Life of Katharine Hepburn* (New York: Norton, 1975; reprint, New York: New American Library, 1976), p. 40.

6. See Edwards, *A Remarkable Woman*, pp. 95–98.

7. Katharine Hepburn, *Me: Stories of My Life* (New York: Alfred A. Knopf, 1991), pp. 144–45.

8. Donald Spoto, *Blue Angel: The Life of Marlene Dietrich* (New York: Doubleday, 1992), p. 124.

9. Even Vito Russo, in his exemplary study of the representation of gays and lesbians in Hollywood, notes with no further commentary (and therefore, one assumes, no disagreement) Robert Aldrich's statement that Arzner's lesbianism made her "one of the boys." Vito Russo, *The Celluloid Closet*, rev. ed., 2d. (New York: Harper & Row, 1987), p. 50.

10. Ibid.

11. Arzner said in her interview with Karyn Kay and Gerald Peary, speaking of the early years of her directing career, that "no one gave me trouble because I was a woman. Men were more helpful than women." See "Interview with Dorothy Arzner," in Claire Johnston, ed., *The Work of Dorothy Arzner: Towards a Feminist Cinema* (London: British Film Institute, 1975), p. 23. But in other contexts, Arzner acknowledged the problems she had with studio heads, especially later in her career. She explicitly told Mary Murphy, for instance, that she was "blackballed" by Louis B. Mayer. See Mary Murphy, "Tribute to an Unsung Pioneer," *Los Angeles Times*, January 24, 1975, p. 16.

12. On butch and femme roles *as* roles, see Sue-Ellen Case, "Toward a Butch-Femme Aesthetic," *Discourse* 11 (Fall-Winter 1988–89): 55–73; especially p. 65, on butch roles: " . . . these penis-related posturings were always acknowledged as roles, not biological birthrights, nor any other essentialist poses." In Judith Butler's words, "within lesbian contexts, the 'identification' with masculinity that appears as butch identity is not a simple assimilation of lesbianism back into the terms of heterosexuality." See *Gender Trouble: Feminism and the Subversion of Identity* (New York and London: Routledge, 1990), p. 123.

13. Postcard from Marion Morgan to Dorothy Arzner, August 20 (no year), Dorothy Arzner Collection, Arts Library—Special Collections, UCLA. Subsequent citations to material from the Dorothy Arzner Collection will be abbreviated "Arzner Collection, UCLA."

14. Postcard from Marion Morgan to Dorothy Arzner, October 15, 1935. Arzner Collection, UCLA.

15. Postcard from Marion Morgan to Dorothy Arzner, no date, Arzner Collection, UCLA.

16. A. Scott Berg, *Goldwyn: A Biography* (New York: Alfred A. Knopf, 1989), p. 238.

17. Review of *Nana, The Hollywood Reporter*, January 4, 1934. Arzner scrapbook, Arzner Collection, UCLA.

18. John Kobal, *People Will Talk* (New York: Alfred A. Knopf, 1985), p. 129. Kobal interviewed Anna Sten, who insisted that *Nana* was a "beautiful film" (p. 133).

19. Louella O. Parsons, "Fans Captivated by Anna Sten at United Artists," *Los Angeles Examiner*, March 1, 1934. Arzner scrapbook, Arzner Collection, UCLA.

20. Louella Parsons, "Dorothy Arzner Made Producer," October 15, 1934. Arzner scrapbook, Arzner Collection, UCLA.

21. Mike Steen, *Hollywood Speaks! An Oral History* (New York: G. P. Putnam's Sons, 1974), p. 76.

22. Mary McCall, presentation at Directors Guild of America Tribute to Dorothy Arzner, January 25, 1975. Tape 2, Directors Guild of America Archives, Los Angeles, California.

23. Ibid.

24. See Kenneth Anger, *Hollywood Babylon II* (New York: Penguin, 1985), 49–63; and Patrick McGilligan, *George Cukor: A Double Life* (New York: St. Martin's Press, 1991), pp. 132–33, 156.

25. Kate Cameron, review of *Craig's Wife, New York Daily News*, October 2, 1936; review

of *Craig's Wife, Modern Screen,* December 1936; Bland Johaneson, review of *Craig's Wife, New York World-Telegram,* October 2, 1936. Arzner scrapbook, Arzner Collection, UCLA.

26. Howard Barnes, review of *Craig's Wife, New York Herald Tribune,* October 2, 1936; Eileen Creelman, review of *Craig's Wife, New York Post,* October 2, 1936. Arzner scrapbook, Arzner Collection, UCLA.

27. In Karyn Kay and Gerald Peary's interview, Arzner says: "I imagined Mr. Craig was dominated somewhat by his mother and therefore fell in love with a woman stronger than he. I thought Mr. Craig should be down on his knees with gratitude because Mrs. Craig made a man of him. When I told Kelly this, he rose to his six foot height, and said, 'That is *not my* play. Walter Craig was a sweet guy and Mrs. Craig was an SOB.' He left. That was the only contact I had with Kelly." See Kay and Peary, "Interview with Dorothy Arzner," p. 27.

28. Virginia Wright, "A Woman under Fire," review of *Craig's Wife, Evening News,* September 25, 1936. Arzner scrapbook, Arzner Collection, UCLA.

29. Bob Thomas, *Joan Crawford: A Biography* (New York: Simon and Schuster, 1978), p. 123.

30. Alexander Walker, *Joan Crawford: The Ultimate Star* (London: Weidenfeld and Nicolson, 1983), p. 116.

31. Jane Ellen Wayne, *Crawford's Men* (New York: Prentice Hall, 1988; reprint, New York: St. Martin's Press, 1990), p. 171; Shaun Considine, *Bette and Joan: The Divine Feud* (New York: Dutton, 1989; reprint, New York: Dell Publishing, 1990), p. 101.

32. Walker, *Joan Crawford: The Ultimate Star,* p. 116.

33. Mary Murphy, "Film Director Dorothy Arzner: Tribute to an Unsung Pioneer," *Los Angeles Times,* January 24, 1975.

34. Howard Barnes, review of *The Bride Wore Red, New York Herald Tribune,* October 2, 1937. Arzner scrapbook, Arzner Collection, UCLA.

35. Review of *The Bride Wore Red, Los Angeles Times,* October 4, 1937. Arzner scrapbook, Arzner Collection, UCLA.

36. Frank S. Nugent, review of *The Bride Wore Red, The New York Times,* October 4, 1937.

37. Letter to Karyn Kay and Gerald Peary, published in *The Velvet Light Trap,* no. 11 (Winter 1974). Arzner is responding to Kay and Peary's article, "Dorothy Arzner's *Dance, Girl, Dance,*" which appeared in the same journal, no. 10 (Fall 1973). Arzner also said in her letter, "It is as if you [Kay and Peary] had functioned from inside my mind when I was making it."

38. Review of *Dance, Girl, Dance, The Hollywood Reporter,* August 26, 1940.

39. Joseph B. Walker and Juanita Walker, *The Light on Her Face* (Hollywood: The American Society of Cinematographers Press, 1991), p. 246.

40. Interview with Dorothy Arzner (1), Oral History Project, UCLA Special Collections.

4. After Hollywood

1. Karyn Kay and Gerald Peary, "Interview with Dorothy Arzner," in Claire Johnston, ed., *The Work of Dorothy Arzner: Towards a Feminist Cinema* (London: British Film Institute, 1975), p. 28.

2. Ibid.

3. Audiotape of Dorothy Arzner, *You Were Meant to Be a Star,* n.d., Directors Guild of America Archives. All further citations in the text are drawn from audiotapes in the DGA collection, Los Angeles.

4. MGM Directors' Biography of Dorothy Arzner, Museum of Modern Art, Film Study Collection, New York.

5. Interview with Dorothy Arzner, (1), Oral History Project, UCLA Special Collections.

6. Different versions of studio biographies of Arzner list different years for the plays; in one bio, 1951 is listed for *The Swallow's Nest*, and in another, 1953.

7. Interview with Dorothy Arzner (1), Oral History Project,˙UCLA Special Collections.

8. Nancy Dowd, "The Woman Director through the Years," *Action*, July-August 1973, p. 18.

9. Francine Parker, "Approaching the Art of Arzner," *Action*, July-August 1973, p. 9.

10. Joseph McBride, "DGA's First Femme Member, Dorothy Arzner, Honored by Directors, Actors," *Variety*, January 27, 1975.

11. Tape of DGA Tribute to Dorothy Arzner, DGA Archives, Los Angeles.

12. Adrienne Rich, "When We Dead Awaken: Writing as Revision," in Adrienne Rich, *On Lies, Secrets, and Silence* (New York: Norton, 1979), p. 35.

13. Molly Haskell, "Women in Pairs," *The Village Voice*, April 28, 1975, p. 78.

14. Claire Johnston, "Dorothy Arzner: Critical Strategies," in Johnston, *The Work of Dorothy Arzner*, p. 4.

15. See Andrew Britton, *Katharine Hepburn: The Thirties and After* (Newcastle upon Tyne: Tyneside Cinema, 1984), p. 74; and Jacquelyn Suter, "Feminine Discourse in *Christopher Strong*," *Camera Obscura*, no. 3–4 (Summer 1979), 135–50.

16. Roland Barthes, *S/Z* trans. Richard Miller (New York: Hill and Wang, 1974).

17. Obituaries in *Variety*, October 10, 1979; *New York Times*, October 12, 1979; *Los Angeles Times*, October 3, 1979.

5. Working Girls

1. See Mary Beth Haralovich, "The Proletarian Woman's Film of the 1930s: Contending with Censorship and Entertainment," *Screen* 31, no. 2 (1990).

2. Screenplay for *Working Girls*, Zoë Akins Collection, UCLA Special Collection, p. B-29.

3. Ibid., p. B-30, B-31.

4. Ibid., p. G-21.

5. *The Bride Wore Red* (discussed below), based on a play by Ferenc Molnár, entitled *The Girl from Trieste*, was supposed to feature a prostitute in the lead; the role was changed to a café singer.

6. Émile Zola, *Nana*, trans. George Holden (New York: Penguin, 1972). For discussions of the gendered economy of *Nana*, see Charles Bernheimer, *Figures of Ill Repute: Representing Prostitution in Nineteenth-Century France* (Cambridge, Mass. and London: Harvard University Press, 1989), chapter 7; Bernice Chitnis, *Reflecting on Nana* (London and New York: Routledge, 1991); Janet Beizer, "The Body in Question: Anatomy, Textuality, and Fetishism in Zola," *L'Esprit Créateur* 29 (Spring 1989): 50–60; Janet Beizer, "Uncovering *Nana*: The Courtesan's New Clothes," *L'Esprit Créateur* 25 (Summer 1985): 45–56.

7. Laura Mulvey, "Visual Pleasure and Narrative Cinema," *Screen* 16 (1975): 6–18.

8. The classic statement on Zola's relevance to the cinema is Sergei Eisenstein, "Lessons from Literature" (1939), in *Film Essays and a Lecture*, trans. and ed. Jay Leyda (New York: Praeger, 1970).

9. See Jane Gaines, "Dorothy Arzner's Trousers," *Jump Cut*, no. 37 (1992), 88–98.

10. Molly Haskell, "Women in Pairs," *The Village Voice*, April 28, 1975, p. 78.

11. Thanks to Terry Moore, who watched *First Comes Courage* with me and suggested the connection with *Casablanca*.

6. Odd Couples

1. It may be accurate, up to a point, to describe Arzner's films as concerned with female, rather than male, oedipal desire, i.e., with how women mature and enter into a social universe. I say "up to a point," because whatever different inflections the term "oedipal" may acquire, it still signifies a scenario of patriarchal authority. To be sure, mediated desire can be thoroughly oedipal as well. But I find the concept more open to the specific plottings of desire that occur in Arzner's work. The classic formulation of mediated desire is found in René Girard, *Deceit, Desire and the Novel: Self and Other in Literary Structure*, trans. Yvonne Freccero (Baltimore: Johns Hopkins University Press, 1972). While Eve Sedgwick's *Between Men: English Literature and Male Homosocial Desire* (New York: Columbia University Press, 1985) is concerned with mediated desire among men, it serves to illustrate how Girard's model is adaptable to a range of desires.

2. Much has been made of Arzner's comment, in her interview with Karyn Kay and Gerald Peary, that she was "more interested in Christopher Strong . . . than in any of the women characters. He was a man 'on the cross.' He loved his wife, and he fell in love with the aviatrix. He was on a rack. I was really more sympathetic with him, but no one seemed to pick that up. Of course, not too many women are sympathetic about the torture the situation might give to a man of upright character" (in Claire Johnston, ed., *The Work of Dorothy Arzner: Towards a Feminist Cinema* [London: British Film Institute, 1975]).

While this interview is an enormously valuable source of information about Arzner and her career, several factors need to be kept in mind. First, the interview was conducted some forty years after *Christopher Strong* was released. Second, throughout the interview Arzner seems somewhat resistant to explicit feminist interpretations of her work; indeed, she appears not to be particularly forthcoming or expansive with details of her career. To conclude from this that Arzner was necessarily "anti-feminist" seems to me to make a very large leap. After several decades of being virtually ignored by film historians and critics, it makes sense that Arzner would be a bit suspicious of the sudden attention. Indeed, Gerald Peary noted this in another story on Arzner, published in 1974: "Today, the requests for an audience with Ms. Dorothy Arzner have started up again, and she is not always so obliging or flattered. . . . 'I've gotten more calls since this women's lib stuff began,' snorted Arzner." Peary describes Arzner as "rather private and introverted." See "Dorothy Arzner: Reluctant Celebrity," *Boston Sunday Globe*, March 24, 1974.

3. Jacquelyn Suter notes that "what could be conventionally referred to as a sub-plot [i.e., the relationship between Harry and Monica] actually functions to work through the problematic that the narrative has set for itself: the existence of a multiple sexual relationship within a social order founded upon monogamy." I am less convinced of the importance of the restoration of monogamy in the film. See Suter, "Feminine Discourse in *Christopher Strong*," *Camera Obscura* 3–4 (1979): 136.

4. Jacquelyn Suter's reading of *Christopher Strong* is based on Cynthia's function as a mediator to restore the patriarchal order of (heterosexual) monogamy. I see Cynthia's mediating function differently, particularly to the extent that the boundaries between subject and object and mediator do not remain fixed in the film. In other words, Cynthia's mediating function seems to me far more unstable than Suter's reading of the film would suggest. See ibid., 135–50.

5. See Kay and Peary, "Interview with Dorothy Arzner," p. 26.

6. Claire Johnston cites this scene as a prime example of how it is the "universe of the male which invites scrutiny, which is rendered strange" in Arzner's work. See "Dorothy Arzner: Critical Strategies," in Johnston, *The Work of Dorothy Arzner*, p. 6. Pauline Kael notes that Cynthia's "acquiescence destroyed her." Kael calls the scene the "intelligent woman's primal post-coital scene. . . . Probably it got there because the movie was written by a woman, Zoë Akins, and directed by a woman, Dorothy Arzner." See *Deeper into Movies* (Boston: Little, Brown and Company, 1972), p. 341.

7. Gilbert Frankau, *Christopher Strong* (New York: E. P. Dutton and Co., 1932), p. 233.

8. Ibid.

9. See Kay and Peary, "Interview with Dorothy Arzner," p. 27.

10. George Kelly, *Craig's Wife* (Boston: Little, Brown and Company, 1926), pp. 17–18.

11. Ibid., p. 18.

12. Julia Lesage, "The Hegemonic Female Fantasy in *An Unmarried Woman* and *Craig's Wife*," *Film Reader* 5 (1982): 89.

13. Ibid., p. 90; Melissa Sue Kort, " 'Spectacular Spinelessness': The Men in Dorothy Arzner's Films," in Janet Todd, ed., *Men by Women*, vol. 2 of *Women and Literature* (n.s.) (New York and London: Holmes and Meier, 1982), p. 197.

7. Dance, Girls, Dance

1. That the cinema had a crucial role to play in this shift has been demonstrated by historians like Kathy Peiss. See her *Cheap Amusements: Working Women and Leisure in Turn-of-the-Century New York* (Philadelphia: Temple University Press, 1986).

2. See Lillian Faderman, *Surpassing the Love of Men: Romantic Friendship and Love between Women from the Renaissance to the Present* (New York: William Morrow & Co., 1981) and *Odd Girls and Twilight Lovers: A History of Lesbian Life in Twentieth-Century America* (New York: Columbia University Press, 1991); and Carroll Smith-Rosenberg, *Disorderly Conduct: Visions of Gender in Victorian America* (New York: Alfred A. Knopf, Inc., 1985).

3. Andrea Weiss, *Vampires and Violets: Lesbians in the Cinema* (London: Jonathan Cape, 1992), p. 14.

4. Warner Fabian, *Unforbidden Fruit* (Cleveland and New York: International Fiction Library, 1928), p. v.

5. The "hard-boiled virgins" of Fabian's novel suggest a response, direct or indirect, to Frances Newman's 1926 feminist novel, *The Hard-Boiled Virgin*, about a woman's struggle for independence and autonomy (New York: Boni & Liveright, 1926).

6. *Unforbidden Fruit*, p. 21.

7. Ibid., p. 64.

8. Ibid., p. 311.

9. Ibid., pp. 317–18.

10. Innocent freshman Verity and serious student Sara are combined to become Helen; Sylvia and Starr, the two heroines, are combined as Stella.

11. See Lillian Faderman's discussion of "Fiction as Weapon" in *Surpassing the Love of Men*, chapter 4.

12. The phrase "female world of love and ritual" is Carroll Smith-Rosenberg's. See "The Female World of Love and Ritual: Relations between Women in Nineteenth-Century America," *Signs* 1 (Autumn 1975): 1–29.

13. See David Stenn, *Clara Bow: Runnin' Wild* (New York: Doubleday, 1988).

14. Miscellaneous Papers, Dorothy Arzner Collection, UCLA Arts Library—Special Collections.

15. The classic essay on *Dance, Girl, Dance* is Claire Johnston, "Dorothy Arzner: Critical Strategies," in Claire Johnston, ed., *The Work of Dorothy Arzner: Towards a Feminist Cinema* (London: British Film Institute, 1975). Other feminist analyses of the film include: Karyn Kay and Gerald Peary, "Dorothy Arzner's *Dance, Girl, Dance*," in Karyn Kay and Gerald Peary, eds., *Women and the Cinema: A Critical Anthology* (New York: Dutton, 1977), pp. 9–25; Lucy Fischer, *Shot/Countershot* (Princeton: Princeton University Press, 1989), pp. 148–54; Barbara Koenig Quart, *Women Directors: The Emergence of a New Cinema* (New York and Westport, Conn.: Praeger, 1988); Giulia Colaizzi, *Womanizing Film: Dorothy Arzner's* Dance, Girl, Dance," Working Papers, Centro de Semiótica y Teoría del Espectáculo, vol. 12 (June 1989); and Samuel Chell, "Dorothy Arzner's *Dance, Girl, Dance*: Regendering the Male Gaze," *Ciné-action*, no. 24–25 (1991): 75–79.

16. The classic statement of this position remains Laura Mulvey, "Visual Pleasure and Narrative Cinema," *Screen* 16 (1975): 6–18.

17. For examples of how the structures of shot reverse shot establish sexual difference in *The Big Sleep*, see Raymond Bellour, "The Obvious and the Code," *Screen* 15 (1974); see also my discussion of the film in *The Woman at the Keyhole* (Bloomington: Indiana University Press, 1990), chapter 1. For examples of literal performances within films, see Mulvey, "Visual Pleasure and Narrative Cinema."

18. Karyn Kay and Gerald Peary report that the character of Bubbles was based on Texas Guinan, a vaudeville performer and entrepreneur "whom Arzner had spotted waving out of her taxi window to everyone in New York." See "Interview with Dorothy Arzner," p. 28. Texas Guinan was the "firebrand hostess of Broadway's high revel during the Prohibition era, who turned New York's nightlife into what she was fond of calling 'an essential and basic industry.' " See Glenn Shirley, *"Hello, Sucker!" The Story of Texas Guinan* (Austin: Eakin Press, 1989), p. v.

19. Script for *Dance, Girl, Dance*. UCLA Arts Library—Special Collections, p. 33.

20. Alexander Doty has suggested the alliterative connection between Basilova and Nazimova; see *Making Things Perfectly Queer* (Minneapolis: University of Minnesota Press, 1993), pp. 31–32.

21. The catfight earns a small place in the 1991 made-for-television movie on Lucille Ball and Desi Arnaz, *Lucy and Desi: Before the Laughter*. In the recreation of the scene, the actress who plays Arzner dresses butch and directs the fight with great gusto.

22. Claire Johnston, "Dorothy Arzner: Critical Strategies," in Johnston, *The Work of Dorothy Arzner*, p. 6.

8. Looking for Dorothy

1. *Wheeling News* (West Va.), Sept. 25, 1927. Arzner scrapbook, Dorothy Arzner Collection, UCLA Arts Library—Special Collections. Subsequent citations to material from the Dorothy Arzner Collection will be abbreviated "Arzner Collection, UCLA." Some citations to clippings in Arzner's scrapbook are incomplete; I provide as much information as is available.

2. "Woman Movie Picture Director," *New York Sun*, September 23, 1930. Arzner scrapbook, Arzner Collection, UCLA.

3. Isaac Julien, quoted in Jim Marks, "Looking for Isaac," *Outweek*, no. 15 (October 1, 1989), p. 31.

4. Arzner scrapbook, Arzner Collection, UCLA.

5. Sumiko Higashi uses the terms "flapper" and "new woman" interchangeably in her study of women in American films of the silent era. According to Higashi, "The flapper looked boyish and acted mannish. According to Victorian standards, women as moral superiors elevated men to the level of their pedestals. The flapper reversed gears and acted like a man, thus making herself more accessible to the opposite sex." See *Virgins, Vamps and Flappers: The American Silent Movie Heroine* (Montreal: Eden Press, 1978), p. 112.

The coexistence of "boyish" or "mannish" traits with sexual availability (to men) runs throughout descriptions of the New Woman, suggesting at the very least that the lesbian implications of this newly independent woman required containment and/or explanation. Carroll Smith-Rosenberg examines the relationship of lesbianism to the New Woman in "Discourses of Sexuality and Subjectivity: The New Woman, 1870–1936," in Martin Bauml Duberman, Martha Vicinus, and George Chauncey, Jr., eds., *Hidden from History: Reclaiming the Gay and Lesbian Past* (New York: New American Library, 1989), 264–80.

6. For a fascinating case study of a group of "New Women" and the role of lesbianism in their community, see Judith Schwarz, *Radical Feminists of HETERODOXY, Greenwich Village 1912–1940*, rev. ed. (Norwich, Vermont: New Victoria Publishers, 1986).

7. See Smith-Rosenberg, "Discourses of Sexuality and Subjectivity."

8. Ann Sylvester, "Make Way for the Ladies," *Picture Play Magazine*, December 1927. Arzner scrapbook, Arzner Collection, UCLA.

9. Marguerite Tazelaar, "Meeting Miss Dorothy Arzner, Screen's Only Woman Director," *Herald Tribune*, November 16, 1930. Arzner scrapbook, Arzner Collection, UCLA.

10. Grace Wilcox, "Hilltop Tenant," *Screen and Radio Weekly*, n.d. (1936). Arzner scrapbook, Arzner Collection, UCLA.

11. "Distaff Side Director," *The New York Times*, Sept. 27, 1936, X, p. 4. Arzner scrapbook, Arzner Collection, UCLA.

12. Sylvester, "Make Way for the Ladies."

13. Frances Juliet Douglas, "Watching the Stars Go By," *The Piqua Daily Call* [?], September 10, 1928. Arzner scrapbook, Arzner Collection, UCLA.

14. Grace Kingsley, "Leave Sex Out, Says Director," *Los Angeles Times*, September 18, 1927. Arzner scrapbook, Arzner Collection, UCLA.

15. Grace Kingsley, "The Only Woman Director," *Screen Hour*, May 1929. Arzner scrapbook, Arzner Collection, UCLA.

16. See Esther Newton, "The Mythic Mannish Lesbian: Radclyffe Hall and the New Woman," *Signs* 9 (Summer 1984): 557–75.

17. Tom O'Connor, *Los Angeles Evening News*, September 30, 1936, Arzner scrapbook, Arzner Collection, UCLA.

18. *Time*, October 12, 1936.

19. "Woman among the Mighty," *New York World Telegram*, November 21, 1936. Arzner scrapbook, Arzner Collection, UCLA.

20. Dudley Early, "Who Is the 'First Lady of the Screen'? The Career of Dorothy Arzner," *Family Circle* 5 (July 6, 1934), 10–11, 16–18. Arzner scrapbook, Arzner Collection, UCLA.

21. Harry T. Brundidge, "Dorothy Arzner, Woman Director," *The St. Louis Star*, 1929, n.d. Arzner scrapbook, Arzner Collection, UCLA.

22. "Dorothy Arzner Is Hollywood's Only Female Film Boss," *The Buffalo Times*, December 9, 1934. Arzner scrapbook, Arzner Collection, UCLA.

23. *Time*, October 12, 1936.

24. An unidentified newsclipping, Arzner scrapbook, Arzner Collection, UCLA.

25. Julie Lang, "Directed by Dorothy Arzner!" *Screenland*, August 1929. Arzner scrapbook, Arzner Collection, UCLA.

26. Mayme Ober Peak, "Only Woman Movie Director," *The Boston Sunday Globe*, December 2, 1928. Arzner scrapbook, Arzner Collection, UCLA.

27. Mary Louise Roberts's reading of Victor Margueritte's 1922 novel *La Garçonne* is concerned with the *garçonne* as a cultural type in the specific context of France; nonetheless, her study is relevant to the development of the androgyne as a type that crossed national borders. See " 'This Civilization No Longer Has Sexes': *La Garçonne* and Cultural Crisis in France after World War I," *Gender and History* 4 (Spring 1992): 49–69. For a relevant discussion of Radclyffe Hall's fashion style and the styles of her era, see Katrina Rolley, "Cutting a Dash: The Dress of Radclyffe Hall and Una Troubridge," *Feminist Review*, no. 35 (Summer 1990): 54–66. See also Katrina Rolley, "Love, Desire and the Pursuit of the Whole: Dress and the Lesbian Couple," in Juliet Ash and Elizabeth Wilson, eds., *Chic Thrills: A Fashion Reader* (Berkeley and Los Angeles: University of California Press, 1993), 30–39.

28. Florabel Muir, "All-Women Film Breeds Nary a Scrap," *Sunday News*, June 19, 1930. Arzner scrapbook, Arzner Collection, UCLA.

29. "A Woman Picture Director," *The St. Louis Post-Dispatch Daily Magazine*, 1929 (n.d.), Arzner scrapbook, Arzner Collection, UCLA.

30. Unidentified news clipping, July 10, 1936. Dorothy Arzner file, Museum of Modern Art, Film Study Collection, New York City.

31. Katrina Rolley notes a similar phenomenon in relationship to Radclyffe Hall: "Radclyffe Hall's modernity resulted from her need to express her sexual identity through 'masculine' dress and appearance. For her, every change in fashion which allowed women to wear clothes formerly designated 'male' was of importance and, since a process of 'masculinization' characterized women's dress during the 1920s, she must often have appeared ultra-fashionable. When, however, a more traditionally 'feminine' look returned, Radclyffe Hall continued to wear clothes which were now acceptable, but by no means fashionable." See Rolley, "Cutting a Dash," p. 57.

32. Unidentified news clipping, August 1929. Arzner scrapbook, Arzner Collection, UCLA.

33. Dorothy Arzner, "A Woman's Touch," *Motion Picture Studio Insider*, July 1937, 20, 46. Arzner scrapbook, Arzner Collection, UCLA.

34. Frederick F. Isaac, "Do Ladies Prefer Brunettes?" *The Sunday Post*, October 20, 1928. Arzner scrapbook, Arzner Collection, UCLA.

35. Mary Murphy, "Film Director Dorothy Arzner: Tribute to an Unsung Pioneer," *Los Angeles Times*, January 24, 1975.

36. Ibid.

37. Here I am summarizing the argument that appears in *The Woman at the Keyhole*, pp. 105–110.

38. Ingrid Sischy, "Jodie Foster: The One and Only," with photographs by Matthew Rolston, *Interview* 21, no. 10 (October 1991): 78–85.

Conclusion

1. See, for example, Arlene Stein, ed., *Sisters, Sexperts, Queers: Beyond the Lesbian Nation* (New York: Penguin Books, 1993).

2. Jennifer Terry, "Theorizing Deviant Historiography," *differences* 3 (1991): 56.

3. Tee Corinne, *Women Who Loved Women* (Pearlchild, 1984).

4. Ibid., p. 7.

5. Katherine V. Forrest, *The Beverly Malibu* (Tallahassee, Florida: Naiad Press, 1989), p. 18. Subsequent citations will be indicated in parentheses in the text.

6. See Eve Kosofsky Sedgwick, *Epistemology of the Closet* (Berkeley and Los Angeles: University of California Press, 1990). On the "romance of the closet," see Blanche Wiesen Cook, *Eleanor Roosevelt,* vol. 1 (New York: Viking Penguin, 1992), p. 14.

7. Alex Doty says of the video that it "implies that most lesbian cultural authorship in mass culture is conducted without reference to directors or even to stars, but rather is achieved by performing 'perverse readings' articulating a text's 'unconscious logic,' 'covert narrative,' or 'homosexual subplots or subtexts'." See *Making Things Perfectly Queer* (Minneapolis: University of Minnesota Press, 1993), p. 113, n. 9.

Filmography

This filmography is adapted from the filmography in Claire Johnston, ed., *The Work of Dorothy Arzner: Towards a Feminist Cinema* (London, British Film Institute, 1975).

1927   *Fashions for Women*

Production Company	Paramount-Famous Players-Lasky
Producers	Adolph Zukor and Jesse Lasky
Script	Percy Heath, from *The Girl of the Hour*, by Paul Armond and Leopold Marchand
Adaptation	Jules Furthman and Herman J. Mankiewicz
Photography	H. Kinley Martin
Choreography	Marion Morgan

CAST:

Esther Ralston	Celeste de Givray and Lola Dauvry
Raymond Hatton	Sam Dupont
Einar Hanson	Raoul de Bercy
Edward Martindel	Duke of Arles
Agostino Borgato	Monsieur Alard
Edward Faust	Monsieur Pettibon
Yvonne Howell	Mimi
Maud Wayne	The Girl
Charles Darvas	Restaurant manager
William Orlamond	Roué

1927   *Ten Modern Commandments*

Production Company	Paramount-Famous Players-Lasky
Producers	Adolph Zukor and Jesse Lasky
Script	Doris Anderson and Paul Gangelin, from a story by Jack Lait
Photography	Alfred Gilks
Editor	Louis D. Lighton
Choreography	Marion Morgan

CAST:

Esther Ralston	Kitty O'Day
Neil Hamilton	Tod Gilbert
Arthur Hoyt	George Disbrow

Jocelyn Lee   Sharon Lee
El Brendel   "Speeding" Shapiro
Roscoe Karns   Benny Burnaway
Romaine Fielding   Zeno
Maud Truax   Aunt Ruby
Rose Burdick   Belle

1927   *Get Your Man*

Production Company   Paramount-Famous Players-Lasky
Producers   Adolph Zukor and Jesse Lasky
Script   Hope Loring, from a play by Louis Verneuil
Photography   Alfred Gilks
Editor   Louis D. Lighton
Tableaux   Marion Morgan

CAST:
Clara Bow   Nancy Worthington
Charles Rogers   Robert de Bellecontre
Josef Swickard   Duc de Bellecontre
Josephine Dunn   Simone de Villeneuve
Frances Raymond   Mrs. Worthington
Harvey Clark   Marquis de Villeneuve

1928   *Manhattan Cocktail*

Production Company   Paramount-Famous Players-Lasky
Producers   Adolph Zukor and Jesse Lasky
Script   Ethel Doherty, from a story by Ernest Vajda
Photography   Harry Fishbeck
Editor   Doris Drought
Choreography   Marion Morgan

CAST:
Nancy Carroll   Babs Clark
Richard Arlen   Fred Tilden
Danny O'Shea   Bob Marky
Paul Lukas   Boris Renov
Lilyan Tashman   Mrs. Renov

1929   *The Wild Party*

Production Company   Paramount-Famous Players-Lasky
Script   E. Lloyd Sheldon, from *Unforbidden Fruit*, by
                         Warner Fabian
Photography   Victor Milner
Editor   Otto Lovering

CAST:

Clara Bow	Stella Ames
Fredric March	James Gilmore
Shirley O'Hara	Helen Owens
Marceline Day	Faith Morgan
Joyce Compton	Eva Tutt
Jack Luden	George
Jack Oakie	Harvey
Phillips Holmes	Phil
Adrienne Dore	
Virginia Thomas	
Jean Lorraine	
Kay Bryant	
Alice Adair	
Renée Whitney	
Amo Ingram	
Marguerite Cramer	
Ben Hendricks, Jr.	

1930   *Sarah and Son*

Production Company	Paramount-Famous Players-Lasky
Script	Zoë Akins, from the novel by Timothy Shea
Photography	Charles Lang
Editor	Verma Willis

CAST:

Ruth Chatterton	Sarah Storm
Fredric March	Howard Vanning
Fuller Mellish, Jr.	Jim Grey
Gilbert Emery	John Ashmore
Doris Lloyd	Mrs. Ashmore
William Stack	Cyril Belloc
Phillipe de Lacy	Bobby

1930   *Paramount on Parade*

Production Company	Paramount
Directors	Dorothy Arzner, Otto Brower, Edmund Goulding, Victor Heerman, Edwin H. Knopf, Rowland V. Lee, Ernst Lubitsch, Lothar Mendes, Victor Schertzinger, Edward Sutherland, Frank Tuttle
Photography	Harry Fishbeck and Victor Milner (some sketches in Technicolor)

Arzner directed the sequence "The Gallows Song—Nichavo," with Richard (Skeets) Gallagher and Dennis King.

1930 *Anybody's Woman*

Production Company   Paramount
Script   Zoë Akins and Doris Anderson, from the story
                          by Gouverneur Morris
Photography   Charles Lang
Editor   Jane Lorring

CAST:
Ruth Chatterton   Pansy Gray
Clive Brook   Neil Dunlap
Paul Lukas   Gustave Saxon
Huntley Gordon   Grant Crosby
Virginia Hammond   Katherine Malcolm
Tom Patricola   Eddie Calcio
Juliette Compton   Ellen
Cecil Cunningham   Dot
Charles Gerrard   Walter Harvey
Harvey Clark   Mr. Tanner
Sidney Bracey   Butler
Gertrude Sutton

1931 *Honor among Lovers*

Production Company   Paramount
Script   Austin Parker, from his own story
Photography   George Folsey
Editor   Helen Turner

CAST:
Claudette Colbert   Julia Traynor
Fredric March   Jerry Stafford
Monroe Owsley   Phillip Craig
Charles Ruggles   Monty Dunn
Ginger Rogers   Doris Brown
Avonne Taylor   Maybelle
Pat O'Brien   Conroy
Janet McLeavy   Margaret
John Kearney   Inspector
Ralph Morgan   Riggs
Jules Epailly   Louis
Leonard Carey   Butler

1931 *Working Girls*

Production Company   Paramount
Script   Zoë Akins, from the play *Blind Mice*, by Vera
                          Casparay and Winifred Lenihan
Photography   Harry Fishbeck
Editor   Jane Lorring

CAST:

Judith Wood	June Thorpe
Dorothy Hall	May Thorpe
Paul Lukas	Dr. Von Schrader
Frances Dee	Louise Adams
Claire Dodd	Jane
Dorothy Stickney	
Alberta Vaughn	
Mary Forbes	

1932   *Merrily We Go to Hell*

Production Company	Paramount
Script	Edwin Justus Mayer, from the novel *I, Jerry, Take Thee, Joan*, by Cleo Lucas
Photography	David Abel
Editor	Jane Lorring

CAST:

Sylvia Sidney	Joan Prentice
Fredric March	Jerry Corbett
Adriane Allen	Claire Hempstead
Richard Gallagher	Buck
Florence Britton	Charlie
Esther Howard	Vi
George Irving	Mr. Prentice
Kent Taylor	Dick Taylor
Charles Coleman	Damery
Leonard Carey	Butler
Milla Davenport	Housekeeper
Robert Greig	Baritone bartender
Rev. Neal Dodd	Minister
Mildred Boyd	June
Cary Grant	Stage actor

1933   *Christopher Strong*

Production Company	RKO
Producers	David Selznick and Pandro Berman
Script	Zoë Akins, from a novel by Gilbert Frankau
Photography	Bert Glennon
Editor	Jane Lorring

CAST:

Katharine Hepburn	Cynthia Darrington
Colin Clive	Christopher Strong
Billie Burke	Elaine Strong
Ralph Forbes	Harry Rawlinson
Helen Chandler	Monica Strong

Irene Brown	Carrie
Gwendolin Logan	Bradford
Desmond Roberts	Bryce Mercer
Jack La Rue	Carlo

1934   *Nana*

Production Company	United Artists
Producer	Samuel Goldwyn
Script	Willard Mack and H. W. Gribble, suggested by Émile Zola's novel
Photography	Gregg Toland
Songs	Richard Rodgers and Lorenz Hart
Editor	Frank Lawrence

CAST:

Anna Sten	Nana
Phillips Holmes	Lt. George Muffat
Lionel Atwill	Col. André Muffat
Richard Bennett	Greiner
Mae Clark	Satin
Muriel Kirland	Mimi
Reginald Owen	Bordenave
Jessie Ralph	Zoë
Lawrence Grant	Grand Duke Alexis

1936   *Craig's Wife*

Production Company	Columbia
Script	Mary C. McCall, Jr., from the play by George Kelly
Photography	Lucien Ballard
Editor	Viola Lawrence

CAST:

Rosalind Russell	Harriet Craig
John Boles	Walter Craig
Billie Burke	Mrs. Frazier
Jane Darwell	Mrs. Harold
Dorothy Wilson	Ethel Landreth
Alma Kruger	Mrs. Austen
Thomas Mitchell	Fergus Passmore
Raymond Walburn	Billy Birkmire
Robert Allen	Gene Fredericks
Elizabeth Risdon	Ms. Landreth
Nydia Westman	Mazie
Kathleen Burke	Adelaide Passmore

1937   *The Bride Wore Red*

Production Company	MGM
Producer	Joseph L. Mankiewicz
Script	Tess Slesinger and Bradbury Foote, from the play *The Girl from Trieste*, by Ferenc Molnár
Photography	George Folsey
Editor	Adrienne Fazan
Music and Lyrics	Franz Waxman and Gus Kahn

CAST:

Joan Crawford	Anni
Franchot Tone	Giulio
Robert Young	Rudi Pal
Billie Burke	Contessa di Meina
Reginald Owen	Admiral Monti
Lynne Carver	Maddelena Monti
George Zucco	Count Armalia
Mary Phillips	Maria
Paul Porcasi	Nobili
Dickie Moore	Pietro
Frank Puglia	Alberto

1940   *Dance, Girl, Dance*

Production Company	RKO
Producers	Erich Pommer and Harry E. Edington
Script	Tess Slesinger and Frank Davis, from the story by Vicki Baum
Photography	Russell Metty
Editor	Robert Wise
Choreography	Ernst Matray

CAST:

Maureen O'Hara	Judy
Louis Hayward	Jimmie Harris
Lucille Ball	Bubbles
Virginia Field	Elinor Harris
Ralph Bellamy	Steve Adams
Maria Ouspenskaya	Madame Basilova
Mary Carlisle	Sally
Katherine Alexander	Ms. Olmstead
Edwar Brophy	Dwarfie
Walter Abel	Judge
Harold Huber	"Hoboken"
Ernest Truex	Bailey 1
Chester Chute	Bailey 2
Lorraine Krueger	Dolly

Lola Jensen	Daisy
Emma Dunn	Ms. Simpson
Sidney Blackmer	Puss in Boots
Vivian Fay	Ballerina
Ludwig Stossel	Caesar
Erno Verebes	Fitch

1943   *First Comes Courage*

Production Company	Columbia
Producer	Harry Joe Brown
Script	Lewis Meltzer and Melvin Levy, from the story *The Commandos*, by Elliott Arnold
Adaptation	George Sklar
Photography	Joseph Walker
Editor	Viola Lawrence

CAST:

Merle Oberon	Nicole Larsen
Brian Aherne	Capt. Allan Lowell
Carl Esmond	Major Paul Dichter
Fritz Leiber	Dr. Aanrud
Erville Alderson	Soren
Erik Rolf	Ole
Reinhold Schunzel	Col. Kurt Von Elser
Isolbel Elsom	Rose Lindstrom

Index

JUDITH MAYNE, Professor of French and Women's Studies at Ohio State University, is the author of *Cinema and Spectatorship*, *The Woman at the Keyhole*, *Kino and the Woman Question: Feminism and Soviet Silent Film*, and *Private Novels, Public Films*.